A PRAGMATIC APPROACH
TO GROUP PSYCHOTHERAPY

A PRAGMATIC APPROACH TO GROUP PSYCHOTHERAPY

Henry I. Spitz, M.D.

Clinical Professor of Psychiatry
Department of Psychiatry
Columbia University
College of Physicians and Surgeons
and
Director, Group Psychotherapy Program
New York State Psychiatric Institute

Susan T. Spitz, A.C.S.W.

Clinical Instructor of Psychiatry
Department of Psychiatry
Columbia University
College of Physicians and Surgeons

BRUNNER/MAZEL
Taylor & Francis Group

USA	Publishing Office:	BRUNNER/MAZEL *A member of the Taylor & Francis Group* 325 Chestnut Street Philadelphia, PA 19106 Tel: (215) 625-8900 Fax: (215) 625-2940
	Distribution Center:	BRUNNER/MAZEL *A member of the Taylor & Francis Group* 47 Runway Road, Suite G Levittown, PA 19057 Tel: (215) 269-0400 Fax: (215) 269-0363
UK		BRUNNER/MAZEL *A member of the Taylor & Francis Group* 1 Gunpowder Square London EC4A 3DE Tel: +44 171 583 0490 Fax: +44 171 583 0581

A PRAGMATIC APPROACH TO GROUP PSYCHOTHERAPY

1 2 3 4 5 6 7 8 9 0

Printed by Braun-Brumfield, Ann Arbor, MI, 1998.

A CIP catalog record for this book is available from the British Library.
⊗ The paper in this publication meets the requirements of the ANSI Standard Z39.48-1984 (Permanence of Paper).

Library of Congress Cataloging-in-Publication Data

Spitz, Henry I., 1941–
    A pragmatic approach to group psychotherapy / Henry I. Spitz and Susan T. Spitz.
        p.   cm.
    ISBN 0-87630-896-5 (alk. paper)
    1. Group psychotherapy.   I. Spitz, Susan T.   II. Title.
    RC488.S6463   1998
    616.89′152—dc21   98-18652
                                                                  CIP

ISBN 0-87630-896-5

To our beloved children, Becky and Jake

Contents

Preface ix

I
GENERAL CLINICAL PRINCIPLES

1   Origins of Group Psychotherapy 3

2   Group Therapy: Definitions and Classification 9

3   Basic Clinical Principles of Group Psychotherapy 19

4   Constructing an Effective Psychotherapy Group 29

5   The Initial Group Session 53

6   Stages of Group Psychotherapy: Therapeutic Issues 71

II
CONTEMPORARY APPLICATIONS
OF GROUP PSYCHOTHERAPY

7   Brief Group Psychotherapy 81

8   Group Approaches to the Treatment of Substance Abuse 93

9   Group Psychotherapy With Couples and Families 107

10 Group Therapy With Medically Ill Patients 125

11 Group Therapy With the Chronic Psychiatric Patient 141

12 Future Directions in Group Psychotherapy 153

References 155

Index 159

Preface

As group therapy nears its 100th anniversary and as we simultaneously approach the next century, the time is an appropriate one to reflect upon past and present developments in the field and to identify future trends.

Group therapy is currently in its third phase of evolution. The first wave, spurred by World War II and the enormous amount of psychological trauma that emerged from the war, created a pressing need for treating the psychiatric casualties of wartime. Experimentation with working in a group setting, as opposed to the conventional individual psychoanalytic milieu, seemed to be a logical attempt to see more people in less time.

The community mental health movement of the 1960s and 1970s, characterized by deinstitutionalization of the chronically mentally ill patient from state hospitals back into the community, presented a similar set of circumstances: a surplus of those in need of psychological help and a shortage of professionally trained therapists to treat them. This gave rise to an exponential increase in the practice of group therapy, particularly in the area of homogeneous groups designed to treat members who shared a common condition. With greater comfort and familiarity in employing group techniques came a corresponding trend toward experimentation with the application of small- and large-group methods to meet the needs of a broad range of patient populations and psychiatric conditions.

The 1990s has been the age of health care reform. With it again has come the pressure to see more people in shorter time frames, but the mandate this time has come from a different source. Managed mental health care and related service models are economically based forms of health care delivery that place a high premium on time and cost efficiency. While the forms of managed care are constantly changing, it is clear that the rate of growth is accelerating. The initial therapeutic impact of managed mental health care and substance abuse treatment has been a high priority placed on brief, symptom-focused treatments. The group version of this trend has been evident in the increased interest in the practice of time-limited group techniques.

Despite its controversial nature, managed care is en route to becoming a major—if not the major—force in influencing patterns of psychotherapeutic practice in the latter part of this century. The emphasis in this book will be on understanding the advances that have taken place in group treatment over the years, regardless of what historical events created or influenced them, and we will focus on what the clinical and research data have identified as reputable and beneficial forms of group psychotherapy. As the book's title implies, the primary concern is pragmatic and is geared to students and practitioners of group therapy who wish to advance their existing base of knowledge and to enhance and broaden their leadership skills.

In order to accomplish this goal, the text is designed to provide a brief historical context against which one can compare and contrast contemporary group methods and identify long-standing trends in the group field. Also, we provide an overview of basic principles of group treatment with specific reference to leadership and membership issues involved in clinical decision making and choice of group interventions.

The focus in the latter part of the volume is on the newer uses of group therapy and an in-depth discussion of the theory, structure, and practice of these innovative group formats. Selected forms of group therapy that are unique, that have been underemphasized in the group literature, and that demonstrate creative adaptation of traditional group theory and technique are the focal points of this section.

With the aforementioned information as background, the text concludes with speculation about groups of the future and about further applications of group treatment to meet the needs of people in a rapidly changing world. Boxed sections have been interspersed throughout the text for purposes of augmenting some of the basic information provided and addressing clinical manifestations of themes described in the various chapters.

I

GENERAL CLINICAL PRINCIPLES

1

Origins of Group Psychotherapy

One of the best ways to facilitate the understanding of contemporary uses of groups to treat psychological disorders is to briefly trace the historical path of the development of the field. In so doing, one can see the foundations for group therapy as well as the rationale for its different uses over time. This is not simply an intellectual foray into the past. When one understands the changes in theory and practice over time, it is possible to join the field of group therapy in its current "flight path" and to identify trends, techniques, and patterns that have stood the test of time. Many of these historical efforts were pioneering in their day and have been modified or adapted to meet the demands of present-day treatment of emotional distress.

Much has been written about the modern historical origins of group psychotherapy. Consensus exists among most group therapists that the embryonic elements of what we currently call group therapy can be traced back to the early 1900s and the work of Joseph Pratt (1907). Pratt was a nonpsychiatric physician treating medical inpatients suffering from tuberculosis. Since isolation from society and prolonged rest periods were the mainstays of the treatment of tuberculosis at that point in medical history, Pratt and others who cared for the sick were faced with the challenge of treating the physical condition and the concomitant task of managing the emotional health of the patient.

In an effort to provide an activity for TB patients who were demoralized as a result of their prolonged convalescence and social isolation, Pratt decided to hold "classes" on the ward to inform patients about the state of what was known about tuberculosis at the time. Quite serendipitously, it was noted that participants in these classes appeared to be less depressed and more cooperative with their individual medical treatment plans.

Pratt's work affords an excellent example of the linkage between "ancient" group history and today's common practices. How different are contemporary psychoeducational groups for the treatment of medically ill patients, people with psychotic disorders or bipolar affective disorders, and those with a variety of family problems in their goals and structure? The components of modern group therapy may be more streamlined, systematized, and even structured into specific protocols or manuals for leading psychoeducational groups, but the bare bones of Pratt's work and those of the practitioner of the 1990s are strikingly similar.

The premise that the threads of the past are visible in the methods in practice today is a helpful orientation to a review of some of the major work that has influenced the field of group therapy. Putting contemporary practice into proper historical perspective gives a valuable context for understanding where the field has come from and where it is likely to be going. This point of view facilitates a better comprehension of the modifications and adaptations of traditional group therapies that have taken place over the course of this century.

EARLY INFLUENCES

Contemporaries of Pratt became aware of his work and began to apply it to different patient populations and in varied clinical settings. Cody Marsh (1931), a minister and psychiatrist, adopted the idea of giving inspirational lectures to psychiatric inpatients and also conducted classes for staff members. Many attribute the early origins of inpatient milieu therapy to Marsh's work.

The 1920s was a period during which several efforts expanded the use of the inherent properties of the group for therapeutic benefit. Trigant Burrow (1927), a psychoanalyst, experimented with the format of "group analysis," liberalizing the conventional practices of dyadic analysis to encompass small-group meetings of patients, family members, and hospital staff. At about the same time, Edward Lazell (1921) lectured to seriously disturbed psychiatric inpatients about Freudian theory and elements of the psychiatric treatment of that era. Lazell noted results similar to those of his predecessors and recommended the use of the didactic model for nearly all categories of hospitalized mental patients.

Alfred Adler (1956) and Rudolph Dreikurs (1959) worked in Europe and expanded Adler's individual therapy model to one of a more collective nature. This system was noteworthy because it advocated including parents in sessions with children who were being seen as patients at the Vienna Child Guidance Center. Dreikurs experimented with the use of group methods in the therapy of both alcoholic patients and general psychiatric patients.

Sigmund Freud (1921) showed interest that went beyond the individual, intrapsychic model common at the time when he became intrigued with the dynamics of large groups. *Group Psychology and the Analysis of the Ego* illuminated much of Freud's view, which was less focused on groups as a method of therapeutic intervention than on the motivation and dynamics of large groups in society.

Modern group techniques subsumed under the heading of psychodrama owe their origins to their founder, Jacob Moreno (1953), whose influence would be enormous in the expansion of the field of group therapy. Moreno's contributions paved the way for several elements that are regular ingredients in modern group practice. Two of the most recognizable points of emphasis are the mobilization and constructive use of intense affect and emotional catharsis in groups and the reactivation of family dynamics and their therapeutic value. Role-playing, alter-ego techniques, and other elements of Moreno's thinking are frequently used in group practice today.

The period encompassing the 1930s up to the onset of World War II included efforts by Paul Schilder (1936) and Louis Wender (1940) that are worthy of note. Both Wender and Schilder understood the untapped potential groups held for the creative expansion of individual psychoanalytic theory and practice. Early efforts at transposing free association, the analysis of transference and resistance, and other staples of classical psychoanalysis to their application in groups characterized the important work done by these pioneering group psychoanalysts.

Samuel Slavson (1943) began work with children in groups. His professional influence on the field of group theory and dynamics was profound in the formative thinking of practitioners in the 1930s through the 1950s. Slavson is generally recognized as one of the founding fathers of contemporary psychodynamically oriented group psychotherapy. His work expanded over the years to include activity group therapy with children and groups involving adolescent delinquents, adults, and families of children who were psychiatrically symptomatic. Slavson was instrumental in the creation of the American Group Psychotherapy Association and the original scientific journals devoted to the group therapies.

THE IMPACT OF WORLD WAR II

In the World War II period, psychotherapists working in the military system, as well as those in civilian life, were deluged with an enormous population in need of psychotherapeutic services and with an array of new psychiatric syndromes that emanated from the war and its physical and psychic carnage. "Shell shock," family disruption and losses, "combat fatigue," the forerunners of present-day posttraumatic stress disorder, and other by-products of war called for immediate and innovative therapies.

The earlier-noted expansion into group work that preceded and paralleled the Second World War offered new options for treating those in need of psychiatric services. Homogeneous groups composed of members who had experienced war-related trauma began to spring up in military hospitals. Self-help groups, outpatient psychotherapy groups, and new efforts designed to combine people with similar conditions in a single therapeutic milieu gave impetus to the expansion of the homogeneous group therapy model both within and outside the military community.

The effort to bridge the span between psychoanalysis and group therapy received great attention through the work of Alexander Wolf and Emanuel Schwartz (1962). Both men believed that it was essential to find group parallels to those techniques they believed were instrumental in helping individuals change through psychoanalysis. In the course of their work, they discovered and composed creative modifications and extensions of the analytic method, capitalizing on the added therapeutic avenues available by having many patients present in the same therapy session.

Wolf and Schwartz originated the leaderless aftersession wherein the group would continue in the absence of the leader and would compare experiences of the two formats in subsequent group meetings. The "go-around" or "round robin," a technique frequently used to open groups, actually began with Wolf's experiments on the use of free association and dream analysis in the group setting.

POST-WORLD WAR II INFLUENCES

At least two social and historical phenomena, the community mental health movement and the Vietnam War, were critical factors in shaping group psychotherapy trends following the post-World War II period. The former effort aimed to reduce the protracted and often inhumane warehousing of psychiatric patients in mental institutions by allowing them to go back to their homes and families. Aside from the economic and political forces that motivated this shift in psychiatric treatment philosophy, the concurrent development of a new generation of psychotropic medications, many of which were being developed in long-acting forms, allowed greater freedom in considering treatment options for seriously impaired psychiatric patients. Contemporary medication groups were born out of this confluence of factors. In addition, therapists became aware of the value of monitoring outpatients in groups as a way of directly observing their interpersonal as well as individual level of function.

The Vietnam War replicated many of the problems seen after World War II and added some new ones. The exponential increase in substance abuse that accompanied the war called upon group therapists to develop effective adaptations of conventional group techniques in order to address drug abuse problems. Large groups, such as therapeutic communities, emerged from this effort. Mutual-help groups derived from 12-step principles, which had long been in existence, experienced a rapid rise in membership and participation. A greater understanding of the components of substance abuse problems led to increased involvement of families in treatment plans, a historical trend directly traceable to Adler and Dreikurs's earlier work.

The other critical postwar influence that had a dramatic presence in group work was the development of family therapy. Nathan Ackerman (1958), a psychoanalyst who was impressed with the power of the family in shaping personality structure, began to see whole families as a means of accelerating diagnosis and intervention in psychological problems. As family therapy grew, so did appreciation of the unique small-group dynamics of working with families. The intersection between group and family therapies is readily apparent in couples groups, multiple-family group psychotherapy, and parenting groups.

The 1960s and 1970s were politically active times, and, as an offshoot of this climate, certain group therapy experiences gained popularity. The encounter and sensitivity movement, designed to use groups as a vehicle for enhanced personal understanding and self-awareness as opposed to a form of psychiatric treatment, flourished during this period. What is perhaps most noteworthy about this point in the life cycle of modern group therapy is that it shed light on the deleterious as well as beneficial aspects of group experiences. Lieberman and Yalom (1972) studied psychological casualties emanating from groups without a membership selection and orientation process and directly related to extremes of group leadership. Their research demonstrated that passive group leaders and "charismatic" group leaders represent the two ends of the leadership spectrum related to poor group outcomes.

Yalom's (1975) later work advocated the usefulness of keeping the focus in the "here and now," based on the assumption that unresolved issues in the lives of group participants will play themselves out in the course of group interactions. The interpersonal manifestations of intrapsychic issues were the tools needed to supply group members with corrective emotional experiences in therapy.

Yalom's scientific rigor and attention to research helped move the group therapy literature away from its subjective and anecdotal form to a more soundly based, documentable view of what actually transpires in groups and what contributes to positive outcomes. Along these lines, Yalom conducted a factor analysis of elements present in groups that have become widely known and used by clinicians. His categorization of "therapeutic" or "curative factors" delineated the natural resources present in all groups that can be harnessed and implemented by group leaders to maximize the chances for success.

THE 1990S

The current decade has been called by many the age of managed care. The emphasis on brevity of treatment and cost containment has led to a wider interest in the use of brief group psychotherapy experiences. The group literature of the 1990s has concerned itself largely with issues related to group treatment outcomes and the stretching of the borders of group therapy to reach untapped patient populations, address differing psychiatric and social conditions, and serve as a vehicle for training and education.

As with many of the earlier-noted trends in the history of group psychotherapy, it appears that circumstance has once again provided a stimulus to which group therapists are responding. While initially there were serious questions regarding the appropriate treatment of patients in time-limited group formats, increased experience with this model is resulting in a clearer appreciation of when, how, and with whom brief group experiences are applicable.

Technical eclecticism is on the rise. The group modality has always been flexible and can accommodate a range of therapeutic interventions. Cognitive, behavioral, family systems, and psychodynamic elements are finding a welcome place in brief group formats. The beneficial spillover of the increased interest in brief group therapies resides in the information that is emerging as this field grows.

Greater clarity is being demanded in defining what therapists actually do in group sessions, what contributes to positive outcomes or creates group dropouts, and how to reproduce methods that appear to work well, along with an emphasis on matching group members with each other and an increased awareness of the value of proper therapist-patient and therapist-group matching.

If past history is any predictor of future trends, then group therapy is currently undergoing yet another metamorphosis. This is likely to result in refined technical interventions, increased understanding of the mechanics and dynamics of groups, and, most important, enhanced provision of sensible and sensitive treatment of patients in groups.

2

Group Therapy:
Definitions and Classification

A clinically oriented definition of group psychotherapy contains several critical elements. A therapy group involves specialized treatment conducted by a professionally trained leader who carefully evaluates and selects members who come together to address their individual psychological problems. Members define themselves as having difficulties that require psychotherapeutic intervention and/or input in order to be successfully resolved. The use of the interpersonal interactions of a group is a central factor in facilitating a process of change in the behavior, self-awareness, and symptoms present in each group member.

Not only is there nothing inherently therapeutic in assembling a random group of individuals, it may in fact be an emotionally hazardous experience. To counter this possibility and to maximize the inherent therapeutic potential of groups, careful attention to group composition and the matching of appropriate leaders to groups is another essential dimension that distinguishes bona fide therapy groups from other experiences transpiring in a group setting and purporting to be "therapeutic."

Since the array of group experiences is so broad, it is essential for the group therapist to have a sense of clarity with respect to the group he or she is leading and where it fits in the overall schema of group work. There are several ways of categorizing groups that help realize this goal. By far the simplest method of gaining an orientation to where a particular group fits in the therapeutic cosmos is to identify the distinguishing characteristics of several major representative group models.

A basic list of commonly used group formats would include the following: psychodynamic group therapy (psychoanalytically oriented group psychotherapy), psychoanalysis in groups, group-centered analytic therapy (group analysis), behavior therapy/cognitive therapy groups, psychodrama groups, self-help/mutual-help groups, structured group experiences, family group therapies, crisis groups, Gestalt therapy groups, confrontational group experiences, transactional analysis groups, existential group therapy, and combined individual and group psychotherapy.

PSYCHODYNAMIC GROUP THERAPY

Psychodynamic group therapy is an insight-oriented form of group psychotherapy that uses and modifies elements of traditional psychoanalysis in conjunction with an analysis of intragroup dynamics. Examination of a member's present life circumstances as well as past history is encouraged. These groups aim at moderate personality reconstruction and generally meet more than once per week.

PSYCHOANALYSIS IN GROUPS

This format is the group counterpart of individual psychoanalysis. Goals are ambitious and include efforts to achieve major changes in personality through the use of a group process involving analysis of transference, resistance, and dreams, along with free association and an extensive interpretation of unconscious conflict. In this model, groups meet as often as three times per week. The leadership posture parallels that of the analyst in dyadic therapies, with no therapist self-disclosure and low levels of therapist activity sufficient to constructing therapeutic group norms and keeping the group centered on its therapeutic goals.

GROUP-CENTERED ANALYTIC THERAPY

Although similar in name only to psychoanalysis in groups, this method is taken in large measure from the work of Wilfred Bion (1977) and involves an effort to use an understanding of the dynamics of the "group as a whole" as the mechanism by which insight and change take place in groups. Currently popular in Europe, group analysis focuses on the in-group transactions of members, an assessment of intragroup tensions, and the reaction of the group to shared stimuli. Leaders decentralize their position and function as participant-observers and interpreters of group phenomena.

BEHAVIOR THERAPY/COGNITIVE THERAPY GROUPS

Groups in this category, which have their theoretical basis in learning theory, attempt to treat psychopathology through application of the principles learned in the group setting. In contrast to other group methods, behavioral groups are largely symptom focused, aiming to change maladaptive behaviors, reduce symptoms, and achieve other, more circumscribed goals. These are often short-term, homogeneously composed groups involving active and directorial group leadership of an educational nature. Common examples are smoking cessation groups, assertiveness training groups, and cognitive therapy groups for depression.

PSYCHODRAMA GROUPS

Psychodrama is a technique developed by J. L. Moreno (1953) in which interpersonal relationships, individual personality conflict, and group dynamics are explored through the use of theatrical methods. The specific elements in the psychodramatic technique are a stage, a subject (patient), a director (therapist), therapeutic aides (auxiliary egos), and an audience. These elements are used in conjunction with a theoretical viewpoint that attempts to promote insight, self-awareness, and individual growth through a group process emphasizing experiential learning and the stimulation of strong emotional experiences.

SELF-HELP/MUTUAL-HELP GROUPS

Groups in this category are leaderless and are composed of members who share a common problem. The goal of the self-help group is to assist participants in understanding and coping with their areas of overlapping concern. These groups are extremely popular and have "therapeutic" benefit for members despite the fact that they are best conceptualized as educational in nature. Members do not define themselves as mentally ill, and there is no treatment contract. Many self-help groups are derived from the 12-step model of Alcoholics Anonymous, although the range of conditions for which mutual help groups are formed extends far beyond substance abuse problems.

STRUCTURED GROUP EXPERIENCES

A wide range of group models, primarily supportive, educational, and non-stressful in nature, are increasingly being used with seriously impaired psychiatric patients both within and outside the hospital. Typical of this group modality are medication groups, problem-solving groups, inpatient community meetings, discussion/education groups, and theme-centered groups. Activity groups, centered around music, art, and poetry as well as physical activities (e.g., dance), are also frequent examples of this modality.

As their label implies, these groups have highly organized boundaries to contain overwhelming emotions and to safeguard the stability of members who may be psychologically fragile. Some of the leadership designs in structured groups are solo, cotherapy, and team leadership composed of several staff members present in the same group experience.

FAMILY GROUP THERAPIES

A variety of methods highlight the intersection between group and family therapies. Inclusion of a point of view derived from general systems and family systems theory adds a dimension to the group that makes it applicable to a wide range of family and marital problems. Groups composed of couples make use of a combination of group and family therapy techniques to address marital issues. Multiple family group psychotherapy features groups (e.g., hospitalized psychiatric patients) composed of several families who share common issues.

CRISIS GROUPS

These are generally short-term group experiences involving the use of peer support, reality testing, and strengthening of preexisting individual defenses to resolve current life crises. Regaining emotional equilibrium through the use of techniques originating in crisis intervention principles forms the core of the group format. After a crisis has been resolved, members are often transferred to another form of therapy more specifically geared to deal with their primary personality diagnosis as opposed to the crisis situation of the moment.

GESTALT THERAPY GROUPS

Gestalt therapy, developed by Fritz Perls (1969), aims to treat the whole person in a biological, perceptual, and interpersonal context. In order to accomplish this, the group concerns itself with the sensory awareness of members in the present rather than information from the past. Gestalt groups commonly make use of exercises, role-playing, and techniques designed to mobilize strong affect and to promote individual growth and development.

CONFRONTATIONAL GROUP EXPERIENCES

Groups of this nature use group pressure in an effort to change maladaptive behaviors members regard as ego syntonic. Most often, these techniques are reserved for interventions with individuals exhibiting intractable, rigid, and long-standing attitudinal and behavioral patterns. Emotional deprivation and intense leader-to-member and member-to-member confrontations are key elements. The substance abuse field has been the main area involving regular use of such group models. Therapeutic community settings for the treatment of addiction (e.g., Synanon, Daytop Village) are perhaps the best-known versions of the confrontational group model.

TRANSACTIONAL ANALYSIS GROUPS

In this group method, which applies theoretical constructs from transactional analysis in a group matrix, each session involves an exclusive focus on intragroup transactions. Observations of group interactions are used to elucidate four major areas deemed critical by exponents of transactional analysis groups: parent, child, and adult ego states; interpersonal game analysis; "life script" analysis; and insight into the motivational basis of members' emotional distress.

Although these groups were at the peak of their popularity in the encounter and sensitivity group climate of the 1960s and 1970s, there are still many active proponents of this orientation. Elements emanating from transactional analysis groups have been found to be of value when incorporated as a component of more technically eclectic group formats.

EXISTENTIAL GROUP THERAPY

This form of group therapy is focused in the present and endeavors to help members with shared concerns about aspects of living. Themes related to death, the meaning of one's life, ambiguous and ambivalent states of mind, personal values, and other aspects common to the human condition are focal points for exploration in these experiential groups.

The existential point of view values appropriate use of confrontational interventions and the development of strong feeling experiences in group sessions. Leaders and members participate in similar ways by sharing insights and emotions that help shed light on existential issues. These groups place a high priority on enhancing effective communication, expressing oneself authentically, and stimulating individual thinking and personal growth.

COMBINED INDIVIDUAL AND GROUP PSYCHOTHERAPY

Many conditions require more than either group or individual therapies alone can supply. The simultaneous treatment of a patient in both one-to-one and group therapy is commonly referred to as "combined therapy." The therapy may be conducted by the same therapist or by two separate therapists. Professional colleagues must regularly communicate with each other to ensure comprehensive coordination of a treatment plan for the patient and to safeguard against "splitting" (playing one therapist against another) when more than one therapist is involved in treating a patient.

A patient with a personality disorder may use individual therapy to focus on intrapsychic issues and can apply the insights gained in therapy and experiment with new modes of behavior in the safe and controlled interpersonal setting of the group. Groups are often concentrated on themes of appropriate interaction with peers and authority figures, constructive expression of intense feelings (e.g., anger), and enhanced reality testing (to counter irrational beliefs and socially deviant behavior).

CLASSIFICATION OF THERAPEUTIC GROUPS

The proliferation of group therapy has been so dramatic that it can be confusing to therapists and patients alike. As a result, it is essential that group leaders have a simple way of thinking about and categorizing their group work. A brief and systematized template for therapists should include at least the following four dimensions of therapy groups: (a) theoretical orientation of the therapist, (b) composition of the group, (c) time factors, and (d) issues related to group size and membership.

Theoretical Orientation

The leader's prevailing therapeutic school of thought directly influences the construction and conduct of the group. While it is critical that group therapists be

BASIC PRINCIPLE 1

It is always safest to assume that groups contain many more differences than initially meet the eye. While it is tempting to categorize groups along the lines of formal definitions, this rarely holds in actual practice. Since there is an ever-increasing trend toward combining elements of several techniques in the same group, the lines between defined schools of group practice are becoming less precise. Still, it is helpful for the group therapist to have a sense of what he or she is drawing upon in constructing each group experience.

For example, a group for women with eating disorders will consist of the following:

- elements from behavioral therapy groups (to gain control over dysfunctional eating patterns)
- psychoeducational elements (to establish a common baseline of accurate information among members and to transmit the findings from the latest research in the field)
- supportive ingredients (to build group cohesion and to promote retention of group members during emotionally trying times in the recovery process)
- psychodynamic techniques (aimed at attaining greater levels of personal understanding in terms of the motives underlying the genesis of eating disorders)
- a family focus (aimed at fostering an appreciation of the role of the family in the creation of symptoms and involving the family in constructive therapeutic interventions)
- an emphasis on homogeneous themes (particularly those related to gender and the pressure on women in contemporary society, along with similarities in the problem sets of group members)
- combined individual therapies (to augment and expedite gains made in therapy)
- confrontational methods (to combat avoidant behavior and resistance to change)
- structured group experiences (such as exercises that enhance personal awareness and bring concealed issues out into the open more readily)
- elements from crisis groups (initially aiming to stabilize a patient and help her make a smooth entry into group therapy)
- co-leadership (to enhance opportunities for role modeling by the therapists, one or both of whom may have had eating disorders themselves)
- simultaneous participation in 12-step-derived self-help groups (such as Overeaters Anonymous) and the primary therapy group.

Even in ostensibly homogeneous groups such as the one just mentioned, the variations among members, leaders, stage of recovery, motivation for treatment, family circumstances, ethnicity, religion, socioeconomic status, level of psychological-mindedness, psychotropic medication status, and a host of other factors are at play in all groups. The astute clinician assesses these variables and creates a treatment plan that covers as many as are relevant to the attainment of individual treatment goals.

flexible in designing their groups, it is usually the case that a leader has a formal or informal theoretical orientation with which he or she feels most comfortable and believes to be an efficacious way to lead a group.

The value of understanding the leader's therapeutic viewpoint is evident in the enhanced ability an informed leader has in communicating clearly and unambiguously with prospective group members. Many people interested in joining groups are anxious and curious about what will actually transpire in group sessions. The leader can allay unnecessary fears by providing an orientation for members. This member orientation relies heavily on the group leader's therapeutic belief system and can be conveyed to new members in a succinct manner.

The advantages of being clear with oneself and with group members are often reflected in a reduction of the group dropout rate, particularly during the period between screening and entry into the group. Information disseminated in a discussion emanating from the group therapist's prevailing theoretical model can help in addressing incoming members' concerns about how active the leader will or will not be, how group therapy is different from individual approaches or other group experiences a member may have had, and why the leader is planning to conduct the group along whatever theoretical model he or she has chosen.

The similarities and differences among several representative psychotherapeutic orientations to group therapy and how they influence actual clinical practice are illustrated in Table 2.1.

Issues Related to Group Composition

The composition of the group is one of the central determinants of its therapeutic destiny. Groups that are composed for specific purposes require a membership likely to facilitate realization of goals.

Perhaps the single most important issue referable to group composition centers around the balance between homogeneous and heterogeneous factors in the selection of members. Most groups are actually heterogeneous with respect to factors such as age, gender, ethnicity, socioeconomic background, history of prior psychotherapy, religion, and vocation. Heterogeneous elements or differences among members set the stage for group interaction, exploration of the baseline group tension arising when members recognize their differences, and an opportunity for learning and emotional growth through observation and interaction with people who have dissimilar behavioral patterns.

Similarities among members (homogeneous factors) are essential in all groups in order to set the stage for the development of group cohesion and the support elements present in therapeutic groups. At times, it makes sense to compose a group that is heavily weighted in the direction of similarities among participants. Brief therapy groups are a prime example of contemporary group approaches that rely on homogeneity of membership. The similarities among members in short-term groups facilitate a more rapid group induction phase, since all members share a common set of life issues, and less ambiguity among members as to why they have been selected for a particular group.

Homogeneous group composition is also evident in the descriptive label attached to a given group. Many groups are described homogeneously in conversation among therapists, denoting the fact that the commonalities among members are necessary if the group's goals are to be accomplished. A few examples of groups that make use of their homogeneous properties are adolescent groups, married couples groups, groups for medically ill individuals, depression groups, groups for drug addiction, groups for adult survivors of abuse, and college student groups.

Table 2.1. Comparison of major group therapy orientations

	Supportive group therapy	Psychodynamic group therapy	Self-help groups	Cognitive/behavioral group therapy
Frequency	1–5 times/week	1–2 times/week	7 days/week	1–3 times/week
Individual screening interview	Usually	Always	None	Always
Group size	8–15 members	5–9 members	No size limits	5–10 members
Goals	Better adaptation to daily living	Reconstruction of personality dynamics	Social support	Relief of specific symptoms
Indications	Crisis situations; severe emotional problems	Neuroses; mild personality disorders	Shared life circumstances and problems	Phobias; anxiety disorders; stress management
Group composition	Homogeneous for level of psychopathology	Balance of similarities and differences	Homogeneous	Homogeneous for similar symptoms
Group focus	"Here and now"; family, vocational, environmental factors	Past and present; intragroup and extragroup dynamics	Education; emotional "sharing"	Training members in specific methods to control symptoms
Use of confrontation	No	Yes	No	Rarely
Therapist activity	Actively structures and leads the group	Active around interpretation	No formal group leader	Very active in teaching skills to group members
Extragroup contacts	Encouraged	Prohibited or discouraged	Encouraged; formal peer sponsorship programs	Discouraged
Transference	Not analyzed	Used extensively	Not analyzed	Not relevant
Therapeutic factors	Cohesion; universality; reality testing; instillation of hope; imparting information	Cohesion; catharsis; family replay; interpersonal learning	Cohesion; universality; education; peer support	Cohesion; universalization; education; reinforcement

Time Factors in Group Therapies

The time factor yields significant information relative to the goals and format of a group. Time, in this context, refers to the actual length of each therapy session and to the duration of the group experience over the course of time. Generally speaking, the group parallel of the "50-minute hour" in individual psychotherapy is the 1.5-hour meeting.

Modifications in the length of each session are made in special circumstances in which a longer or shorter time element is more tailored to the needs of the group. A case in point is the 1-hour or 45-minute meeting of a group of hospitalized psychotic patients. A 90-minute meeting is probably beyond the adaptive capacity of most seriously impaired psychiatric inpatients.

Session time extensions are not as commonly used today. Historically, extensions were used in unique circumstances when it was believed that a longer time period would help in breaking down maladaptive defenses of group members. Fatigue, a group climate of emotional withholding, and increased opportunities to see many repetitions of rigid interactional patterns formed part of the rationale for expanding the time frame of the session.

Time-extended groups can range in duration from 3-hour double sessions to weekend-long "marathon" sessions. Many nonpsychotherapeutic groups have co-opted the group therapy model and used the time extension of sessions to further their particular interests. Large groups such as E.S.T., Lifespring, and other "self-actualization" models usually incorporate longer sessions into their programs. Despite the enthusiasm voiced by proponents of time-extended models, there is no scientific evidence that increasing the time frame of a group increases its benefit. Moreover, there is a literature that clearly points to the dangers of time-extended groups, particularly when a group is large in size (e.g., 20 to 100 participants) and there is no pregroup screening for psychiatric illness or vulnerability.

Issues Related to Group Membership

The critical variables concerning group membership are whether or not the group is open or closed to new membership during its therapeutic course and the size of the group.

Fixed membership (closed) groups begin and end with the same membership. If patients drop out, they are not replaced, since this interferes with the group process in a way that is counter to the group goals. Open membership groups are usually longer term groups involving a turnover in membership. When members leave, either through dropping out or successfully completing their therapeutic agenda, they are replaced.

Broadly speaking, brief therapy groups with fixed memberships are geared toward symptom removal, acquisition of specific interpersonal skills, common life cycle or adult developmental issues experienced by members, and a set of similar psychological problems present in all group members. Open-ended, longer term groups that accept new members have more ambitious goals approximating those of psychodynamically oriented individual psychotherapy. Groups in this category strive for the acquisition of intrapsychic and interpersonal insight, place value on the understanding of members' past experiences, attempt to increase self-awareness and empathy for others, and explore group manifestations of significant family behaviors and attitudes.

Group size is the other treatment consideration that helps define the scope of a group. According to the group literature, interactional groups led by a single therapist ideally range from five to nine members. Groups of fewer than five members are too small and lack the potential for interaction. Groups of more than nine are viewed as too large to permit effective group management and to keep a group theme in focus as a result of the competition among members, many of whom have urgent issues to discuss.

Groups can be of larger size when there is more than one leader or when the purpose is something other than interactional group psychotherapy. In groups that commonly involve co-leadership (couples groups, adolescent groups) or those led by teams composed of more than two therapists (multiple family groups), the therapeutic workload can be divided among group leaders, thereby permitting a larger group constituency.

Large groups for educational or training purposes or for purposes of disseminating standardized information to patients can be much larger in size as well. The inpatient community meeting is perhaps the best-known example of this group type. With all ward staff and patients together, therapists can address administrative issues, manage potential crisis situations that occur while patients are hospitalized, conduct didactic sessions (e.g., on topics such as new psychotropic medications), and monitor the progress of individuals as measured by their ability, or lack thereof, to participate in large group meetings.

Once the therapist has arrived at a satisfactory understanding of the location of his or her group along the spectrum outlined here (i.e., theoretical model, group composition, time factors, and group size), the actual process of accumulating, evaluating, and preparing prospective group members can begin on a firm foundation. Subsequent chapters are pragmatically focused. Tracking the path taken by therapist and group member in the actual clinical course of a group from start to finish affords an ideal means of explicating what transpires and creates a process that leads to a successful therapeutic experience for the patient and a meaningful professional experience for the therapist.

3

Basic Clinical Principles
of Group Psychotherapy

Prior to a discussion of the application of group techniques, it is necessary to consider a few general principles that influence psychotherapy groups. All effective groups share a minimum of three critical elements:

1. A group leader who possesses an ability to be appropriately active in the group. The form and timing of the leader's activity vary according to the composition of the group but must be based on a firm grounding in group theory and in individual and group dynamics.
2. Careful attention to pregroup evaluation, selection, and preparation of prospective group members.
3. Sound group composition and organization, along with a clear sense of the goals of the group. A therapeutic plan that implements the process of change is an essential component in helping to actualize the goals formulated for both the group as a whole and each individual member.

In order to reach a point of success in group treatment, each group therapist is charged with the task of thoughtfully creating an experience that will be helpful to all participants. There are several avenues available to the group leader in the service of simplifying his or her mission. One of the most basic, but crucial, starting points lies within the group leader's understanding of what is unique about psychotherapy groups and what "natural therapeutic resources" are available to the therapeutic endeavor.

Yalom (1985) developed a simple and widely used system to conceptualize the therapeutic properties of groups. He conducted a factor analysis of a long list of inherent group properties and categorized those elements that were similar or clustered together naturally into a brief format that he termed the "curative factors" present in groups. A group leader's understanding of therapeutic factors through the use of Yalom's criteria or some other model is a sine qua non for the eventual success of any psychotherapy group.

An understanding of the therapeutic factors present in groups helps clarify basic group dynamics. The focus in this section is on the value to the leader who appreciates the application of these elements in composing and conducting groups. In that spirit, it is helpful to review the therapeutic factors with an emphasis on their utility in facilitating the task of group leadership for the practicing clinician.

Groups are valuable as a mechanism for the dissemination of information. The form this takes is widespread in contemporary group practice. In psychoeducational groups (e.g., those composed of patients with schizophrenia or major affective disorder), there is a didactic component to help educate patients, families, and significant others about the primary psychiatric condition. Sex education groups and preventive group work for substance abuse also rely heavily on the principle of education through the group as a preventive measure.

With increased appreciation of the use of groups in the treatment of medically ill patients has come a greater respect for the value of educating people about health- and illness-related issues. AIDS awareness groups and homogeneous groups for postmyocardial infarction patients are two present-day examples of this therapeutic factor in action. Education on the causes, course, and treatment of medical conditions is a central ingredient in the psychotherapeutic management of patients with physical illness. Techniques such as stress management, relaxation training, and information about diet, nutrition, and safe exercise are regular instructional elements in such groups.

It is interesting to note that the use of teaching through the small and large group is widely accepted today. Historically, this was not the case. Objections came from those with a predominantly psychoanalytic orientation, who feared that a leadership posture of educator would interfere with the development of transference and other membership experiences deemed essential for psychoanalytic work. Modern group therapy, even that of a psychoanalytically oriented nature, has come to respect the value of having an informed group membership. Education of a group by mental health and/or medical personnel does not obliterate anxiety completely, nor does it prevent the development of strong feelings between members and therapists. Rather, an informed group can more rapidly focus on its task, not becoming detoured owing to misconceptions, myths, and fears originating out of ignorance.

The therapeutic value of instilling hope in group members, the second of Yalom's curative factors, cannot be overemphasized. The sense of realistic hopefulness that emanates from a strong sense of positive group morale is invaluable to many group members. A cardinal feature noted among depressed patients in particular is their sense of futility about the future. If, for example, a new patient suffering from depression presents a despairing picture of her or his life to the group, other members who themselves have been depressed and are at the point of recovery can have immense therapeutic impact in a way that no leader can: by sharing their personal experiences with the new member.

One caveat about the role played by hope is that it must never be equated with giving group members false reassurance. In spite of a leader's good intentions, reassurance that is not predicated on a sound clinical basis can be harmful to patients. Unfortunate examples abound in which leaders, in the spirit of trying to "cheer patients up" or as a countertransferential response to their own feelings of therapeutic futility, take an unrealistically optimistic stance, unwittingly setting members up for eventual disappointment when the rosy promises are not realized.

Realistic support, hope for positive change, and promises of good treatment outcomes must be offered sparingly and based only on documentable clinical data. Otherwise, there is the risk for endorsement of what some have cynically labeled "cheerleader" therapy. The hopeful feelings that emerge from strong cohesion in a group with clear goals and strong leadership represent a phenomenon quite different from false reassurance.

The feeling of universality that comes from being a part of a group in which others struggle with the same problems is yet another potential resource present in all groups. One of the immediate benefits to members that comes from recognition of the universal nature of emotional difficulties is the accompanying sense of destigmatization of people who are defined as psychologically impaired. Participation as a member of a group counters feelings of low self-esteem, uniqueness, or freakishness and allows members to feel less isolated. Patients with serious mental or medical illness often report the sense of acceptance and relief from feelings of shame or embarrassment that comes from being in a therapeutic setting with others who share similar conditions.

Psychiatric patients who are withdrawn and, as a consequence, lack an interpersonal network can be helped to establish embryonic emotional bonds with other people who find themselves in similar life circumstances. Depressed patients, psychotic patients, and group members with a schizoid personality style are commonly the types of people who find the similarities among group members to be of comfort.

Therapeutic group experiences involve a sense of altruism as well. The therapeutic benefit that accompanies one person's ability to help another is visible in virtually every group meeting. For many people, the therapy group becomes the first place in their lives where they experience their interpersonal impact on others. Those with low self-esteem and poor self-images tend to minimize or negate the effect they have on other people. The group offers an opportunity for people to see their influence on others.

The mechanisms by which altruism manifests itself in group therapy can take the form of advice giving, sharing of personal experiences, and modeling of altruistic behavior on the part of an empathic group leader. The advantages of altruistic behavior are considerable; as in the case of instillation of hope, however, a word of caution is also in order. The potential pitfall of excessive reliance on altruism as a central therapeutic goal is that there are specific clinical situations in which this may backfire.

The most common example occurs when leaders decide to include a higher functioning member in a lower functioning group. Initially, the member benefits from the help and comfort he or she can give to the other group members. The posture of this member is more leaderlike than memberlike and creates a lopsidedness to the group experience for all concerned. When functioning more like a cotherapist by default, the altruistic member can give but cannot receive from the group. While this is less visible in the early stages of the group, sooner or later the altruistic member or the group leader begins to question how much benefit can be derived from the persistence of this group imbalance.

When discontent is member initiated, it often comes in the form of the following question: "I know I can be helpful to others, but what am I going to get from the group?" At times, the leader will confront members who hide behind altruism as a defense against accepting their patient role in the group. In either case, group leaders have to be on the alert for errors made in composing groups that result in a "one-way street" for altruistic group members.

Sometimes changes in the actual group composition are required to rectify the situation. The leader must make an astute clinical judgment as to whether the altruistic stance represents resistance to the group and, if so, whether to handle it by interpretation, confrontation, or some combination of the two. In this instance, the member would be retained in the group, and the issue of the patient's rigid role definition (exemplified by the one-dimensional altruistic posture) would be worked through as part of his or her group agenda. If, on the other hand, the impasse originated from a leadership error in composing the group, the circumstance is probably best dealt with by removing the altruistic member, referring him or her to a more suitably composed group, and resolving the issues attached to the departure of the member with the remaining group members.

The replay of feelings stemming from the families of origin of group members provides the substrate upon which many psychodynamic groups are built. There are countless possibilities for the reactivation of unresolved family issues stimulated by the emergence of new relationships in the group. Commonly accepted views such as the therapy group as a "second chance family" attest to the power group experiences hold for the evocation of difficulties that are in-group dramatizations of the family legacies of group members.

Developing social skills forms an inherent part of every group. Whether it is the primary goal of the group or simply a positive by-product of groups with broader agendas, the acquisition of greater comfort in interpersonal settings is at the heart of the advantages of group therapies over many other psychotherapeutic interventions. Responsibly constructed groups offer an opportunity for patients to be involved in an ongoing experience with other people in a setting that is safe and controlled. Groups can provide increased opportunities for reality testing through consensus on particular issues. Similarly, the added options for interpersonal feedback result in group members having a greater ability to obtain a cross section of responses to their perceptions and productions.

The clinical value of the social dimension of group therapy can be seen on several fronts in actual clinical practice. In work with seriously impaired psychiatric patients, socialization groups can be essential to the recovery and rehabilitative process. Chronically psychotic patients can be placed in social support groups that provide them with a sense of being interpersonally anchored during emotionally trying times. Specific social skills training modules of a behaviorally oriented nature can easily be incorporated into in-hospital or outpatient groups of chronic psychiatric patients.

Higher functioning group patients make use of the social atmosphere present in groups. For many, the group is a place where they can discover and practice appropriate modes of social interaction that are then transposed into the lives of members outside of the group. Here again, as with many of the other therapeutic factors noted earlier in this chapter, the leader must be clear on the form, frequency, and content of the social interactions among group members to avoid misuse of this core dimension of groups.

Socialization outside of the formal group session can function in concert with group goals or can be viewed as acting-out behavior, depending on the group in which it occurs. In outpatient groups of severely ill patients, members are encouraged to exchange addresses and phone numbers so that they can "check in" with one another prior to a group session and, in a situation in which one member feels too immobilized to attend, make arrangements to accompany the depressed

BASIC PRINCIPLE 2

Always be aware that there are *multiple* simultaneous levels of transference operating in any therapy group. An unparalleled value of group therapy is that it enhances work with family issues on many levels. In psychodynamically oriented groups, family analysis provides the mainstay of many group interventions. As an example, the insight-oriented group leader works on the multiple dimensions of transference that manifest themselves through the group interaction. Three predominant modes of working with transference in psychodynamic groups are as follows:

1. *Horizontal transference:* This refers to feelings on the part of group members toward one another. These peer-based emotions usually have their origin in sibling relations in the primary family. Members who express anger toward fellow group members may well be projecting competitive feelings based in their sibling relationships onto the interaction in the "here and now" of the group.
2. *Vertical transference:* Intense reactions of members to the group leader are referred to as transferences that occur in a vertical direction. Understandably, although these can be some of the most powerful emotions expressed in the group interplay, they usually predate the group and are traceable to feelings originally aimed at parents. Unresolved issues with power, control, and authority are commonly worked on at the level of vertical transference.
3. *Therapist countertransference:* Since ongoing groups catalyze powerful emotions in members, the group climate is often supercharged with affect. No one in the group, including the leader, is immune to these group pressures. The therapist's variation on the transference theme is called countertransference.

When groups complain that their leader is too passive or when the leader is under attack, strong emotions are certain to be stirred in the therapist. Leaders' awareness of their own reactions and ability to differentiate group phenomena from their personal blind spots form the basis for their reaction to the group process. When leaders are clear as to the origins of feelings directed at them, they are in a position to add another dimension to the group by therapeutically using their countertransference.

A clinical case in point is as follows. A leader who was new to groups was excessively concerned about being "liked" by the group. In the initial phase of the group, the leader unwittingly steered participants away from any themes that would challenge his competence or arouse anger, and he was overly careful about using confrontational interventions for fear that this practice would make him appear "punitive and hostile." Upon reflection, the leader realized that the origin of his need to be idealized by the group antedated this therapy situation. His own past (including a set of parents who withheld approval and taught that negative emotions were to be avoided at all costs) was dovetailing with group interactions and made him vulnerable to this countertransferential pitfall.

The point of understanding the varied ways in which family-based emotions manifest themselves in the group is to help members resolve the emotional loose ends that interfere with the satisfactory conduct of their lives in the present. If this is to occur, it is not sufficient for the leader to merely unmask or decode intragroup transference phenomena. This is only the first step in a process that aims to create attitudinal and behavioral change for members in a more realistic way.

Once a member finds out that he or she is carrying excessive amounts of unexpressed anger originating from a dysfunctional family model, the leader has to structure the group so that the member gains an ability to learn appropriate modes of expression of anger, locate appropriate targets for such feelings, and develop enough empathy to appreciate the impact of what he or she is expressing on the feelings of the recipient.

The ability to combine insight into one's problems with the experiential aspects of learning that occur through group interaction, along with an alternative mode of conflict resolution, distinguishes an emotional experience in the group from a therapeutic experience that extends to the patient's life outside the group.

member to the meeting. In contrast to this constructive use of extramural socialization among group members are instances in which contact outside the group runs counter to group goals.

An example of improper use of social contact outside of the group is as follows. Two members of a men's substance abuse group, one early in recovery and the other with longer term sobriety, went out for dinner after a group meeting. The second member described his desire to have a drink before dinner and ordered one. He justified this by stating that his real problem drugs were marijuana and cocaine, both of which he had not used for 2 years. Alcohol, he felt, was in a different and milder category, and he felt "entitled" to a social drink on rare occasions. This was profoundly upsetting to the newer group member, who looked up to the "elder statesman" of the group and felt disappointed and alarmed by his casual attitude toward alcohol consumption.

This example is an illustration of socialization between group members being used in a fashion completely at variance with the norms and purpose of a substance abuse group. In maintaining control over group behavior, the leader must have a ready reference point to discriminate between the therapeutic potential of social elements in the group and those undermining behaviors that are rationalized as being therapeutic in a true social sense. Rapid intervention is critical in situations in which members mask unresolved individual and/or group issues under the guise of "socializing." Options for managing problems in terms of the social dimension of the group are discussed later in this volume when group leadership is the focus.

Another advantage of group therapy is apparent in the opportunity for group members to be exposed to the thinking and actions of others who differ from themselves. This increases the options for learning through observation in the group. Members are encouraged to borrow from one another in the hope of expanding their interpersonal repertoire.

Role modeling by the group leader is a common example of the employment of this principle. Equally important is the role of peers in the group. Members regularly "try out" behaviors demonstrated by the leader and other group members, tailoring these behaviors to fit their own needs. Withdrawn, schizoid, or inhibited members can make valuable use of what they see demonstrated by others in the group. When Yalom consolidated his list of therapeutic factors, he referred to this phenomenon as imitative behavior. The term is an apt one since it simultaneously identifies a key aspect of groups and describes the process by which it takes place. Group members initially tend to observe the leader and may first show signs of imitative behavior mirroring that of the leader. The desirable elements of this process become apparent when members imitate aspects of the leader's posture in the group. Members who become more self-reflective, more empathic, and less likely to act precipitously are echoing therapist behaviors that are in concert with the group's norms.

A humorous, but unmistakable, example of the presence of imitative behavior in action occurred in a men's group. This long-term outpatient group was co-led by two male therapists, both of whom happened to have full beards and smoked cigars. Not long into the life of this group, an "epidemic of hirsutism" and rampant cigar smoking broke out among six of the eight members. There was no doubt about the origin of these new actions taken by group members. On a more serious level, this example merely makes concrete what happens in both overt and subtle ways in groups in which members therapeutically borrow from the broad range of options personified in the group.

Psychodynamic psychotherapists of all theoretical persuasions value insight and learning as essential to the process of therapy. Group therapy expands opportunities for the acquisition of insight and for enhanced learning. Many feel that these factors form the cornerstone for personality change in psychotherapy. The situation is complex enough when working with one person in individual therapy. In groups, the level of complexity increases as a result of the presence of many members; however, the therapeutic avenues for change that are available to the attentive group therapist increase as well.

Learning in groups takes place on several simultaneous levels. This is most easily illustrated in the psychodynamically oriented, open-ended group format. Group members have the chance to learn about the motivational basis for their behavior, acquire insight into the familial origins of their current problems, and have a rare chance for experiential learning through their ongoing relationships with the group members and the group leader.

Greater personal awareness comes about through the multiple levels of transference present in groups and from the interpretations and feedback from other members and the leader. While many of the components of how patients acquire knowledge through the group process are difficult to define, suffice it to say that the amount of input available to participants is enormous. In groups where the acquisition of intrapsychic and interpersonal insight is a major goal, the group setting offers a unique confluence of therapeutic resources that contribute toward this end.

Group cohesion is the glue that bonds members together for a common purpose. Cohesion is essential to all group experiences and is particularly important in the early stages of the group. The positive feeling that develops toward the group and its members forms the foundation for group cohesion. Strictly speaking, group cohesion is not a change unto itself but, as Yalom initially noted, a precondition for change without which the subsequent stages necessary for group development will be aborted.

The attainment of rapid group cohesion is a necessity in brief group therapy. In longer term groups, cohesion sets the stage for support, emotional sharing, and self-disclosure. In groups composed of seriously ill psychiatric patients, an embryonic feeling of group cohesion permits members to tolerate the stresses and anxieties they experience during sessions. In all groups, the value of sound group cohesion cannot be underestimated.

Good group therapists are clear on what constitutes group cohesion. Group cohesiveness acts as a layer of protection for members, functioning like an emotional shock absorber and counterbalancing inappropriate or ill-timed interactions. There are times, however, when other group phenomena mimic cohesion.

In the instance of a couples group, it is often difficult to distinguish genuine group cohesiveness from other similar processes. It is safe to assume that almost all members entering a new group have considerable apprehension about the experience. In groups composed of dyads, the preexisting relationship between partners may be dysfunctional but is familiar to them. In response to anxieties related to group entry, many couples hide behind their relationship as an avoidance mechanism. In other words, it feels more comfortable to "huddle" with the partner behind the protection of the relationship than to risk exposure in the group. Huddling in fear, a form of pseudocohesion, is a resistance to group involvement. Since the group consists of people involved in established relationships, it is more difficult for the leader to differentiate whether or not true cohesion has been attained or if couples are merely seeking safety by closing ranks with each other.

When a state of true cohesion has been reached in a couples group, there are signposts for the leader that help document this process. The communication patterns in cohesive couples groups cease to be restricted from partner to partner within the confines of the relationship (side-to-side communication) and are introduced into the arena of the whole group. When cohesion is present, members talk across relationship lines (interactive communication) and, in so doing, make their relationship open for observation and discussion in the group.

A clinical rule of thumb is that the leader should not engage in anxiety-promoting interventions until a firm sense of group cohesion exists. To do so is to risk premature dropouts from the group and/or damage to the therapeutic alliance between members and the therapist. Once true group cohesiveness is in place, the peer support elements from member to member bolster participants and create a group climate of low risk for untoward emotional reactions. Time invested in establishing cohesive binds among group members is invaluable to the leader in plotting a successful treatment course.

One final resource that forms a central component of many group experiences is the power of therapy groups to unleash affect. Emotional catharsis in groups parallels its individual psychotherapeutic counterpart, except it is often more intense. Because of the presence of a leader and other members, an individual in group therapy receives a type of interpersonal response that is not possible in traditional individual approaches. Interaction with other members can lead to an escalating pattern of emotional expression in the group session. Depending on the purpose and composition of the group, this affective intensification can be either a benefit or a hazard to the therapeutic process.

In groups where members rely heavily on psychological defense mechanisms such as intellectualization, isolation of affect, and denial, mobilization and proper channeling of affect is an integral part of the therapeutic agenda. The converse is the case in groups with members who have histories of poor impulse control, emotional dysregulation, mood swings, and a history of overwhelmingly strong affect leading to a worsening of their psychological state.

Group leaders must be cautious not to get caught in the trap of believing that the primary goal of group therapy is to release pent-up emotions. This caricature of group therapy ignores the importance of the balance between intellectual understanding and emotional experience in producing therapeutic results. A dramatic clinical example illustrates the potential harm of lopsided emphasis on emotional expression or a "letting it all hang out" approach to group treatment.

In an outpatient group of recently discharged hospitalized psychiatric patients, the following scene took place between two group members. One of these individuals was a schizophrenic female patient who lived at home with 20 cats. Another group member complained bitterly that the "cat lady" went on endlessly talking about her animals and that this was getting "boring" and she did not want to listen to any more of it. Upon hearing this, the first patient took immediate offense and became visibly upset and started shaking. She responded by communicating a direct threat to the second member, stating her intention to bring a large pair of scissors to the next group meeting and stab the member who made the insensitive remark.

The group was frightened and in a state of shock. They turned to the co-leaders for help at this critical juncture. Efforts on the leaders' parts to reduce the emotional intensity in the session were unsuccessful, and the schizophrenic patient remained severely agitated when it was time to end the session. The therapists asked the patient to remain after the meeting in the hopes of decompressing some of the overwhelming rage that had consumed her. These efforts were to no avail, and it was necessary to rehospitalize the woman directly from the group session.

Stimulating affect for affect's sake alone is a common misapplication of the therapeutic value of mobilizing, labeling, and appropriately expressing feelings of all kinds in therapeutic groups. Anger and intimacy form the two poles of the spectrum of feelings many group members need to work on as part of their therapeutic plan. The group leader who is not fearful of affect, is aware of what it triggers in his or her own life, and can plan controlled and safe interventions for participants offers members of the group the promise of a true therapeutic emotional experience.

The therapeutic or curative factors potentially present in therapy groups represent one of many systematized ways of helping leaders comprehend the components of group experiences. One of the advantages for the therapist in conceptualizing the key factors available in the group is that it allows for more effective treatment planning. Group therapists can construct a therapeutic climate that draws upon the therapeutic factors deemed most relevant to the goals of the group. The combination of ingredients in a treatment recipe created by the group leader is influenced by the group's composition, the context in which the group is conducted, the overarching group purpose, and the theoretical school of thought of the therapist.

Once the group leader has a grasp of essential group properties and group dynamics, the next step in the clinical setting is to evaluate and assemble a group of people who make sense as participants in a common experience that will help them in dealing with whatever life issues prompted their desire for psychological assistance. How the group therapist operationalizes his or her understanding of basic group principles and converts that knowledge into the composition of an effective psychotherapy group is the next logical step in clinical work.

Chapter 4 addresses the ''nuts and bolts'' issues involved in evaluating and preparing new members for entry into the group, screening out people for whom group therapy may be poorly timed or contraindicated, and composing a group that is most likely to achieve its purpose. The role of the leader, so essential to this process, is highlighted. Membership issues that bear upon group selection and composition also form a component of the material to follow.

4

Constructing an Effective Psychotherapy Group

The first step in constructing a psychotherapy group is the initial interview of a prospective group member.

INITIAL INTERVIEW ISSUES

The first contact with a candidate for group therapy is similar to that with an individual psychotherapy patient. The therapist is charged with the task of collecting a great deal of information in a short span of time. The group therapy interview includes an individual evaluation along with an assessment of interpersonal skills. In this respect, the initial interview requires that the therapist have a format in mind in order to glean as much relevant information as possible from the patient in the time allotted.

In an ideal clinical situation, the therapist has the option of deciding how many meetings are necessary to perform a complete evaluation and has the time available as necessary. Realistically, most therapists in actual clinical practice do not have the luxury of limitless time and are restricted to a single session in which they must screen, select, and prepare incoming group members.

Depending on the clinical context, the evaluator may or may not be the person who will also be leading the group. Many outpatient clinic settings involve a separate subdivision that manages initial intake and disposition of patients. Under these circumstances, the initial interview is conducted by someone other than the group leader. There are many advantages and several important disadvantages attached to this commonly employed model.

The independent evaluator has the freedom to pursue almost any topic with the patient in the first interview. This permits the evaluator to include elements of a stress interview as part of the process if such items would be helpful in making a more specific referral for treatment. The problem that unfortunately exists in many clinic and institutional settings that use an independent evaluator as the initial interviewer is that not all evaluators are as familiar with group therapies as they are with individual therapies. In fact, it is not uncommon for a skilled interviewer with an individual therapy orientation to tend to refer ''healthier'' patients to long-term psychodynamic individual psychotherapy. Many higher functioning patients who would do well in groups are funneled off to therapies other than group, and lower functioning patients become the bulk of those referred for group treatment.

Two significant problems that may emerge as an offshoot of the independent evaluator model are a "downward drift" of more seriously impaired patients into group therapy and a skewed view of the proper indications for referral to groups. Both of these issues are troublesome from the standpoint of treatment and education.

Reserving group referral for patients who have a history of being refractory to other psychotherapeutic interventions and for those who have a history of poor interpersonal function runs the risk of reinforcing inaccurate beliefs about the narrowness of the applicability of group psychotherapy. Such a practice is also a poor model for staff and trainees who are new to groups. It sends a clear, but unfounded, message that group therapy is not a first-line treatment for people with mild to moderate psychological problems.

If the evaluator is also going to be the group leader, the added pressure of establishing a rapport with the patient becomes one of the aspects of the first interview as well. The use of confrontation and anxiety-evoking interview techniques is kept to a minimum or omitted when the evaluator and therapist are the same person. Although obtaining relevant patient information is a central goal of the initial interview, data collection cannot be done at the expense of forming a collaborative interaction when first meeting a potential group member.

In terms of the actual conduct of the first interview for group therapy, it is mandatory to include some rough gauge of the patient's interpersonal function, both historically and currently. The simplest way to do this is to take a chronological history of group functioning in the patient's life to date. In other words, how has the person fared in everyday situations in which interpersonal effort is required?

Sequentially, the group history begins with a careful family history, since the family is the primary group experience for all people. The family focus is weighted toward understanding the quality of the patient's relationships with parents, siblings, and extended family. Significant points to look for in the assessment of family relationships include how the family handles issues of power and control, independence and dependence, trust, and emotional closeness and distance, along with the family's communication patterns. Similarly, does the family demonstrate a capacity for empathy with others? Do they model collaboration in their transactions? How are competitive feelings handled? What conspicuous deficits or challenges are unique to the family (i.e., medical illness, significant losses, parental separation and divorce, and issues related to physical, sexual, or substance abuse)?

The next area of inquiry relates to the theme of peer group relationships. Exploration of the sibling subsystem in the original family is a logical starting point for this issue, which also extends into peer group relationships in childhood and adolescence. The taking of an educational history, of which academic performance is only one part, often provides needed information about the level of capacity for peer relatedness in the prospective group member. Questions concerning friendships, social isolation, being a "team player," and the like give the interviewer a feel for the patient's ease in or aversion to making connections with contemporaries.

A review of a patient's employment history is invariably part of a good initial interview. Here again, the emphasis for purposes of group placement is less on the type of work done and more on the characteristic interpersonal behaviors tapped in

---

BASIC PRINCIPLE 3

Never evaluate an individual for group therapy without taking a history of group function.

---

a work atmosphere. Repeated difficulty taking direction, conflicts with authority, a sense of being undervalued relative to coworkers, and the capacity for assuming a leadership role are examples of the type of group-relevant information emanating from an appreciation of the role of work in a person's life.

An estimate of the prospective member's ability to form meaningful relationships is another dimension of the first group therapy interview. The capacity for forming and maintaining friendships and romantic/sexual relationships is a very telling area with direct applicability to a person's ability to relate to others. Difficulties with relationships are one of the most common reasons why patients seek group therapy and professionals make referrals for group treatment.

The group history also involves examination of any other "natural" groups in which the patient has participated. Inquiring about school, military service, religious affiliations, membership on an athletic team, volunteer work, and any other unique group involvement will usually lead to significant information about the patient's experiences in groups.

One final note is necessary on the subject of the group history. Therapists who take a careful group history often find themselves in the position of noting gaps and deficits in a prospective member's ability to get along in groups. When this is the case, the clinician can use such information to make a good recommendation for group placement. Two extremes can be illustrated. One is the patient with a poor history of group functioning who, although he or she could benefit from group therapy, does not possess the skills needed to join an interactional group. Such patients do well to have their initial group experience be either an orientation group or a time-limited social skills training group. If they successfully complete the recommended group, they are often ready to have a second-stage disposition placing them in a higher functioning group.

The other side of the issue is the patient who has a history of relatively good group functioning. The question that arises with such patients is how a particular group will be of benefit to them. This situation often occurs with patients who have had good experiences in individual therapy but lack a real-life network in which to apply the insights gained in their individual work. Groups are an excellent vehicle for people who need to apply the awareness obtained from previous psychotherapeutic efforts.

A therapist who fails to thoroughly explore a prospective member's life experiences in terms of group participation invites trouble in selecting a good group and creates avoidable pitfalls in the ongoing conduct of the group itself. Taking a history of group functioning is a quick, easy, and cost-effective technique for avoiding these problems.

DIAGNOSTIC CONSIDERATIONS

The initial group psychotherapy interview contains elements that are unique and others that are part of the comprehensive assessment of any patient. The most obvious similarity between interviews for individual psychotherapy and those for group therapy is the task of establishing a working clinical diagnosis. Toward this end, the use of a standardized system of diagnosis is helpful in evaluating a patient and in communicating in a common language with other health care professionals.

The American Psychiatric Association's *Diagnostic and Statistical Manual of Mental Disorders* (4th edition) (*DSM-IV*) is the most well-known and widely used diagnostic classification system. One major goal of the initial group therapy interview is to form a diagnostic impression of the patient conceptualized along the lines of the terminology used in the *DSM-IV*. The diagnosis arrived at in the interview may be helpful in several ways. In terms of composing homogeneous groups, the diagnosis is often the essential commonality shared among group members. When treatment planning is discussed with staff members, outside referral sources, and third-party payers, use of the language of the *DSM-IV* helps avoid miscommunication and misunderstanding referable to patient diagnosis. Having a standard initial diagnosis is useful in assessing change over the course of subsequent therapy.

For group therapists, there is a need to augment traditional diagnosis with some measure of interpersonal style. While extremely comprehensive in scope, the *DSM-IV*'s end product is a diagnostic label; a personality classification; a mention of current stressful life events and any coexisting physical or medical conditions; and a global assessment of function score. The *DSM-IV* does not provide an appreciation of the subtleties involved in diagnosing large groups of people.

Interpersonal style denotes the interactional component accompanying any diagnostic entity. In practice, therapists are familiar with potential group patients who carry a diagnosis of borderline personality disorder. This group of patients is known for the problems they create in psychotherapy. Acting out, suicidality, eroticizing or psychoticizing transference relationships with the therapist, overvaluing and devaluing of others, and excessive use of splitting and projective identification are just a few of the treatment concerns for this patient population. It behooves the group therapist to make distinctions among potential group members who bear the same diagnostic label.

Some borderline patients are not particularly at risk for active suicidal behavior, while others will make the threat of suicide the battlefield on which they test their therapist and group. Many borderline patients who present some of the treatment issues just noted are *less* anxious in groups and function on a stronger plane. The dilution of intensity of transference to the leader that occurs through sharing the same therapist in groups, coupled with the built-in capacity for reality testing that groups invariably offer, tends to diminish the extreme behaviors of many borderline patients.

When patients diagnosed with personality disorders are judged solely on their individual therapeutic records, many are screened out as unsuitable for group therapy. This is clearly the case with some patients who fit the diagnosis, but there are many others similarly labeled who would not only do well in groups but would

---

BASIC PRINCIPLE 4

Always add an interpersonal assessment to any individual diagnostic evaluation of a prospective patient for group therapy.

---

add an air of spontaneity, introduce an injection of affect into a stagnant group, and sufficiently value membership in a group that they would work hard to comply with group norms and goals.

Paranoid patients are another group in which diagnosis alone is insufficient for making sound judgments in terms of suitability for group therapy. There are paranoid patients who are aggressive, litigious, and threatening. There are also those who are quite disturbed but more withdrawn in their posture. The image that comes to mind is one of a large outpatient schizophrenic group in which a single paranoid member attends regularly but always sits outside the group circle, wears his sunglasses (with silver reflective lenses), and has his raincoat on and buttoned up to the neck.

The following two examples are of common diagnoses calling for different treatment plans. Patient A would be disruptive in a group, probably needs to have an updated evaluation for medication, and might even require inpatient placement, but his current level of functioning would seem to preclude outpatient group membership. Patient B, who might be as, if not more, disorganized in his thinking, possesses the ability to attend therapy consistently, does not disrupt or sabotage the group effort, and is not threatening to others. This individual might do very well in an outpatient medication and life issues group dealing practically with the difficulties members encounter in life outside the hospital.

Combining formal diagnosis with interpersonal style considerations makes the task of selecting patients for groups a much easier one for the group leader and broadens the range of group options open to the patient seeking treatment.

SELECTION OF PATIENTS

Selection of patients for groups is inextricably linked to the issue of group composition. The therapist must choose members who meet the individual criteria for participation but must also have an idea of which patients will interact well with others. Selecting group members and composing a group that makes sense is the foundation for eventual positive or negative outcomes in group treatment. Many clinical problems that emerge in the therapeutic process are directly traceable to errors made in the member selection and composition phase of the therapy group.

Piper and McCallum (1994) reviewed the group literature on patient selection and noted an important change in emphasis with respect to selection criteria for group therapy. According to these authors, "More recently, the trend has been toward matching specific selection criteria with particular forms of group therapy.

That trend reflects the idea that characteristics of groups, for example, theoretical approaches, goals, and techniques, have implications for the type of patients that should be selected'' (p. 1).

Piper and McCallum's observations echo the sentiment noted earlier: The leader is well advised to conceptualize the selection and composition process as one entity. The therapist performing the evaluation should ask two simultaneous questions: Is this individual suitable for group therapy? and, if so, what particular constellation of patients will maximize the chance of meeting the patient's treatment goals?

This point of view has emerged as a response to dissatisfaction with traditional forms of selecting patients for groups without incorporating an appreciation of the group they will enter. Historically, the conventional method of patient selection relied heavily on a list of inclusion and exclusion criteria. In actual practice, group therapists began with a list of exclusion criteria for patients with qualities deemed unsuitable for group work and selected the individuals who did not meet these criteria.

While quite crude by contemporary standards, this was the prevailing method of patient selection well into the late 1960s. In this schema, patients considered to be inappropriate candidates for group therapy were those who were (a) acutely psychotic, (b) actively suicidal or homicidal, (c) marginally psychologically compensated such that confrontation and mobilization of affect in groups might worsen their condition, (d) non-English speaking, (e) in acute crisis situations, and (f) suffering from some form of organic mental disease that would make group participation impossible. This is a prime example of the ''default'' model of patient selection. Quite understandably, this imprecise method of selection led to high dropout rates and to many instances of patient and therapist dissatisfaction with the group experience.

In more recent efforts, attempts have been made to create a more positively based group selection method that defines specific criteria for inclusion in groups. A representative sampling of group inclusion criteria synthesized from the literature on patient selection includes the following: The chief complaint contains an interpersonal component; the patient demonstrates positive motivation for change; the patient is able to perform the tasks of the group; the patient shows some evidence of being able to empathize with other people; there is a basic understanding of the purpose of the group and a commitment to participate on a regular basis; there is evidence of psychological-mindedness or the ability to be self-reflective; and there is a reasonably realistic set of expectations about what can be accomplished in the group.

Inclusion criteria become even more refined when group considerations are added to the selection procedure. For example, in short-term therapy groups, the person must be dealing with a circumscribed psychological problem or life issue that is specific to the group and lends itself to resolution in a brief therapeutic time frame. Similarly, patients being considered for long-term supportive group psychotherapy might have to present a history of chronic mental illness (possibly including prior unsuccessful psychotherapy experiences), a pattern of treatment noncompliance, problems with psychotropic medication stabilization, and an uncertainty about their ability to commit to a program of a long-term nature.

In conjunction with the use of formal lists of inclusion and exclusion standards for groups, it is helpful to explore several areas during the initial interview that help in selecting patients and composing groups. These themes bring the formal clinical inclusion criteria to life and often form the basis for a decision to include or exclude a prospective member. The best way to conceptualize this for the therapist is to design a standard set of questions to pose to each prospective member so that all members are evaluated equally along these parameters. This helps avoid selecting members who would not fit in with the group.

We have found several questions helpful in terms of the selection and group composition phase of therapy. These questions are discussed in the sections to follow.

Why Are You Considering Group Therapy?

Responses range widely in answer to this question. Some people have been in individual therapy and want to remain in therapy, but they hope to shift the focus to the relationships in their lives. Others have friends or relatives who have been in group therapy and report positive experiences with the group format.

The rationale for some is economic; group therapy is more affordable than its individual counterpart. This common rationale is one that invites further clarification. Economic factors are not sufficient in themselves as the primary motive for seeking group treatment. Even if group therapy is the only affordable treatment available, there must be specific inclusion criteria accompanying economic concerns.

In another common answer to this question, the patient indicates that he or she does not know why group therapy referral has been initiated. Patients' self-doubts and misconceptions about groups may emerge when the therapist pursues this avenue. Many people think that group therapy is the therapeutic end of the line and that referral to such therapy means that someone has given up on them. Others mistakenly think that they are joining a group to make friends and establish romantic relationships with group members. While group therapy engenders many of the same positive feelings found in close real-life relationships, it is not "matchmaking" in the conventional sense. What matching does occur is in the spirit of matching a patient to an appropriate group and matching a therapist to a group with which he or she is compatible.

Why Are You Thinking of Group Therapy at This Point in Time?

The timing of group entry in a patient's life is another important consideration for the therapist conducting screening and evaluation. Crisis situations often propel people into a search for psychotherapeutic help. The nature of the crisis itself will provide information relevant to the decision regarding group placement or another form of therapy.

Experiences of current, historical, or anticipated loss are common focal points for people in crisis. The rupture of significant attachment bonds through death, divorce, geographical relocation, and other life circumstances leaves people with a major interpersonal gap in their lives. These crisis points often suggest a type of group therapy that is self-evident. Bereavement groups for those confronted with the complexities resulting from the death of a significant other, support groups for people experiencing divorce, and groups for people who have recently lost their jobs are but a few options for those in crisis over an emotional loss.

Another regular motive for seeking group therapy at a particular time may come from a sense of frustration at a lack of progress in coping with an important area of individual and/or interpersonal functioning. Many people seek group therapy because they understand that groups can furnish a wealth of information in a short period, which may help them get "unstuck" in their lives.

People who have reached a stage of despair concerning their inability to find, form, and sustain a love relationship often think about joining groups. The timing of their decision may seem to be late in the game, but for many people the cumulative effect of being alone, feeling like a failure in this aspect of life, and the demoralization and depressive feelings that result from chronic unsuccessful relationship patterns cause a sense of immediacy about finding a new way to deal with these problems.

Issues of loss are often coupled with other life events, the sum total of which surpasses the patient's threshold for tolerance and results in a constructive desire to inquire about group therapy. Substance abuse is an area where multiple issues related to crisis, loss, and other problems of living are seen simultaneously. When a person who is abusing drugs makes a decision to give up the addiction, he or she will require an integrated treatment plan that involves group therapy as a major feature if not the centerpiece.

There are many reasons why an addicted person may seek treatment at some specific point in time and for multiple motives. For example, when a substance abuser cuts his or her ties to the drug-using subculture, he or she immediately becomes interpersonally isolated. What frequently accompanies this picture is a family history of hopelessness and despair such that the addicted person cannot turn to family members for help. The lifestyle required to support a significant drug habit is survival governed. As a consequence, the emotional debris of broken friendships, sociopathic behavior, and breaches of trust leave behind an empty interpersonal trail. What usually remains is an isolated, physically ill, psychologically symptomatic person in need of immediate help, and the individual typically copes by pondering a return to drug use.

Such patients, troubled as they may seem, are often excellent candidates for immediate group placement in the initial phase of treatment. This may seem somewhat paradoxical in light of what has been stated earlier about exclusion criteria for group therapy, but a more detailed explication of the rationale for placing the substance abuser in a group will explain the apparent inconsistencies.

Supplying a network and a social support system through the use of a therapy group has the instant advantage of countering the sense of isolation so keenly felt by substance abusers early in the process of recovery. Furthermore, the group is not merely a substitute peer vehicle but, rather, a group of peers who are drug free. This helps the addict gain a more rapid sense of emotional equilibrium and counters her or his sense of futility in terms of rebuilding relationships with "normal" people.

Most substance abusers are also encouraged to attend self-help groups along the lines of the 12-step model of Alcoholics Anonymous. This additional group experience is recommended as a daily part of the patient's routine. Regular participation in a psychotherapy group and a mutual-help group constructively occupies the time of many who use drugs as an escape from feelings of boredom and who lack a sense of direction in life.

Groups offer positive role models in the form of other addicts who are successfully mastering their substance abuse problems. Many in the group can share experiences, give useful advice, identify with the position of the addict's struggle to become drug free, and provide a conditional climate of acceptance as long as the new group member is making legitimate efforts to engage with his or her drug-use-related problems.

The decision to place a patient in a group for substance abusers demonstrates an active example of the use of many of the therapeutic factors involved in clinical practice. The destigmatization that results from identification with others changes the self-perception of the patient from that of a "junkie" to that of a person in recovery. This enhances self-esteem and diminishes feelings of depression. Being part of a group lends a spirit of community and a sense of shared purpose toward common goals. This results in feelings of inclusion at a time when someone feels marginalized. The wealth of up-to-date information imparted by the group leader and members provides the new member with an enhanced base of accurate knowledge about his or her condition.

The "reality check" that comes through the group interchanges helps reduce the use of denial and avoidance in the member and allows fellow group members to experience the benefits of their altruism. Seeing others in advanced stages of recovery spurs realistic hopefulness for problem resolution. Participation in a group over time provides regular socialization experiences and reinforces a sense of commonalties among members.

Being part of a cohesive group repairs family damage (e.g., deficient boundary and limit setting, scapegoating of a family member, inappropriately using parental power) while simultaneously modeling self-reliance and reliance on peers as two underdeveloped resources in the addict's emotional life that can be strengthened. The learning curve for a new member of a substance abuse group can be dramatic. This phenomenon provides new material for the patient to think about instead of the deadening experience of repeatedly obsessing about issues with no resolution of the problem. Groups offer intellectual and emotional stimulation to new members, who are often depressed and devoid of innovative ways of thinking about the resolution of their emotional conflicts.

In sum, answers to the question "Why are you considering group therapy?" are invariably multifactorial in nature. Assessment must therefore include a range of information relevant to suitability and timing of placement of patients in groups. The situations described in this section illustrate the complex of intrapsychic, familial, social, interpersonal, physiological, and biochemical factors that, when taken into account collectively, can improve the prospects of making a good clinical choice for patients seeking psychological intervention.

What Is the Context in Which the Patient's
Current Problems Exist?

In a manner much like the initial interview for family therapy, group therapists are well advised to think about the patient's presenting symptoms in the context of her or his current life circumstances. This social-systems-based line of inquiry yields essential information relating to the patient's current level of motivation for therapy. The sentiment that therapists can supply many things in therapy, but motivation must come from the patients is as true for group therapy as it is for any other form of psychotherapy.

A simple question in the initial interview such as "Who's idea was it that you be in group therapy?" will open the door to pursuit of the answer to the question of treatment readiness. In ideal circumstances, the response will be an unambivalent one in which it is clear that the patient originated this idea. It is surprising how often motives other than the patient's form the basis for a referral to group therapy.

The three most frequent sources of motivation outside the patient are the family, another therapist, and an outside agency, of which schools and courts are the most likely points of origin. It is a priority in evaluating patients for group therapy to assess their degree of motivation. The unspoken questions in the therapist's mind should be as follows: Is the patient a substitute for someone else who needs treatment? Who benefits from the patient being in therapy? and Whose agenda is being satisfied by recommending that the patient be in group treatment?

Many examples in the family life of patients disclose the "true" basis for seeking group therapy. Family therapists are regularly presented with clinical situations in which parental marital conflict is detoured through a psychologically symptomatic child who is presented as the identified patient in need of help. Couples with troubled relationships are often more comfortable labeling the problem as one residing in their child so that they can escape the scrutiny of therapy for themselves. The child may comply with the parents' view that he or she needs therapy, since the threat of a marital breakup may be more anxiety laden. In response, the child takes a "sacrificial" position, opting for the lesser of two evils, and offers himself or herself up for therapy.

While the child may have diagnosable psychological problems such as academic failure, eating disorders, substance abuse, and separation/individuation issues, it serves the parents' unconscious agenda to have the child, rather than themselves, in psychiatric treatment. In such instances, group therapists are well advised not to be naive or short-sighted; instead, they should view the presentation of a "motivated" young adult not as a good candidate for group therapy but as a member of a family system in which the parents are resistant to marital and/or family therapy. A couples group for the parents and a multiple family group for the entire family are the only forms of group therapy that would sufficiently address the problems of such a family. Either choice would counteract the family's desire to mask family problems behind a child-centered issue.

Reaction to the question of the genesis of the patient's current interest in joining a group often comes not from the patient but from a therapist who has suggested evaluation for group therapy. Many of these situations are "benign" and are just as they appear: A knowledgeable therapist who either does not conduct group therapy or who sees a clear indication based on the patient's clinical course has made an appropriate referral for the next phase of ongoing treatment. There are, however, numerous similar circumstances in which the issues are not as simple as they appear on the surface. Therapists who wish to rid themselves of difficult patients may misuse groups as a convenient and face-saving dumping ground for doing so. Patients with personality disorders and those who have not been sufficiently responsive to individual therapy may be shunted over to group therapy by therapists who are frustrated or "burned out" from working with a particular individual.

Even therapists who are well meaning and have their patient's best interests at heart may make inappropriate referrals for group therapy. This may be based, to some extent, on less fluency with group treatment on the referral source's part, resulting in an unrealistic appraisal of what groups can do. A case in point occurred when a patient referred himself for a consultation concerning group therapy for his excessive anxiety, which escalated in dating situations with women. He volunteered that he had expressed his desire to be in a group in order to work on relationship issues but was discouraged from doing so by his individual therapist.

His therapist was unfamiliar with group treatment and told the patient that such therapy was not relevant to the treatment of the patient's social anxiety: "Group therapy is mainly for alcoholics and drug addicts. Since you are neither, I don't see how group therapy can help you, but go for a consultation if you feel you must." The therapist was sincere, but seriously misinformed, in his beliefs about group treatment but was open enough to allow his patient to explore and eventually participate quite successfully in long-term combined individual and group therapies.

Finally, the impetus for group referral may come from an independent source with which a patient has significant contact. Children and adolescents are often noted to be having trouble with peers in school, behaving in a disruptive way in class, exhibiting extremely shy and withdrawn postures, or having difficulty with a particular teacher. Many times a referral for psychotherapy (group, family, or individual) may be entirely appropriate. On occasion, referral to group therapy is used as a disciplinary action or as a default mechanism by a teacher who is feeling overburdened. Similarly, court-mandated treatment as an extension of the punitive aspects of a case results in understandably unmotivated or negativistic prospective group members.

While even the most positive motivation for therapy does not come without some trepidation on the group member's part, the picture is clinically quite different from some of the earlier-noted examples of other elements masquerading as strong positive interest in group therapy. By asking "Why group?" "Why now?" and "What motivates your interest in group therapy?" the therapist can ascertain whether or not the setting, timing, and personal incentives are present in a form that will allow a patient to capitalize on all of the advantages groups can offer.

PREGROUP PREPARATION OF MEMBERS

Once a patient has been screened, diagnosed, and evaluated and the conclusion reached that he or she is a good group candidate, one final step remains prior to beginning the actual group: All prospective group members must receive a pregroup orientation. The importance of providing an orientation for incoming group members cannot be underscored enough.

What was sensed empirically for many years by seasoned group therapists has now been scientifically studied and found to be supported by research data. Piper et al. (1992), Spitz (1984), and others have emphasized the critical role of including a patient preparation component in the phase of group therapy preceding the first session.

The benefits to patients and therapists that emanate from thoughtful pregroup patient preparation include reductions in group dropout rates, enhanced ease of group management for the leader, less anxiety about group entry for new members, a clear sense of the purpose of the group and the therapeutic route that will be taken to arrive at the group's goals, and an accelerated start to the therapeutic process.

In practical terms, there are many ways to prepare new group members, ranging from informal discussions with patients to structured pretraining programs (Piper et al., 1982), distribution of written orientation manuals, use of videotapes of simulated group sessions, and group orientations involving many new group members simultaneously. Regardless of the format of the group orientation, the group leader is well advised to include an organized preparation component as a routine part of the pregroup phase of group therapy.

Members with a clear understanding of the group's mission and clear knowledge concerning its goals enter the group in a state of greater "readiness to work" on their target goals and are less preoccupied with issues that commonly distract, detour, or delay the onset of the therapeutic process (Spitz, 1996). The early sessions of the group are less consumed by questions about group therapy, these issues already having been addressed in the orientation phase. Patients also experience less of a sense of goal incompatibility between themselves and other group members, since all members have been given the same briefing prior to attending the initial group meeting.

Preparation of the patient before initiation of the group should be regarded not only as a necessary orientation tool but as an opportunity for further screening and evaluation. In going through the different elements contained in the group orientation, the therapist may discover patient attributes that were not apparent during the initial screening process. This new information can form the basis for a therapist's decision to reconsider the wisdom of including the patient in the group as planned. Illustrations of this process are incorporated throughout this section as the specific components of the pregroup orientation are discussed in more detail.

Of the many options available to group leaders, we favor a format that is comprehensive but not excessively time consuming. The pregroup orientation checklist is a model that offers economy of time but not at the expense of quality of patient care. Despite the fact that the components of the pregroup orientation are discussed in considerable detail here, the actual time necessary to apply the system is never more than one session and, more commonly, is closer to half a session.

Fifteen items make up the pregroup orientation checklist. Depending on the type of group and the personality of the incoming member, group leaders have the option to focus in more depth on those areas covered in the list that may be most specific to the group and the patient in question and focus less on topics that are not as applicable to the situation.

Goals and General Purpose of the Group

In keeping with the tenets of good group practice, the therapist must clearly state the purpose of the group the patient will be entering, including an explanation of goals. Goals that are vague or too ambitious should be avoided in favor of goals that are patient specific.

As an example, consider a patient who has been evaluated and diagnosed as having posttraumatic stress disorder (PTSD). The treatment plan is to have this patient join a brief therapy group homogeneously composed of members dealing with PTSD. The leader can inform members that the goals of the group will be to teach members what is known about the natural course of this condition and to help members overcome the obstacles posed by PTSD that interfere with their ability to return to work.

When stating goals in this form, the therapist communicates several things to the patient. First, the patient gets a sense that there will be an educational component to the group experience. Second, there is a target goal. The goal is not the resolution of all life issues influenced by PTSD but a more circumscribed focus aimed at addressing specific problems posed by PTSD that intrude in such a way as to make reentry into the workplace a problematic issue. Finally, the unmistakable message is communicated to the patient that behavior change is the ultimate goal of the group.

Since there are many roads to behavior change, the benefits derived from group therapy usually result from cognitive, behavioral, psychodynamic, and educational aspects of the group working in concert to produce change. The endpoint for members of PTSD groups is an improved level of life functioning enabling them to resume their customary vocational activities.

Composition of the Group

The therapist tries to convey a picture of the group the patient will be entering without disclosing information that violates the confidentiality of other group members. The purpose of this portion of the orientation is to allay fears that are avoidable and serve only to complicate group entry. The goal is to provide the member with an understanding of who will be in the group, why specific members have been selected, and what the size of the group will be.

Other group members are not identified by name, but symptom similarities are highlighted. This reinforces the statements made about the group's goals and helps the new member develop a realistic preview of what kind of people he or she will be working with in the group. What this actually accomplishes is a head start on the group process. With a picture of the group in the mind's eye of the patient, the therapeutic wheels begin to turn. Patients start to develop fantasies and feelings about a group that has not yet officially begun. By the time the first meeting takes place, members are actively involved in the life of the group. This expedition of the entry phase is a part of what allows groups of shorter duration to accomplish significant goals in a limited time frame.

In a group for people with depression, the leader makes a simple statement to incoming members about the composition of the group. A typical example is the following:

You will be joining a group of people who all have been depressed, some of whom are taking antidepressant medications, and the focus of the group will be understanding the influence of depression on the important relationships in your life. Another purpose of the group is to help members learn better ways to cope with being depressed periodically. The group will be composed of men and women ranging in age from their early 30s to their 50s, and everyone in the group is having difficulty interacting or getting along with one or more significant people in their lives. The group will be open to new members and will have an average of eight members at any given time.

Role of the Group Leader

A key concern for new members of any group is what to expect from the group leader. Members who are accustomed to individual psychotherapy may be anxious about sharing the therapist with other group members, puzzled about how help can come from others who themselves have significant emotional problems, and wondering how much reliance they can have on the group leader.

Those who have previously been involved in groups will want to know how the leader's style will be similar to or different from the style of leadership to which they are accustomed. This is particularly true in circumstances in which the patient has been in traditional, long-term psychoanalytically oriented group psychotherapy and is making a transfer to a brief therapy group.

Many people have never before been in group or individual psychotherapy and share many of the common myths, fears, and misconceptions surrounding group therapy, particularly in the area of the role the leader will assume. Will the leader be an ally or an adversary? Will the leader protect me if I come under attack? Do group leaders talk about their own experiences in the group? These and a host of other worries of the uninitiated psychotherapy patient are regularly addressed in this segment of the pregroup orientation session.

Patients in certain diagnostic categories are exquisitely sensitive to the actions of the group therapist. The most common examples involve patients with borderline or narcissistic personality structures who often dislike the idea of group therapy entirely. The prospect of sharing both the group leader and the group spotlight with others is viewed negatively by people who are accustomed to having sole possession of an individual therapist. On occasion, a prospective group member will balk during this part of the pregroup orientation and try to engage the leader in a collusive alliance in which the member will be ensured a ''special'' role vis-à-vis the therapist. This request is impossible for any leader to honor if he or she is to maintain a sense of fairness to all group members.

Perhaps more important, this patient behavior during the orientation may signal trouble unnoticed in the initial interview. This is an illustration of the point made earlier concerning use of the pregroup orientation as an extension of the evaluation process. Circumstances in which an incoming group member protests vigorously about an aspect of the group as explained in the orientation should immediately alert the group leader that perhaps this patient is not ready or able to participate in the group as planned. In such cases, the treatment plan is reviewed, and an alternative therapeutic disposition can be made.

What the group leader actually tells members in the orientation dialogue is aimed at addressing common patient concerns about leadership activity versus passivity, how the relationship with the leader in the group relates to the kind of help patients can expect from group therapy, how structured the group will be, whether the group leader will be available for individual sessions outside the group, and a host of recognizable pretherapy fears that affect new patients in groups.

A sample of how the group leader might encapsulate information about the leader's role in the group is contained in the following prototypical orientation speech:

You may be concerned about what my participation in the group will be. I plan to be very active at first, in getting the group "launched" and setting a climate in the group where people can get down to work on their problems quickly. In this group, I will try to keep the group on course toward its goals and I will try to make myself available to answer questions arising in the sessions. In addition, I plan to suggest certain exercises, "homework," and other things which will require your active participation in and outside of group meetings for their eventual success.

Observing and Recording Group Meetings

There are settings and circumstances that may call for groups to be observed. In training programs, observation and recording of group sessions are primarily used for the benefit of teaching therapists a particular technique or method. There are also times when recording, especially videotaping of meetings, is used as part of the group therapy itself, as well as a vehicle for training, supervision, and quality control.

Observation of any kind must be handled openly before the first session and with the patients' informed consent. If a group session is being observed from behind a one-way mirror, the leader should inform the group *prior to* implementing this plan. Furthermore, the leader is obliged to inform the group members who the observers are and what their presence is designed to accomplish. Members are also given the choice of going behind the mirror and meeting the professional staff observers if they so desire.

When videotaping of the group is being used as a therapeutic tool, its purpose and rationale are explained to prospective group members. Videotaping has proven to be a valuable adjunct in instances in which the group is composed of members with eating disorders, body image distortions, public speaking anxiety, interpersonal communication problems, and social inhibition, as well as in other circumstances in which direct observational data concerning group members' attitudes and unrealistic self-perceptions can be useful. It can also assist in behavioral rehearsal and reinforcement of adaptive behavior. Some of these issues can be clarified through the use of videotape playback, and the progress of therapy can be hastened by the instant reality check that videotaping provides in many of these problem areas.

Groups can also be documented by the taking of notes in session. This is not a method we recommend. Verbatim or detailed "process notes" of the kind used by trainees in individual psychotherapy supervision are undesirable in group therapy. The kind of effort required to document all that goes on in group sessions is of such magnitude that it occupies too much of the leader's time in an unproductive way. The leader who does this risks being seen as removed from the group, as disinterested in the group, or as a remote scientist rather than a group participant.

Therapists who insist on extensive note-taking in group sessions are usually new to group therapy, anxious, and/or obsessive in their own personalities. Recording the significant group events for the group as a whole and for individual members can be accomplished quite simply by making notations immediately after the group session has ended. The advantages of this approach to recording the group experience are that group material is fresh, therapists get into the habit of reviewing each session by having to think about it and put it in writing, and a strategy or therapeutic plan for the next meeting is easier to conceptualize.

Arrangement of the Therapy Setting

While it might seem superfluous to inform a patient of where the actual therapy session will be conducted, there are many instances in which omitting this aspect of the pregroup orientation can be a mistake. When working with seriously disturbed, suspicious, paranoid patients or with group members who display excessive amounts of anticipatory anxiety, a simple statement about—and a short visit to—the room in which the group will be meeting may help allay fears.

During or after the visit to the group therapy room, it is generally a good idea to ask the incoming group member how it felt to see the room. Most people will report some sense of relief, but some will describe the experience in terms that are clinically revealing. For example, after a visit to a large therapy space, one person may say "The room feels claustrophobic to me," while another may say "The chairs seem so close to each other; can people actually touch you in the group meeting?" It is advisable to include a brief statement about the physical location and arrangement of the therapy room or to arrange a visit for the comfort and ease of entry of new members and for whatever serendipitous behavioral information it might yield.

Group Time Factors

The time frame of a group correlates directly with the group's purpose. The orientation session includes remarks about the time frame of the group a person is about to enter. Time will vary according to the group's goals. As a general rule, short-term groups have a fixed time limit and focus on changing maladaptive behaviors. Ongoing or open-ended groups are more ambitious and aspire to reach many of the same goals as individual psychotherapy. Personality and attitudinal shifts, as well as behavioral change, are part of the long-term group model.

Within the framework of the duration of the group are considerations about the optimum time frame for each individual group session. Patients should be aware of the time limits set in advance of the group's initial meeting. If a member is unclear about the reason for the group's particular time frame, a satisfactory explanation is provided in the pregroup orientation.

A cognitive/behavioral group, for example, may meet for 1-hour sessions over the course of 12 weeks. What is unique to many behaviorally oriented groups is that they meet more than once per week. The incoming patient has to be informed that the group meets two or three times per week because special techniques need to be taught or because practice and repetition are valuable in reinforcing behavioral gains made in the group. Habit control groups for smoking cessation and weight loss groups are two common examples of groups that are likely to require meetings more frequently than once a week.

Another popular group format in which time plays an important role is the bereavement group. In a loss group conducted along the lines of Piper et al.'s (1992) model, members are selected because they are having difficulty functioning in some central life area owing to their present psychological status in relationship to the loss they have sustained. The pregroup orientation of these members helps them understand concepts of protracted or pathological grief and offers the group as a way of helping them attain greater understanding and resolution of the conflicts underlying their difficulties. Each member is told that the group will meet once a week for 12 weeks and that each meeting will be 90 minutes in duration.

Loss and Addition of Group Members

All groups require a sufficient number of members to reach their objectives.

Brief therapy groups. Some groups, usually those of a shorter term nature, begin and end with the same members. If, in the course of the time, members drop out of brief therapy groups, they are not replaced. The limited time frame virtually precludes the addition of new group members once the group has started. Many short-term therapy groups have a structured protocol for the conduct of each session, and groups of this type do not allow for changes in membership.

The rationale for placing strong emphasis on the pregroup orientation phase is apparent in short-term groups. Since retention of membership is essential to realization of the group's goals, well-prepared members are less likely to leave the group, and the group leader can rely on a much more stable group nucleus with which to work. Members are told in the orientation that the original group members will remain throughout the group experience and that no new members will be added. The advantage of taking this stance is twofold: It increases the chances of there being the necessary number of members for the work of the group and communicates to members that they share responsibility for determining their own therapeutic destiny.

The expressed advantages of fixed membership groups are that longer term groups often convey no sense of urgency about change, the problem of having a shifting group membership over time is averted, programmatic formats are easier to implement when all of the members are at the same stage in their understanding of the program, the group does not have to stall or back up in order to orient new members, and the leader can focus on target goals and not be distracted by having to manage group members who are at different levels of development as a product of their entering the group at different points in time. These factors, along with a host of others, allow for ease of group management and a greater possibility of the group reaching its goals in a limited time period.

Long-term groups. Open membership groups assume that members will be leaving the group over the course of its existence. The two primary ways in which members leave a group are premature termination and realization of their treatment goals, which obviates the need for further group work. In either case, gaps are left in the group, and the leader must decide whether and when open slots in the group should be filled by bringing in new members.

Issues of timing are important when considering additions to a group. In most cases, long-term dynamically oriented groups do not seek immediate replacements for a departed member. When a member leaves the group, whatever the reason, it is experienced as a loss by the group membership. The leader needs to allow time for the group to deal with the issues ushered in by the loss of a member. Powerful emotional themes related to death, abandonment, separation, and loss are but a few of the feelings that accompany the exit of a longtime group member.

The therapeutic factor of family reenactment is invariably mobilized when there is a break in the ranks of a group. The dynamically inclined therapist leading a long-term group can make extraordinarily productive use of this moment. When, for example, a member has successfully completed her or his therapeutic agenda and leaves the group, all members experience something. The range of reactions catalyzed when a member leaves the group is legion. These emotions, most of which are historically based, are replayed in the group and are available for therapeutic exploration.

Competitive feelings abound wherein members who remain in the group experience a sense of resentment that they are still working on their problems while someone else has made more progress and is graduating from the group. Prior experiences with the loss of a loved one; reactivation of feelings of emotional or actual physical abandonment by parents; remnants of earlier, unresolved separations; and a fear that the group will fall apart and end are commonplace. To ''plug in'' a new member prematurely precludes the option of working on these critical issues for patients in long-term psychodynamically oriented group psychotherapy.

Consequently, the therapist needs to anticipate the comings and goings of group members and prepare incoming members for the fact that there will be turnover in membership over time. Neglecting to address issues related to the loss and addition of group members invites avoidable problems in the ongoing conduct of the group. Insecure members often misperceive a new group member as a replacement for themselves, or they believe that they have failed or are in some way inadequate, so the leader has to bring in new people to keep the group going. Needless to say, these very troublesome feelings alter the group's stated course. Such issues need not come up as obstacles at all if the leader is careful about adequately addressing the theme of adding and losing members as a routine part of the pregroup orientation interview.

Rules About Attendance

All groups strive to establish regular attendance as a central group norm. When a person misses a group meeting, he or she is in the dark about the events that transpired during the session. Group therapists are faced with the decision of whether or not to fill the absent member in on what was missed or to move on as planned. Even though it may be naive of the leader to expect that each member will be able to attend every session, it still is a primary leadership responsibility to advocate and model regular group attendance. In so doing, the leader makes a position statement about the seriousness and importance of the group and how vital each person is to the endeavor.

The related issues of avoiding lateness and having members call prior to the session if they are going to be absent are also discussed in this phase of the pregroup orientation. Members in groups in which absences and lateness are accepted tend to devalue the group experience; lose confidence in the leader, whom they regard as weak, passive, or inadequate; and feel like they are participating in a failed endeavor. All of these factors are, at the very least, demoralizing, but they may actually be injurious to patients who come to group therapy with preexisting feelings of low self-esteem, a sense of personal failure, and a reasonable expectation that their lives will be enhanced, not made worse, by joining a therapy group.

While regular attendance is essential, there are certain circumstances that call for modification of this part of the therapeutic contract. In work with seriously impaired patients, rigid restrictions on attendance may result in patients attempting to comply with a task that is beyond their adaptive capacity. Therapists who work with schizophrenic outpatient groups may modify this portion of the group preparation module to allow for a certain amount of irregularity in attendance as long as the patient can make an attachment to the group and remain with it over time. Such patients may have poor per-session attendance records, but those who regard themselves as members of the group or members of the program do well over the longer life span of the group.

Higher functioning patients can be held to a higher standard of attendance. However, to confront a psychotic group member about missing a session invariably backfires. Instead of encouraging and reinforcing regular meeting attendance, the therapist who takes a rigid or guilt-inducing stance in the name of speaking for group rules is often unwittingly driving away lower functioning members. This theme is amplified in Chapter 11, which deals with the application of group therapy with chronic psychiatric patients. For purposes of the pregroup preparation of incoming members, the group leader must decide in advance what the policy on attendance will be and orient all members in a uniform way.

Fees and Billing Procedures

The mechanism by which therapy will be paid for is included in the orientation session. In the current climate of managed mental health care, the intricacies of reimbursement for treatment have added another dimension to the preparation of patients for group therapy. Issues of precertification for sessions, proper referral procedures, and compliance with the criteria set forth by the managed care organization form the essentials of this process.

Many members are uncertain about their benefits, confused about copayment provisions of certain plans, uninformed about how the actual process of payment for treatment is supposed to be handled, or generally intimidated or in the dark in regard to health care coverage. It has become a part of the pregroup preparation of members for the group therapist to go over the details of payment for therapy. Therapists should feel free to consult directly with managed care companies if they are in doubt, and they can also encourage group members to call or write to their overseeing bodies to obtain answers to any questions regarding the financing of their group therapy.

Aside from the administrative and managerial advantages this affords, it also sets an early therapeutic tone of collaboration between leader and member born out of a mutual effort to understand and work within the confines of managed care. Specific issues such as the case review and appeal processes can be included in the patient preparation protocol.

The question of fees has obvious clinical implications. Group leaders must decide whether it suits the goals of the group to have a standard fee for group therapy or whether, in cases in which finances are an issue for a group member, there should be fee adjustments. Whatever choice is made, it is important for the leader to spell out the policy regarding fees to each incoming member. In psychodynamic groups, the fee is often the reality focus for issues other than monetary ones. For example, it is common in groups in which members pay different fees for group members to feel that the therapist prefers those who are charged the lowest fees. This is an in-group replay of unresolved family issues of parental preference for one sibling over another displaced onto what appear to be practical matters involving money. The alert group leader can differentiate genuine issues about money from other psychodynamic and group process issues if he or she takes care to explain to each member the policy for group fees during the orientation meeting.

Coordination of Other Therapies

Group therapy is frequently part of a broader treatment plan for patients. The group leader is responsible for coordinating the treatment of each group member. In the pregroup orientation session, the therapist goes over other concurrent or potential treatment efforts and discusses how each will be handled. This aspect of pregroup member preparation encompasses several important considerations.

If the group member is also in another form of psychotherapy (usually individual, couples, or family therapy), the group leader must obtain permission from the patient to contact the other therapist(s) involved in the patient's care at any point the group leader deems necessary. In this way, not only can the group therapist's database of information about the patient be expanded, but some potentially troublesome clinical issues that can arise when patients are being seen by more than one therapist can be avoided or dealt with expeditiously. The classic example of this kind is seen in patients with borderline personality disorders, who commonly use splitting as a defense against anxiety. When more than one therapist sees the borderline patient, there must be an open channel of communication between therapists to guard against the patient's tendency to use splitting as a means to "divide and conquer" the therapists and thereby sabotage treatment efforts.

The two other areas to be covered in this section of the orientation concern medication management and provisions for hospitalization of patients. If someone other than the group leader is prescribing psychotropic medication for a member, the leader must have clear knowledge of the drug regimen. At the same time, the clinician providing the medication can obtain valuable information referable to the patient's response to drug therapy as demonstrated by the patient's individual and interpersonal actions in the group.

When a group member has a history of prior psychiatric hospitalization or has a condition that becomes unstable at times, then a plan for how, when, and by whom the patient will be hospitalized must be agreed upon. Patients who become overtly psychotic in group sessions may require admission to an inpatient facility directly from the group. In these instances, the understanding conveyed to the patient in the pregroup orientation is that the group leader will oversee the decision to hospitalize anyone from the group. The group therapist must be sure that the patient understands the plan and is in accord with it in order to avoid group crisis situations for which no appropriate contingency plan has been made.

Extragroup Socialization

Conventional groups, especially those with a psychodynamic point of view, actively discourage or prohibit contact among members outside of group sessions. This policy is designed to counteract the dangers that can arise when the group leader is not present. Subgroups or cliques that exclude certain group members, business or professional affiliations that spring from the group, and romantic and sexual relationships that develop between members are a few of the countertherapeutic results that may follow extramural socialization among group participants.

While it is tempting to make what appear to be sound clinical policy decisions concerning contact among members outside the group, there are always exceptions to the rule. In some groups, the leader may *encourage* contact among members for reasons consistent with group goals. A ''buddy system'' in a group of patients who are lower functioning is an example of extragroup contact designed to be an extension of the therapeutic group process. In such systems, group members are paired together and usually arrive at sessions and go home together. Given that social isolation, loneliness, and regular group attendance are problems for these patients, creation of a group-generated plan that involves all members is qualitatively quite different from spontaneous or planned outside contacts among members of higher level groups. The latter is almost always an example of enactment of some issue outside the confines of the group, where it would have to be openly addressed.

In some substance abuse groups, the case can be made for a telephone network among members outside of group sessions. The purpose is to give members who are at risk of lapsing back into drug use an alternative option whereby they can call a sober group member who will support their healthy efforts to resist using drugs.

Whatever the group therapist decides is in the best interests of the group regarding extramural contact among group members, the pregroup orientation, rather than the established group, is the time and place to discuss this subject in some detail. Here again, the group leader may encounter prospective group members who are unable to agree to adhere to this portion of the therapeutic contract. These individuals may have to be screened out on the basis of their high-risk potential for undermining the group effort through misuse of relationships with other members.

Modifications of the Group Contract

The reason for including this category concerns the rare but significant instance in which something in a patient's life could potentially be at cross purposes with his or her effective participation in the group. In one pregroup session, a prospective member stated, almost as an afterthought, that he had a construction job that would require him to work at different work sites periodically. When asked how this would affect his ability to attend group sessions, he replied that he thought he would probably have to miss one session each month.

While he met the other criteria for the group he was about to enter, his response to this question revealed a side of his life that automatically disqualified him as a member. Many people in groups have scheduling constraints; however, it is always a mistake for the leader to accept a member when it is clear that this individual will have a regular pattern of absences. Individual requests to change the meeting time or date of the group based solely on a single member's personal limitations regarding scheduling should be denied. The time, date, and meeting place are nonnegotiable items unless, for some reason, the therapist must alter arrangements because of his or her professional commitments.

While this may seem somewhat undemocratic, the problems that occur when group meeting times are changed to accommodate one member, episodic absence is accepted, or other deviations from the standard group design are allowed can be of such magnitude as to threaten the viability of the entire group experience.

Confidentiality

"Confidentiality is to psychotherapy as a sterile operating field is to a surgeon" (Lewin, 1996). Effective psychotherapy of any kind cannot take place in the absence of assurance of strict confidentiality. Incoming members are notified of the gravity of the confidentiality rule and are asked whether or not they feel they can adhere to it. Breaches of confidentiality are grounds for immediate dismissal of a member from the group. Any incoming member who cannot commit to strict confidentiality in the initial interview is excluded from joining the group.

Confidentiality takes on added meaning in group therapy, since members have the ability to take information about other people out of the group. In order to protect the confidentiality of all group members, the leader must draw a clear distinction between gossip and the constructive use of information originating in the group.

If the group is conducted under the umbrella of managed care, the therapist should also explain what kind of information will be released about the patient to the managed care company. Concerns about dissemination of patient information are increasing with the greater impact of managed care on clinical practice. The orientation meeting is an ideal place to openly discuss possible ramifications with respect to sharing information about patients with outside sources.

Rules about confidentiality should be restated in the initial group session and again at any point in therapy at which potentially sensitive material is discussed.

Questions and Answers

The preparation session includes a portion in which patients are allowed to ask any questions related to the group they are joining or about any aspect of group therapy in general. It is best to leave time for questions near the end of the meeting, after the other checklist items have been explained.

The significance of allowing for a question-and-answer period cannot be over-looked. On the simplest level, it affords an opportunity for the group leader to gain a sense of the tone of the pregroup orientation meeting. It also allows the group member and the leader time to go over any areas of confusion or misunderstanding concerning the content of the session.

Since many people enter group therapy with preconceived notions concerning what actually happens in group sessions, the pregroup interview encourages the expression of doubts, fears, and irrational beliefs about the upcoming group. The therapist can clarify myths and misconceptions and help ease many of the avoidable anxieties attendant to the process of being a new member of a therapy group.

In spite of the group leader's attempts at reassurance and clarification, many prospective members remain uneasy, mistrustful, or worried about aspects of the group. Persistent behavior or responses that indicate reluctance, a continuing sense of mistrust, a fear of being attacked in the group, and concerns about humiliation, public exposure, and embarrassment are clues to the leader about the patient's particular difficulty with entry into the group. In a more classical psychodynamic sense, another way of viewing the patient's negative reactions in the interview is to view them as forecasters of the kinds of resistances that person is likely to demonstrate in the interpersonal milieu of the group.

The therapeutic process actually begins in the initial interview session. Early warning signals about fears and resistances on the part of new members can be engaged during the screening interview. The result of this effort is a tangible demonstration to the patient of the therapist's interest in facilitating both group entry and retention in the group.

Barriers to Group Participation

The last subject on the checklist is cast in the form of the following question: "Is there anything unique about your life situation that might interfere with your ability to join, remain in, or participate in the entire group experience?" This catchall question is designed to elicit practical barriers to regular group involvement such as job constraints, medical illness, pregnancy, family circumstances, and other concrete factors that might arise during the course of the group and intrude upon consistent attendance at meetings.

The question is also used for another reason. It is deliberately vague enough so that prospective members may offer valuable information not elicited elsewhere in the preparation session that can have a direct bearing on their suitability as new group members. One prospective group member, in a striking response to this question, made the following statement: "I think that your group's meeting time

---

BASIC PRINCIPLE 5

The orientation of incoming members before the first group session is essential to the eventual success of group therapy.

---

conflicts with my *other* group's time!'' On further inquiry, it became clear that this woman was ''comparison shopping'' for therapy and was not ready at the time to make a serious commitment to any group.

The foregoing checklist is presented as a guide, not as dogma. There are undoubtedly additional items that other therapists would place on the list and other specific groups that would call for the inclusion of group-specific preparation issues. Therapists are encouraged to develop their own pregroup orientation schedules relating directly to the group work they will be doing.

While it seems perfectly natural to take a patient through a preparatory session prior to the start of the group, it is still surprising to note how frequently this step is omitted or abbreviated by busy clinicians. Regardless of the form the procedure takes (e.g., individual interview, psychoeducational waiting list group, written orientation manual), the orientation phase is the foundation of the group experience and cannot be omitted if one is to expect positive outcomes in a psychotherapy group.

Once the orientation phase is complete, a time and starting date are set for the entire group or for a new member who is entering an established group. In a new group, the next event in therapy is the first group meeting.

5

The Initial Group Session

The initial group session sets the tone for the group work to follow. There are many aspects of initial sessions, from the mundane to the profound, that require thought and planning on the part of the group leader. The hard work that has gone into the evaluation and preparation of incoming members begins to bear fruit in the initial meeting of the group.

To the extent that the group therapist can anticipate the issues likely to emerge in initial group sessions, the task of leading the group is simplified. There are administrative and managerial functions as well as psychological themes to address in the first meeting of a group. In many respects, the initial group session is the source of greatest anxiety for both group leaders and group members. The leader can minimize his or her own apprehensions by focusing on the components of the central group goals: setting a therapeutic group climate and helping the group to coalesce.

This chapter is directed to the role of the group therapist and provides an overview of most of the considerations confronting group leaders as they embark on the start of a new group. When the leader has carefully thought through the group goals, the interventions in the first group meeting have a unifying theme. Most of the therapist's behavior in the first meeting is designed to set the stage for implementation of the goals for each member and for the group as a whole. When the group therapist has a clear sense of focus and purpose, he or she can take charge of the group experience from the very beginning and steer it in the most productive direction.

Groups cannot be expected to self-regulate initially. The leader must design a group model wherein members will develop good group habits. At a later stage, when positive norms have been established and the group is cohesive, many groups can take a large share of the responsibility for the change that will occur through the group. The group will never reach this stage unless the leader is active in the first session in setting an atmosphere within which change is most likely to flourish. How the leader goes about accomplishing this task in actual clinical practice forms the basis of the discussion that follows.

LEADERSHIP ISSUES

General Principles

Group therapists must wear many hats. They provide emotional support and an analytic and objective perspective, function as gatekeepers and positive role models, and serve an administrative function. Furthermore, they stimulate group interaction, build morale, and provide an overriding sense of meaning to the often confusing times in the life of the group. In light of these multifaceted responsibilities, it is no surprise that therapists experience appreciable anxiety prior to the initiation of a group. If the job of the therapist can be broken down into an analysis of its component parts, the task of starting the group becomes much less formidable.

It may be of some comfort to the new group leader to realize that the therapeutic process has actually already begun with the earlier contacts with group members in the pregroup phase. During the evaluation of patients and the orientation of those selected for group membership, patients are also making observations about the group leader. The first session is "first" only in the sense that it will be the first meeting of the new entity, the therapy group. The leader has had significant contact with individual members prior to the first group meeting. This is helpful because one of the main objectives for the leader in Session 1 is simply to restate the group's ground rules, already discussed with each member individually, to the entire group.

Since the evaluation and orientation process has been standardized for all members, there should be no problem reiterating the guidelines as an initial organizing maneuver at the start of the first meeting. This serves the dual purpose of establishing an initial framework for the therapy and reinforcing the role of the leader as orchestrator of the group experience. Initial "opening moves" (discussed later) can vary; at some point very early in any first group meeting, however, a recitation of the group rules by the leader is standard fare. Members expect this, and it provides the leader an acceptable way to begin the group session.

In both short- and long-term groups, the leader has to keep the group on task from the outset. This function is accomplished in brief groups by the limits of time and the adjunctive use of structured protocols or a session-by-session plan that builds in safeguards against the tendency to drift away from the work of the group during times of anxiety. In long-term groups, the leader has to rely on clinical judgment to identify when the group is getting away from its stated goals. Especially in psychodynamic groups, the group therapist has more time and greater options available for dealing with the manifestations of resistances to central group tasks.

The leader of the psychodynamic group can help members understand how and why they are tempted to avoid engaging with emotionally charged issues that arise in the course of therapy. By use of interpretation, the leader can illustrate what members do to avoid conflict and can link present group behavior with past personal experiences, thus providing an enhanced level of insight for the member or the group as a whole. In the case of the psychoanalytically oriented group, the therapist has the freedom to use many of the elements derived from psychonanalytic techniques to keep the group centered. Through the analysis of intragroup transferences, the use of dream material, an emphasis on exploration of self and group phenomena, the consistent encouragement of self-disclosure, and the understanding of resistances, the leader is equipped to point out and modify barriers to resolution of problems in the group.

In the first group session, the leader not only presents to the group, but also personifies through his or her own posture, the behaviors and attitudes that are to become the group's norms. A leadership attitude that encourages members to be open in disclosing their thoughts and feelings, encourages free interaction among members and toward the leader, invites high degrees of group involvement and self-revelation, models active participation, and puts a high premium on understanding others as well as understanding oneself immediately sets a tone conducive to the generation of positive group norms.

It is wise for the leader to always be thinking ahead. Even though there are more "chores" to be done in the first session than in any other (except, possibly, the very last group meeting), the therapist has to add anticipation to his or her list of items to be implemented in that session. Thinking ahead refers to the ability of the group leader to simultaneously conduct the session and observe group interaction with an eye toward upcoming individual or group roadblocks.

Fears are present in every first meeting of a group. What specific members fear may vary somewhat, but the leader is on safe ground in looking for direct and indirect expressions of those fears as a common focal point for discussion in a first group meeting. When members are able to be open about their fears of groups, several common themes emerge. Most people are concerned with being attacked by others or making fools of themselves by sounding stupid or inarticulate when they speak. Also, they are frightened that their perceived inadequacies will be exposed in the public forum of the group.

For these reasons, the group leader can think ahead prior to the first session as to how ample doses of reassurance and support can be woven into the fabric of the group to ensure that no member feels at risk in a therapeutic setting. Simple statements as obvious as "It is normal for everyone to feel nervous in a first group meeting" will go a long way toward reducing start-up anxieties in group members and getting the group launched through discussions of what each member is specifically concerned about. When a leader takes this stance, it reinforces healthy boundary lines between patient and therapist and allows the leader to establish his or her role from the inception of the group experience. The support elements required by every group are initiated by the leader in typical first-session encounters such as the one just described.

Specific Considerations of the First Group Meeting

A number of issues remain to be considered before the leader steps into the room and begins the initial session. Although some of the topics were discussed in the section on pregroup orientation, there are still choices the leader must make prior to Session 1 that directly influence the direction the group will take.

The room itself and its arrangement will be the first thing members notice upon arriving at the first session. Many issues are tied to the structure of the therapy setting, and the leader must be aware of them. One everyday example includes the seating arrangement. Ideally, chairs should be freely moveable so that members can seat themselves in ways that provide nonverbal cues regarding their emerging relationships in the group. The "John Wayne model"—get the wagons (chairs) in a circle—is, by far, the most common physical arrangement of group therapy rooms.

It is recommended that, in the first session, the leader enter the room *after* all members are present and seated. In this way, it is possible to observe who sits next

BASIC PRINCIPLE 6

When planning a group intervention, think about three potential avenues of interaction: intrapsychic, interpersonal, and whole group. As early as the first group session, the multiple levels of interaction are evident in the group. The three levels that are present in any group are as follows.

1. *Individual/intrapsychic:* This is the dimension of the inner psychological life of each member in the group. The thoughts, feelings, fantasies, dreams, transferences, and any other manifestations of the unique aspects in the minds of each group member compose this level of potential group exploration.
2. *Interpersonal/group:* Traditionally, this refers to the transactions between group members during ongoing sessions. The interpersonal interaction in the present or "here and now" of the group is the operative venue for witnessing important group events.
3. *The "group-as-a-whole":* The homogenized response of the entire group or the group consensus is what is subsumed under the notion of the whole-group level of interaction. It is the stratum formed by the sum of group interchanges, resulting in a common group identity.

The group therapist who is aware of these three levels of group life is in an ideal position to plan a strategy for subsequent sessions by choosing which level, at a given point in time, is the most effective for intervention.

The following vignette illustrates the value of thinking on a three-dimensional level, even in the first group meeting. In the initial session of an open-ended outpatient group dealing with unsuccessful relationship themes, one member noted that she wasn't sure this was the "right group" for her. It was too early in the group's existence for this belief to be based on anything that had transpired in the group transactions themselves. The leader was alert to the threat this statement posed to the successful initiation of the new group and thought it through on the three levels just noted.

On the individual level, the group member in question was demonstrating her anxiety about relationships when faced with the actuality of meeting the people with whom she would be having a therapeutic relationship in the group. Historically, or intrapsychicacally, being in the first group meeting mobilized her lifelong self-doubts and feelings that people would eventually let her down. This sprung from a set of beliefs her mother and father had taught her: that the world was a dangerous place, that people can't be trusted, and that she really didn't have the toughness necessary to handle herself in relationships with anyone outside the family.

On the interpersonal level, it was apparent that she had developed an avoidant pattern as a coping mechanism for her feelings of vulnerability. Merely being in a group forced her to contend with the prospect that escape was not going to be a viable option for her in a psychotherapeutic context. When two of her fellow members attempted to welcome her to the group, she misperceived their actions as "manipulative" and self-serving. She withdrew in response to their overtures and slid back into the more familiar posture of interpersonal withdrawal.

At the level of the whole group, the leader had immediate concern for the impact of this patient's fears on the integrity of the group, since they were expressed in the form of questioning the appropriateness of the leader's judgment in selecting this group for her. The risk was that her doubts would amplify existing doubts on the parts of other group members, and the initial group meeting would be characterized by an air of fear, suspicion, and confusion.

Since this was an initial session and group cohesion had not yet had a chance to develop, the leader avoided a direct confrontation with the patient, instead choosing to generalize to the level of the theme of fears about joining a new group. This intervention accomplished

(continued)

BASIC PRINCIPLE 6 (continued)

several purposes. First, it interrupted the possibility of contagious emotional responses in others in the group, which invariably results in escalation of anxiety and a group that is difficult to reassure or control. Second, by not singling out the member who voiced the objection, the group leader was able to use the emphasis on similarities among group members to counter both the patient's and other group members' trepidation about the start of the group. Third, since the patient had a strong tendency to isolate herself interpersonally, the leader sought a means by which she could be included and realize that she was not unique in her concerns about whether or not this was the right group for her. Fourth, by handling the situation nonpunitively and avoiding sharp individual confrontations, the leader was able to model the acceptability of expressing negative feelings in the group and how quickly peer support appears to help diminish extremes of negative affect.

---

to whom, who always needs to be seated next to the leader, who moves his or her chair away from the group circle, and how seating arrangements change over time. Changes in or rigidity of seating patterns reflect behavioral data concerning alliances, subgroups, and splits and changes in intragroup relationships. Progress in therapy can also be demonstrated through subtle changes in seating patterns. Dependent group members who feel secure in early sessions only if they can sit close to the leader will show signs of individuation and autonomy, eventually choosing to take a chair further away from the leader's seat.

The arrangement of the room also relates to issues of psychological diagnosis. In high-functioning interactive groups, there should be no physical barriers (e.g., tables) inhibiting free expression and clear visibility among members. In groups in which members need protection from themselves or others, the converse is the case. Tables, the larger the better, afford a layer of emotional and literal protection from the tendency of patients with impulse control problems to act out their aggressive feelings. In groups in which members have a history of violent behavior, careful arrangement of the room (and seeing that the room is located within easy access to security personnel, particularly in hospitals or prisons) is essential.

Decisions about whether or not members will be allowed to smoke or eat during sessions are preinitial session decisions as well. We prohibit smoking in all group sessions. It is hard to imagine a good reason for allowing patients to smoke in psychotherapy. Since the whole enterprise is predicated on improving members' lives, it is a stark contradiction for a therapist to permit someone to do something self-destructive while in a therapy session. Many times pressure comes from patients who object to this restriction, stating that they will not be able to tolerate being in the group unless they can smoke. This is not negotiable. Patients are told that the worst that can happen to them is that they will become more anxious if they do not smoke, and a therapist's office is the best place to be if they feel overwhelmingly anxious. The goal of therapy is to teach people alternative, non-self-defeating ways to cope with dysphoric feelings through the use of a therapy group.

Food is on the list of pretherapy considerations because a case can be made for not only allowing but encouraging members to eat during group sessions! The precedent for this began in the 1970s, when injectable neuroleptic medications became available for the treatment of psychotic patients. It served the interests of patients and staff alike to administer and monitor medication by seeing groups of patients rather than holding individual sessions. The development of "coffee" groups (Masnick et al., 1974) was the first large-scale effort to attempt to involve psychotic outpatients in group psychotherapy.

The premise was largely behavioral in origin. It was postulated that, if patients were given coffee and doughnuts and gathered in a large informal group while waiting to see the psychopharmacologist, the seeds of social interaction could be sewn. The coffee group used food as an antianxiety agent to offset the apprehension most of the patients had about being with other people. The focus of the meeting was not on "psychotherapy," a concept that would scare away most prospective participants, but on a more efficient way to obtain medication and to have something to eat while waiting to see the doctor.

In point of fact, what emerged was a meeting led by a staff social worker that consisted of members milling around and making embryonic social contact with other people. This had not occurred spontaneously in clinics where patients sat around, simultaneously but noninteractively, waiting for their appointment with the doctor. The result of this pioneering effort was that psychotic patients had a much greater capacity for-and tolerance of-group situations if they were chaperoned during the experience and given food as a focal point to offset their uncertainty about how to interact spontaneously with others. Later in this volume, when groups for psychotic members are discussed, many of the same principles from the coffee groups will be apparent in daily clinical work with this patient population.

Another pregroup decision for the group therapist that seems deceptively simple is how to address members and how members will be addressing the leader. Traditional psychotherapies have taught us to use a titled basis when relating initially to patients in psychotherapy. Since the group model more closely approximates a social/familial model, the precedent for both presumes a degree of familiarity or intimacy in which people call each other by their first names. The leader must decide in advance of the first session which mode of address is most consonant with group goals.

Some patients desperately need to see their leader as a therapist and as an authority figure, and they need to refer to the therapist as "Dr.," "Ms.," or "Mr." or by another formal title. Others, often those in the same group, will have equivalent reasons for being on a first-name basis with the leader. Whatever choice the leader makes has inevitable clinical repercussions. The clinical implications of the system chosen to start the group are the focal point for this commentary.

A safe assumption for all group leaders is that members' expressed preference for what to be called and what to call the therapist is no accident, and this bit of clinical information is important. Several cases involving problems related to the "name calling" issue delineate the breadth of this seemingly innocuous aspect of a first group session.

In one group, a new member began the group by asserting, "Before we get started, I just want to make one thing very clear. I intend to call the therapist by his first name no matter what the rest of you do.'' The group was taken aback by the suddenness and forcefulness of this man's position. What was relevant from a group management standpoint was that the member was telegraphing many things in his brief but powerful opening statement. This was the first sign of his problems with authority, a lifelong issue for him and one of the major reasons group therapy had been recommended. In addition, he segregated himself from the other group members by taking a position before he conferred with them. In so doing, he demonstrated a glimpse of his interpersonal problems, including a lack of trust in others, an inability to collaborate with peers, and an ''I am above the law'' posture that was emblematic of his stance in his life outside the group, where he felt he was not accountable to any universal standards or rules.

In a supportive therapy group led by a male-female therapy team, the therapists gently, but perhaps naively, opened the group by saying, ''Feel free to call us anything you feel comfortable with.'' One group member immediately responded with ''How about Mommy and Daddy!'' Here again, the issue of how people address each other is often one of the first clues of how patients go about negotiating new interpersonal situations, what they fear, and, particularly in this case, their unmet expectations and hopes for what they can gain from a therapy group.

When cotherapists lead a group, the situation becomes more complex. Usually colleagues are on a first name basis with each other; when they lead a group, however, they are often called by their titles by the group members. This artificial distinction, born out of a sense of respect for all group participants, may inadvertently backfire. Communication between co-leaders can become problematic. Do cotherapists address themselves by title to the group and by first names when they talk to each other in sessions? If so, this creates a two-tiered system that excludes group members. If one co-leader is an MD or PhD, the group can call that leader ''Doctor''; what happens, however, if the other leader is from another discipline that does not carry the doctor title? ''Doctor Smith and his cotherapist Martha'' gives the group the wrong message. It implies that the therapists are primary (the doctor) and secondary (the therapist without the title) rather than equal in their leadership functions. This model, sarcastically called the ''Tarzan and Jane'' model of co-leadership, is to be avoided at all costs.

Some of the problems that can result from the leader's lack of attention to the issue of how to address members and leaders in the group include the following.

1. *Crisis creation.* A group member who wishes to divide the cotherapists or wants to have unblocked access to one leader will create a crisis situation for which it appears that only one of the leaders can be helpful. Medication pseudocrises are staged by people who subscribe to the notion that the physician is the primary therapist and the important leader to have access to.

2. *Denial of the patient role.* Members who are too quick to be on a first name basis with the therapist are resisting their role as a member in the group. Many times these patients not only use first names but also adopt a posture that is more leaderlike than memberlike. Therapists who work alone have to be careful not to be seduced into using such patients as substitute cotherapists.

3. *Prolonged use of titles.* Over the course of therapy in open-ended groups, a major part of the therapeutic menu is the resolution of lingering familial

BASIC PRINCIPLE 7

Cotherapists must have an ongoing dialogue following group sessions. This practice avoids pitfalls that can occur as a by-product of having two group leaders. Cotherapy is valued as a source of support for therapists who lead groups. It can, however, be problematic. The term "co" must represent equal, not adjunct, with respect to leadership roles in the group. The yardstick by which equality needs to be measured is the unique contribution each therapist has to offer the group. Interdisciplinary cotherapy teams often get tripped up by groups that restrict their views of the co-leaders to concrete differences between the two individuals.

Gender, age, professional discipline, position in the hierarchy of the parent institution, ethnicity, and degree of participation are often the substrates upon which group members form their assumptions about the relative power and worth of each group leader. Older leaders, for instance, are more likely to be seen as parental figures and consequently are attributed more power than their younger counterparts. Similarly, the cotherapist who is more active, directive, and verbal in sessions is assumed to be the main or primary therapist.

In groups that include members with borderline personality disorders, the tendency to use the defense of splitting is pronounced. The presence of a two-therapist model forms a fertile field for splitting defenses. Anxious borderline patients often seize upon the realistic differences between cotherapists and use them to keep the group focus off of themselves. Invariably, they attempt to undermine the therapeutic process by presenting the differences between leaders as a source of confusion and contradiction. In so doing, they have successfully deflected the group focus from themselves onto the leaders. By attempting to drive a wedge through the cotherapy relationship, these patients are using the principle of "divide and conquer" in the arena of group therapy.

An example occurred in a mixed adult outpatient group in which a member with a borderline personality disorder was made anxious by any show of unity between the leaders. As a child of divorce and a witness to constant parental fighting, he was unfamiliar and hence mistrustful of any show of solidarity between individuals of opposite sexes. He went to great lengths to undermine the unified posture of the therapists, saying, in one session, "The two of you have no separate identities. You always act and talk as though you agree on everything. What about the fact that you are a man and she is a woman? I get conflicting and confusing messages from the two of you, even though you pretend to be in agreement. I think you are plotting a strategy to trick us into trusting you, but I see through it."

Since a desire to disempower cotherapists is not restricted to members with borderline personality disorders, it behooves the cotherapy team to have a mechanism they can use to understand the state of the co-leader relationship at any point in the life of the group. Just as groups pass through predictable developmental stages, so do cotherapy relationships. It is critical, in terms of both ease of group management and personal comfort, that both leaders understand where their working relationship falls along the developmental spectrum of cotherapy paradigms.

In instances in which cotherapists are colleagues who choose to work together, there is an initial enthusiasm about having found each other and a sense of optimism about the prospects for a rewarding experience. This initial "honeymoon" phase of cotherapy relationships is not necessarily present in settings where teams are assigned by someone else in the clinical setting. These "clinically arranged marriages" can be risky. Involuntary cotherapy pairings require an initial stage of getting acquainted and experiencing the pros and cons of working with a colleague for the first time. If this preaffiliation stage is successfully negotiated, the pair proceeds to a honeymoon phase similar to that in which co-leaders have elected to team up.

A stage of joint function follows. In this phase, the cotherapists present a "united front" to the group. Communication by the leaders most commonly begins with "we," and there is little, if any, evidence of differences between the therapists. This "pseudomutual" stance

(continued)

BASIC PRINCIPLE 7 (continued)

is unrealistic and denies the individuality of each leader. It is often adopted as a way for therapists who are new to cotherapy or new to working with each other to handle anxieties by minimizing their differences.

Obviously, this is not the ultimate model leaders want to present to members about how two adults collaborate. In order to move to the next stage, the therapists must make an effort to openly differ and acknowledge realistic ways in which they are not the same. In dealing with their differences, they model for the group how to differ respectfully, how to express contrary opinions without undermining a partner, and how there is room in life to view a situation in more than one way.

Group members benefit from this corrective model of adult collaboration modeled by the co-leaders' efforts to refine their relationship as the group progresses. Members who come from families in which there is strict loyalty to one parent over the other learn that it is possible to have a simultaneous and noncompetitive relationship with two other adults.

Effective handling of the differences between leaders results in a final stage of cotherapy relationships: individuation and balance. At this point, the group is clear that the leaders have two distinct identities and can call upon the qualities of each in solving the problems for which they entered group therapy.

Cotherapists who are aware of the developmental stage of their therapeutic relationship can sense retrogressions to earlier stages in response to events in the group. For example, when sibling issues are at the forefront of the group, there is often a reverberation of competitive feelings between the leaders in response to this group theme. When the leaders can discuss these reactions openly in their joint meetings outside of group sessions, they add an extra dimension to the group experience that is not present with a therapist working alone. The changes in the cotherapy relationship now become an emotional barometer that is reactive to, and reflective of, central group processes.

Finally, it is wise for cotherapists to assume that all group members have a perception or fantasy about the real-life relationship between the leaders outside of the group. Male-female teams are often perceived as having a "therapeutic marriage" entailing a romantic and sexual relationship with each other. Senior and junior staff teams are frequently viewed as parent-child dyads. Training co-leaders of a similar age or stage of training evoke sibling or peer perceptions or transferences. The point is that it is the way in which the co-leaders are experienced in the minds of the members, rather than their true relationship to one another, that shapes the reactions, misperceptions, and interactions of members to co-leaders.

---

problems. For many, the ability to relinquish the need to call the therapist by his or her title is the result of taxing work done in the group that may be reflective of resolution of family themes. Although the shift from title to first name between member and leader may be difficult, it is a desired aim in group treatment. Owing to the psychodynamic significance invested by each member in the therapist, this process unfolds at different rates. The therapist must be able to distinguish between a patient who has unresolved issues and is not yet ready to make the transition and a patient who is actually further along but is apprehensive about being on familiar terms with the therapist.

One useful method for starting the group in a way that will both facilitate group interaction and preserve the possibilities for examining the therapeutic significance of the naming process is for the leader to start the session by introducing himself or

The "go-around" or "round robin" technique—asking members to comment in succession—is often used in initial group sessions or during the course of an ongoing group. While this is its most common contemporary use, the technique has important and lesser known historical origins.

Alexander Wolf, a psychoanalyst who pioneered the application of analytic methods to the group setting, experimented with modifying conventional tools of individual psychoanalysis to the group milieu. In the course of his work, Wolf looked for ways to use dream analysis in groups. He began sessions by asking for one group member to report a recent dream. Then, instead of having the dreamer associate to his or her dream, Wolf asked each group member to share associations to the dream.

What emerged was an array of thoughts, feelings, other dream elements, comments, and a host of unique and valuable material for promoting group interaction. The dreamer did not necessarily receive an interpretation for the dream, but the dream was the catalyst around which group interchange began. Quite serendipitously, Wolf discovered that modifications such as these would allow for the use rather than abandonment of the basic principles of individual psychoanalysis.

Wolf went on to do similar work involving the analysis of transference and resistance, free association, exploration of unconscious conflict, and many other standard tools of the analytic method. His basic position was that, if properly modified, much of the standard armamentarium of individual analysis would find a useful place in analytic group psychotherapy. Wolf's landmark work and his later collaboration with his friend and colleague, Emanual Schwartz, earned him the title of the father of group psychoanalysis and resulted in the publication of the classic text *Psychoanalysis in Groups.*

herself by title and full name. This allows group members the choice of a variety of names to use when talking to or about the therapist in group sessions. The choice made by the member is important to note, because it provides clues about the person's entry posture into the group. Dealing with issues related to what people call each other and the therapist is not ordinarily part of an initial session unless the situation is of such magnitude that it threatens the viability of the group. The leader makes a mental note for use in later sessions if it will provide a useful substrate for addressing patient issues manifesting themselves in the form of group interactions around the theme of how people address others.

Starting the Initial Session

It is essential to begin the first session on time. Even though there may be members who straggle, get lost, forget, or are chronically late to everything in their lives, the stance of the therapist must be one of promptness. Group leaders must practice what they preach; it is unreasonable to expect members to comply with a set of standards to which the leaders do not subscribe. If certain members are not present at the designated starting time, the leader can offer an explanation for their absence if, indeed, he or she knows why they are not in attendance.

The therapist facilitates introductions by introducing himself or herself and asking members to state their first names in turn. Depending on the nature of the group, the introductions can be combined with members' initial problem statement

Table 5.1. Therapeutic guidelines for substance abuse groups

1. The goal of the group is to help oneself and others abstain from drug and alcohol use.
2. Each member must be prepared to be totally honest about past or present drug use.
3. An absolute commitment is made to refrain from using any mind- or mood-altering substances.
4. Regular attendance is mandatory. Excessive absences are destructive to the group and its mission.
5. No one may come to the group while actively under the influence of drugs or alcohol.
6. "Slips" (i.e., using drugs in the course of the group) will initially be treated as potential learning experiences. However, repeated slips are self-defeating and may require different treatment, such as hospitalization or a stay in a drug rehabilitation program.
7. All group members agree to have random urine testing for the presence of drugs done at the discretion of the group leader.
8. Members are asked not to socialize with each other outside of group sessions.
9. The group leader has the permission of each group member to be in contact with family members or with any other therapists who may be involved in his or her care.
10. Absolute confidentiality is a nonnegotiable core element of the group. Violations of the confidentiality agreement are grounds for dismissal from the group.

or reason for being in the group. "Please state your first name and say something about why you are in the group" is a typical opening statement.

Once everyone in the group has spoken, the leader briefly restates the group ground rules discussed with each member in the orientation phase. Ground rules are group specific and are designed for two primary purposes: to anticipate potential issues that could undermine group therapy and to begin to establish the desired group norms from the beginning. Table 5.1 (Spitz & Rosecan, 1987) illustrates a prototypical set of group standards for a substance abuse group.

What follows depends on the time frame of the group, the degree of psychopathology present in the group members, and the theoretical orientation of the group leader. In short-term groups, the leader takes charge of the session and begins the therapeutic program that will govern the group for its entire length. Groups with severely impaired members require support and structure from the leader in order to make members feel at ease in the new group. Leaders with a psychodynamic orientation may say nothing after the initial go-around and see what the group does spontaneously. Some leaders will use the period immediately following the ice-breaking phase to elicit reactions from group members about how they are feeling about being in the group.

In describing a first session (or any phase of group therapy), the intent is not to be formulaic in recommending interventions. These recommendations are meant as guidelines that are flexible enough that they can be tailored to comfortably fit the therapeutic style of the leader. It is best to view the ideas presented regarding leadership as a therapeutic road map allowing for many different routes to the same treatment destination. The suggestions are offered in a spirit meant to free group therapists, not to handcuff them by implying any sense of rigid adherence to the clinical interventions illustrated.

Common Initial Session Themes

The next step involves management of the bulk of the initial session. Another suggestion that may help the leader organize a plan for the meeting is to anticipate and identify the group themes that almost always accompany a first session. The search for commonalities among members is an integral part of a first group meeting. As noted earlier, this represents the very beginning of the forces that will shape group cohesion.

The search for common elements shared by group members is also a way in which members deal with the theme of inclusion versus exclusion in groups. The unspoken feeling is "Will I be accepted by the group? If we share enough in common, I will feel reassured that my chances of getting rejected are decreased." Groups that encourage open discussion in a first session will involve extensive conversation centering around the ways in which members share characteristics. Work themes, where people live, prior therapy experiences, similar psychological symptoms, and shared side effects from medications are all recognizable initial session group themes.

The issue of trust is a core first-session concern. Members worry that they will not be able to openly express themselves and be certain of an appropriate response from fellow group members. Members also listen carefully in the first meeting for signs that others may not be as committed to the group or as motivated to be helpful to others as they are. This, too, is a component of the trust issue presented in the first session. Trust always includes the group therapist as well. Members need to know that the leader understands them, will not let them be the victims of scapegoating, is capable of leading the group, is not arbitrary or punitive, and can handle the ongoing problems that will arise.

Another constant in first group sessions is variation on the themes of independence and dependence. These themes may show themselves in the form of members' attempts to have one-to-one dialogues with the leader, as though the other group members were not present. Alternatively, some members may act in counterphobic ways by denying the leader's importance and even suggesting that the group can lead itself. The initial impact of being in the group and tangibly seeing that the leader has to be shared results in dependency issues coming to the fore. Group members struggle with the dilemma of how they will establish a special niche for themselves so that the leader recognizes their needs and will be sufficiently attentive to them.

Testing of the leader, another in-group expression of anxieties felt in a first meeting, is also an extremely common initial session theme. Here, too, the forms this theme may take are interesting. Incessant, direct questioning of the leader is perhaps the most obvious form of testing. Sometimes, the questioning is less for clarification and more confrontational. It is as though the member is presenting a challenge to the leader to see whether the leader is equal to the task.

Another group phenomenon that reflects the theme of testing the leader occurs when the group permits one member to describe his or her individual issues at length. The member is usually all too pleased to have this much of the therapist's undivided attention. The group colludes in this process for two reasons. First, when members let someone else take center stage, they are spared the anxiety of being the group focus themselves. Second, the group members are observing how the leader handles a problem situation presented by one member as a preview of how they think the leader might handle one of their own when they choose to self-disclose in the group.

Common First-Session Patient Roles

Since the first group session is a tense time for virtually everyone in the group, members assume roles in the group that reflect how they try to negotiate new interpersonal and therapeutic situations. The group leader who is aware of the postures taken by different members is in a better position to plan a treatment strategy for the group. The assumption of in-group roles roughly corresponds to the kinds of resistances members will demonstrate to quell their fears about change in therapy. In a first session only, identification of these roles takes place as a private process on the part of the therapist. Since it is entirely appropriate for people who are anxious to lapse into roles that are familiar, albeit maladaptive, the leader must permit members to work their way into the group in whichever role they adopt.

The leader has an initial impression of the roles taken by each group member. This information is saved for use in future sessions should rigidity of roles interfere with individual or group progress. Roles or postures that frequently appear from the start of a group can be extreme. Two extremes on the continuum of verbal production are the silent member and the monopolizing member. Silent members handle their fears of the group by observing rather than participating. Often, other new members are made uncomfortable by the silence and try to draw the silent member out by asking questions. The member either responds and becomes more involved in the group or retains his or her silent posture at all costs, usually with explanations such as "I'm a shy person," "I'm not ready or comfortable talking about myself just yet," or "I'd rather watch what goes on and jump in when I have something to say." The group therapist respects and does not challenge these defenses in a first group meeting. As the group progresses, unidimensional defenses and rigid roles become open for exploration as part of the patient's therapeutic agenda.

When a new member monopolizes a good portion of the initial session, this individual is controlling his or her anxiety by talking excessively. Group members are often legitimately confused about the differences between a social situation and a group therapy meeting. Members have to be educated and given permission by the therapist to interrupt members who are digressing or obsessing. Members who monopolize are the symptom bearers for those in the group not comfortable with spontaneous interaction among all of the participants. Nonverbal, noninterrupting members are equally involved in the enabling of a monopolizer in dominating group time. The group leader can provide a guide for future sessions by offering to group members the following psychotherapeutic maxim: "In group therapy it may not be polite to interrupt someone in the middle of a sentence, but it is fine to interrupt someone in the middle of a paragraph!"

Describing one's symptoms at length is another opening posture for which a therapeutic plan must be devised. Symptom description, like social chatter (another common first-session resistance to self-disclosure), tends to keep the group imbedded in a certain level of superficiality and, over time, thwarts the development of a detailed focus on relevant group issues. The introduction of humor can also be extremely therapeutic in groups; however, when a member takes the role of the joker or court jester in the group, this too derails conversations that are proceeding into uncomfortable emotional territory. The humor is seductive for member and leader alike, but it is the leader's obligation to balance the constructive use of humor against its countertherapeutic use as a sabotaging maneuver.

Challenges to the leader are seen less commonly but are important first-session behaviors. Two primary forms are arguing with the leader and directly confronting the leader. People who are argumentative in their lives reproduce this behavior in the group. Because the group leader is an emotionally supercharged figure, the argumentative member may focus on the therapist in a first session. Other group members are not immune to the challenge of the confrontational member, but when this occurs in a first meeting it usually is an indirect message to the therapist. Creating conflicts or disputes between group members may be motivated by a member's desire to place the therapist in a position in which he or she (like a judge, referee, or parent) must make a ruling about the issue at hand. If the leader does so, the group member who initiated the argument looks carefully to see whose "side" the leader takes.

Direct confrontation of the leader in the form of an attack or questioning the leader's competence is also one of the many faces resistance and fears may take. Members who accuse the leader of being too active or too passive, showing favoritism, being arbitrary, insensitive, or judgmental are often voicing their own fears about negative consequences resulting from misuse of the therapist's perceived power in the group. Confronting the leader in these ways is a final manifestation of initial anxiety about the group the member has just entered. The unspoken communication to the group therapist is something along the lines of the following: "Are you competent, strong, and experienced enough to be relied upon to take care of the group?"

Leadership challenges in the early stages of the group are best seen as indirect requests for reassurance. The leader who mistakenly enters into a power struggle with a provocative or testing group member usually "fails the test" and becomes embroiled in an avoidable tug of war with a fearful patient.

Scapegoating of a member is another initial group process that occasionally hampers the start of a new group. It is tempting for new group members who are apprehensive to seize upon a statement or behavior of another group member onto which they can displace their emotions. Scapegoating of a group member is a familiar form this process takes. Scapegoating is never a therapeutic event, no matter when it surfaces in a group; as such, it constitutes a group emergency. For this reason, the rule of not confronting members' roles or resistances in a first group meeting is overridden in instances of scapegoating. The group leader cannot knowingly participate in or sanction any group process that causes harm to a member.

Patients who have self-defeating, masochistic interpersonal relationships have an uncanny knack of inviting attack upon themselves, even in group situations in which the participants are not known to them. Certainly, this is a high-priority item in their group therapy. However, if the scapegoating process is not interrupted by an active leadership stance, such individuals may drop out of the group, be so traumatized that they will never again try any group therapy, or suffer serious damage to their self-esteem.

Finally, helpful information for the group therapist is present on the nonverbal as well as the verbal level of the group. In the first meeting, it is a good idea for the leader to note significant patterns of behavior communicated through actions rather than words. This may be the first glimpse of important issues that will require attention in the group as it evolves. Consider the following vignette from an initial meeting of a couples group. A man in the group complained bitterly that his wife was undemonstrative and never displayed any overt signs of affection. In the initial group session, the group theme quickly turned to the subject of how different couples handle angry feelings in their relationships. Suddenly, this man who had been quite vocal in expressing himself was conspicuously silent. Nothing in the verbal content of the session could account for his silence.

Fortunately, the group session was videotaped and, upon review of the tape, the group leader noticed that each time the topic of anger was introduced, this man's wife moved closer to him and held his hand. Her family history was replete with incidents of physical abuse and verbal shouting matches without conflict resolution, and her parents believed that it was ''sinful'' for children to be angry in a family. She grew into an adult who was virtually phobic about being exposed to conflict or to anger-inducing situations.

The husband was so desperate to have positive contact with his wife that he immediately shut off any expression of anger in exchange for her gestures of apparent connection with him. What looked like affection was really a mechanism for extinguishing or controlling angry feelings in a partner. This central relationship dynamic, which was to form the mainstay of their group work, was communicated nonverbally in the first group meeting!

Ending the First Session

Just as a group session must start on time, it must end promptly. At the end of a first group meeting, it is a good idea to allow some time before members leave to get a sense of closure on the meeting. The end of the first session may be seen as a termination in miniature. Brief therapy formats differ slightly from their longer term counterparts in regard to the manner in which the first session ends. Both share the goal of debriefing members and preparing them for the next session. The two models differ in the techniques used to accomplish these ends.

In brief therapy groups, especially those of a cognitive or behavioral nature, the first meeting ends with homework. An out-of-session task is assigned for members to complete before the next group session. For example, in a behaviorally oriented weight control group, the leader assigns the task of keeping a food diary for the upcoming week. The task is explained to the group in plain language so that members cannot come back to the next session claiming that they did not do the diary because they did not understand what was required of them. A representative example of the phrasing for this task is as follows: ''For the next session, it is important that each of you keep a food diary. What this means is a record of when you eat, what you eat, and what your main emotions were at the time you felt motivated to eat. We will review the diaries in the next group session.''

Since time is of the essence in short-term groups, the therapeutic process has to begin in the first session. Closing the session with a concrete task demystifies the therapy experience for members. They know what to expect in the next meeting and tangibly see that they are going to be actively involved in their own therapeutic progress through their efforts outside of formal group sessions.

Leaders of long-term groups are not as directorial in regard to managing the end of the first session. There are many positive ways to conclude the first meeting in open-ended group formats. A popular technique involves informing the members that the session will be ending shortly and asking them to again engage in a go-around as they did at the start of the session, this time sharing their feelings and reactions as to what the first meeting was like for them. The group leader usually follows this with a summary based on the content of the members' responses. In an initial meeting, the therapist's summation emphasizes the positive aspects of what occurred. If members took mild risks in revealing things about themselves, if they demonstrated empathic responses to others, and if the group stayed on course, the therapist reinforces these behaviors, which he or she wishes to become permanent fixtures in the group, through the use of a summary statement. Even in psychodynamic groups, interpretations are avoided in favor of supportive and reassuring comments. Therapists need to program the group to understand when the session is coming to a close. A session summary by the leader is one closing ''signature'' that can be used to get the group into the habit of stopping on time. If the group becomes too accustomed to the leader doing the work of summarizing the session, the group leader can ask a member to make the closing observations. In this way, the group does not become lazy and let the therapist do all of the thinking about what has transpired. End-of-session summaries are the psychodynamic parallel of the message given in brief groups that no matter the group design, patients have an active role in determining their therapeutic course.

In groups with seriously ill psychiatric patients, the session summary is sometimes recorded in written form and read aloud at the start of the following group meeting. The rationale for doing this is severalfold. For example, it provides a sense of continuity from session to session for members who often have difficulty seeing such connections on their own. In addition, the written summaries are kept in a book, and the group develops a sense of having its own history and a document that concretely shows evidence of their successful participation. Summaries can be used over time to demonstrate progress to patients, who can compare where they were with where they are now. Starting each group with the reading of the notes of the last session supplies a structured beginning and a routine for patients who are in need of these elements in their lives.

Ending first meetings of higher functioning groups with the request for verbal feedback from members allows the group leader to evaluate how the session has gone, note what roles members take in their initial entry into the group, and what obstacles to progress, or resistances, each member and the group may face in future sessions. This information is essential to successful treatment planning in group therapy.

Before leaving the subject of the initial group session, some comments are in order. The first session has been studied extensively and been given great and deserved attention. What is virtually absent from the group literature is any emphasis on the second group session.

After the first meeting has been held and members have experienced what it is actually like to be in a group, as contrasted with how they thought it would be, there is usually a second-stage reaction to group membership. The leader can get therapeutic mileage from an appreciation of where each member is after the first session is over. Some members will be greatly relieved and reassured by what they saw in Session 1. Hopeful about the prospects for change, feeling that there are kindred spirits in the world who grapple with the same stresses in life, and buoyed by the enthusiasm of the group leader, many members are much less anxious about attending the next meeting. As a result, their posture in the second session may differ dramatically from that in the first. Patients with high degrees of anticipatory anxiety often demonstrate the process just described.

People who are highly competitive, those who possess paranoid traits, and those who have profound social anxiety are not as likely to have such a rapid positive response to the first session. They usually wait longer to increase their involvement with the group. In this respect, their second session role may look much like their role in Session 1.

In either case, the group leader needs to pay attention to the shifting interpersonal roles taken by members of the group. Retreats back to an earlier posture may signal that a critical issue has surfaced for a group member and that the member is at an immediate loss on how to handle it. Experimentation with new roles exhibited by other group members may begin as early as Session 2 of the group. Borrowing some of the leader's qualities can also be in evidence in the second group meeting. Threats to leave the group and questioning of the group's value often crop up in the second group session. In order to get on with the tasks of the group, this introduction of doubt and skepticism must be dealt with before it becomes part of the group's ongoing climate. Session 2 is a frequent forum wherein fear-driven reservations are voiced vigorously.

If the group leader thinks of the group experience as a continuum rather than a series of sequential sessions separate from each other, it is more likely that he or she will be aware of potential threats to the attainment of goals as they occur. The initial session is another step along this continuum that began with the pregroup interactions with group members. Once the first session is completed and the group has officially begun, what logically follows from this point of view are the successive stages of group development, the subject of Chapter 6.

6

Stages of Group Psychotherapy: Therapeutic Issues

All group therapies are interpersonal processes that occur over time. As such, groups progress through a series of developmental stages in the course of their existence. Much like a human infant evolves from a primitive being requiring immediate satisfaction into a mature adult who has the capacity for tolerating frustration, seeing beyond the moment, and making use of collected life experiences, groups also pass through definable phases on their way to maturity.

These stages of development of therapeutic groups are overlapping and indistinct in clinical practice. Group therapists who write about phases of groups arbitrarily divide them into distinct entities to distinguish one from another. Regardless of the system any group leader uses to conceptualize the stage of his or her group, it is essential to have an idea of where the group is in its therapeutic journey. The major advantage for group leaders who are familiar with stages of development in groups is that treatment planning is made much easier.

The goal of understanding the stage of a group's development is to enable the group leader to make stage-specific treatment interventions. The more appropriate an intervention is to the phase of the group, the more likely it is that two things will happen. First, the opportunities for advancing the goals of the group and the individuals in it are enhanced dramatically. Second, and equally if not more important, is that stage-specific interventions reduce the chance of untoward reactions among group members.

Many psychiatric casualties emanating from group therapy experiences can be directly traced to mistakes involving the timing of the techniques chosen by a leader who is not sufficiently aware of where the group is at the time of the intervention chosen. Precedent for this observation is not the unique province of group therapy. Psychoanalysts have observed for years that it is best to analyze a patient's resistances before dealing with the content of his or her productions. Behaviorists have noted the importance of achieving a state of relaxation prior to encouraging action in areas of phobic magnitude for patients. Systems-oriented family therapists value a nonintrusive therapeutic posture until they have worked with a family long enough to be sure of how the system operates. Therapists from diverse clinical orientations have noted the importance of avoiding premature interventions that the patient is not yet ready to handle.

There are many parallels to this premise in group psychotherapy. This chapter highlights examples of the use and misuse of clinical interventions at various stages of group development.

CLASSIFICATION OF STAGES OF GROUP THERAPY

While it is tempting to generalize about the stages groups go through, any method of classification must consider the time frame and clinical goals of the group. In the broadest sense, members of groups engage with the generic themes of affiliating with others, defining the rules for power and control, resolving issues of dependency, achieving adult intimacy, creating a healthy set of interpersonal boundaries, establishing a sense of individuality and autonomy, and dealing with the separation and loss themes ushered in by the termination of the group.

Interpersonal/"Here-and-Now" Model

There are significant differences between the form and length of group stages in brief and long-term therapy groups. In an open-ended, interpersonal group model along the lines of Yalom's (1985) interactional outpatient format, one can see stage-specific tasks indicating the point the group has reached in therapy. In Yalom's words:

A group goes through an initial stage of orientation, characterized by a search for structure and goals, by much dependency on the leader, and by much concern about the group boundaries. Next, a group encounters a stage of conflict, as it deals with issues of interpersonal dominance. Thereafter, the group becomes increasingly concerned with inter-member harmony and affection, while inter-member differences are often submerged in the service of group cohesiveness. Much later, the mature work group emerges, which is characterized by high cohesiveness, considerable interpersonal and intrapersonal investigation, and full commitment to the primary task of the group and each of the members. (1985, pp. 299–300)

In Yalom's model, these stages are followed by a termination period with its own associated dynamic issues. When Yalom's prototypical group is compared with a psychodynamically oriented model, it is easy to see areas of consensus and difference.

Traditional Psychodynamic/Analytic Model

The initial stage of a time-unlimited psychodynamic group is that of a process of preaffiliation among members within which they experience themes of emerging trust and a tentative commitment to the group. Members are more leader focused and less inclined to interact with each other. The hallmark of the second stage is an emphasis on interpersonal issues. Group dynamics are manifested through power struggles with other group members, challenges to the leader, a high risk of dropout, the emerging seeds of group cohesion and group norms, and competitive and aggressive behavior.

Following the successful management of the early stages of the group, the next phase to appear is one in which the subject of closeness and distance in relationships dominates the group's attention. This stage is emotionally intense and can be a stormy time for the leader and the group. Members risk exposure through greater self-disclosure and often communicate their needs for emotional nurturing from the group. Transference relationships in the group solidify and become more available for group exploration. Powerful affect is experienced and begins to be expressed regularly by members during this stage.

The phase that follows involves the task of membership differentiation. Once group cohesion has been firmly established, group members are more comfortable in examining their differences. Up to this point, the emphasis has been more on similarities in the service of building group cohesiveness. Since members have gone through a period of experiencing identifications with one another and have felt the positive impact of peer support, they are more comfortable in venturing out into areas in which they are dissimilar. Greater spontaneity of expression, high levels of member-to-member support, and respect and tolerance for differences are distinctive elements of this stage of the group.

The last stage deals with the feelings generated by the ending of the group. Themes of separation and loss are common. In response to these painful emotions, members often revert to earlier, more primitive defenses. The reappearance of excessive use of denial in refusing to accept that the group is actually stopping, regressive behavior, or the recrudescence of symptoms or problems that appeared to be well in hand are familiar reactions of members struggling with the termination of the group. As is the case with most groups, a review of each member's progress and an assessment of what, if any, further treatment is needed take place during the termination stage.

Brief Group Therapy Model

Several proponents of the model of brief group psychotherapy have applied their expertise to a definition of the stages of development in time-limited groups. MacKenzie's (1990) six-phase classification system of group stages consists of engagement, differentiation, individuation, intimacy, mutuality, and termination. His orientation is predicated on the assumption that "developmental stages and social roles together constitute a theoretical infrastructure for organizing group phenomena" (MacKenzie, 1990, p. 47). In this model, each group stage has its unique therapeutic challenge, and the therapy is specific in that there is a strong emphasis on the particular stage of development of the group.

Piper, McCallum, and Azim (1992), in their work involving a 12-session psychodynamically oriented group therapy format for people who have experienced a major loss in their lives, evolved a simple group staging model that divides the entire group experience into clusters of sessions defined as beginning, middle, and end stages. Stage-specific tasks and methods to implement these steps are clearly spelled out for the leader. As an example, one goal of Sessions 4 through 8 is to help members see their stereotypical roles taken in response to loss. The leader deliberately avoids direct gratification of the expression of these feelings and instead uses interpretive interventions to mobilize concealed affect related to the losses sustained by group members.

Budman and Gurman (1988) approach the staging of groups from an adult developmental perspective in which the focus of group therapy remains on the individual developmental task for each member. The groups are homogeneous in composition with respect to life cycle stage and age, thus facilitating the use of common themes to accelerate the pace of the group. The resultant system of phase classification of is as follows: starting the group, early therapy, middle of the group, late therapy, termination, and follow-up.

Elsewhere, Spitz (1996) has proposed a staging schema for brief groups in the context of managed care. This model incorporates stage-related considerations that are factored into treatment planning owing to the unique demands of group therapy conducted in the managed mental health care setting. The pregroup phase adds some administrative tasks to the ordinary pregroup preparation of the patient described earlier in this volume. Before the group begins, the therapist checks to see that precertification has been obtained and often reviews the initial treatment plan with the managed care representative.

The induction into group stage follows next and is used as an added means of assessing how effectively the group has been composed. Stage 3 in this system is the establishment of rapid group cohesion. Since time is at a premium, the sooner the group can coalesce, the sooner the participants can begin the therapeutic process.

The fourth stage (and the one most difficult to describe) is the working group phase. This period in the group is usually the longest in terms of time. The ''work'' in this stage is roughly equivalent to the working through phase of traditional individual or group therapies. In psychodynamic groups, the insight gained in therapy is put into action via the interpersonal transactions of the group. In cognitive or behaviorally oriented groups, the principles taught are applied both in the group and in the lives of members outside the group. Typical of the working or middle phase of therapy are the inevitable ambivalent feelings members experience as change begins to occur. The working group stage presents many opportunities for growth along with coexisting forces pulling members in the direction of sameness and rigidity.

Stage 5 is one of individuation and differentiation. This stage is virtually identical to the corresponding phase in MacKenzie's classification except that managed care may intrude into the therapeutic process. In this phase, a treatment plan may come up for review for recertification purposes. The group leader has to factor in the stage of the group's development in order to intelligently discuss the progress of any group member whose treatment is up for review. When there is still significant work to be done in therapy, the leader must communicate this clearly in the treatment plan and goals to ensure further authorization for group treatment. The therapeutic work of Stage 5 strengthens the group members for the final stage: termination.

Clinical Significance of Group Stages

In the three models of staging groups (or some combination of the three, as seen in technically eclectic group leadership), an effective group leader requires a working knowledge of the stages of group treatment. Identifying group stages gives the therapist control over the group and prevents it from getting sidetracked. While this is applicable to all groups, it is of particular importance to keep the group on task in groups with shorter time frames. Brief groups lack the luxury of open-ended time present in their long-term counterparts and are not able to accomplish their stated goals unless the leader sticks to the original therapeutic plan. There no time to do extensive repair work in short-term group formats.

Having an idea of what stage the group is in gives the group therapist an advantage insofar as there are predictable behaviors related to different stages of the group. This allows for advance planning, along with eventual ease of management of potential therapeutic pitfalls in the group or threats to the group's continued existence. The leader has to be prepared to be active in any meeting, whether the group is of long or short duration. Staging the group helps in terms of anticipation of the stage-related issues that are likely to emerge in future sessions.

Throughout all group stages, an essential quality of a good leader is the ability to be self-reflective. The reactions a leader experiences in the group provide another avenue for understanding what stage of development the group is going through. When competitive feelings are induced in the leader, it is often in response to unresolved sibling, parental, or other interpersonal issues that are being worked out in the group. When the leader can make use of his or her own reactions or countertransferences to what has transpired in the group, it increases the probability that these group themes can be brought up as "grist" for the therapeutic mill. Knowing what issues are commonly linked to each developmental stage of a group lessens the chance of the leader getting caught up in his or her own responses and helps keep the group focus on the members and their goals.

In essence, stages of group development are an integral part of any group. They can be harder to identify in shorter term groups but are of enormous therapeutic help to the group leader, providing a systematized way of looking at the issue of group stages.

Application of Stage-Specific Interventions

The termination phase of a group offers a fertile field for demonstrating the usefulness of knowledge of where the group stands in its development. Endings in groups are dependent on the nature of the group. In brief, fixed membership groups, the entire group terminates in unison. In long-term groups, the termination phase is often heralded by the first member who introduces the notion of preparing to leave the group.

The differences between long-term and brief group management of termination issues are illustrated in Table 6.1.

There are many powerful therapeutic issues embedded in termination. Sensitive management of termination issues on the part of the group leader can help members negotiate this trying phase. In brief groups, there is an acute and immediate awareness on everyone's part that the group is ending. Even in the first session of a brief group, termination issues can be identified. This is not the case in open-ended, time-unlimited groups, where there is much less of a sense of urgency about the conclusion of the group.

The pressure on the group leader to extend the time frame of a brief group can be intense. The conventional wisdom in brief therapies has been (and continues to be) to stay with the original therapy plan at all costs. It is inevitable that there will be unresolved issues and emotional loose ends in most groups. The termination date in brief groups is nonnegotiable. The group leader must distinguish between

Table 6.1. Comparison of the termination stage: long-term and brief group therapy

	Long-term group	Short-term group
Length of time	Many sessions; "ritualization" and long preparation phase	Shorter, more sudden termination
Awareness of group ending	Late in the life of the group	Immediate and ongoing
Group cohesion	Stronger, longer duration of cohesion	Shorter, intense sense of cohesion
Common themes	Separation, death, loss	Separation, death, sense of unfinished business in the group
Timing of termination	Members end singly when individual goals have been met	Entire group ends at the same time
Transference	"Familylike"; central to the technique in psychodynamic groups	Present but not as developed as in long-term groups; usually not a central component of a brief group
Group focus	Shifting focus over time	Persistent focus on original group goal
Therapist risks	Countertransference reactions	Extending the ending date of the group
Follow-up	Done in instances where significant problems remain for a member	Always done as part of the last phase of the group

unresolved individual problems that do not surface until the termination phase and those that are reactive in nature and triggered by the ending of the group. Therapists who succumb to group pressure to extend the time frame of the group usually lose credibility and find their position as group leader weakened.

In most long-term groups, individual members terminate or graduate from the group at different times. Ordinarily, an individual termination date is set well in advance of the member's leaving, and individual and group issues related to the termination are discussed and analyzed as necessary. Leaders of long-term groups who are aware that termination of one member brings with it many issues for all members can begin to identify these issues and help the group understand them.

In one group, a member announced that she felt ready to plan her departure from therapy. This single statement evoked the following clinical issues related to termination in groups.

1. Members began to question her "readiness" to leave. The group leader had to determine whether this was a defensive maneuver on the part of individuals made anxious by the prospect of losing a valued group member or whether the members sensed that significant problems remained to be resolved and the member was leaving prematurely to avoid dealing with these problems.

2. A number of other group members voiced a similar desire to set a termination date for themselves. When one member of a group indicates the desire to leave the group, the other members take a quick emotional inventory. Many discover that they feel uncomfortable remaining in the group. At times, an epidemic of threats to leave the group ensues through the mechanism of emotional contagion, which "seizes" many apprehensive, envious, or competitive group members.

3. Members suggested that it would be a great idea to have a party to celebrate the graduation of the member from the group. In some groups, usually those composed of patients who want to strengthen or develop their social skills, a going-away party may be an ideal vehicle for putting certain group goals into action. The vast majority of groups, especially those toward the psychodynamic end of the psychotherapeutic spectrum, would actively discourage this suggestion. Parties are often misused to mask a variety of negative feelings on the part of remaining group members. Separation fears, sensitivity to loss, angry feelings, concerns about not measuring up as well as others, concerns about "public" (in front of others in the group) displays of sadness, worry about being seen as emotionally immature, and a host of other difficult emotions can be camouflaged behind the false gaiety of a party for a departing member.

4. One member said he would be unable to attend the departing member's last session. Nothing would realistically prevent him from coming, despite the fact that he attributed his inability to attend to scheduling conflicts with a course he was planning to take in the future. Termination evokes such exquisitely painful feelings for some members, who must physically absent themselves from witnessing the event.

These are but a few of the stage-specific clinical considerations raised by patients in the termination phase of group psychotherapy. Long-term therapy means long-term relationships among group members. The threat of prospective rupture of significant interpersonal bonds developed in the group causes a rash of ambivalent feelings among the group membership. These feelings require exploration, not cosmetic cover. When the group leader knows that a group is at a certain stage, the task of guiding members through these troubled emotional waters becomes simplified. What could be a traumatic time for a patient can turn into a maturational experience when the group leader is cognizant of the important emotional issues attached to each stage of group therapy.

II

CONTEMPORARY APPLICATIONS OF GROUP PSYCHOTHERAPY

7

Brief Group Psychotherapy

Psychotherapy has always been an evolving field, one that is sensitive to changes in the cultural climate, reactive to the lessons learned from history, cognizant of world events, aware of developments in scientific research, open to new systems of diagnosis of emotional illness, and focused on updating theory and clinical techniques in the spirit of providing a level of care that is relevant, effective, and capable of being incorporated into new health care delivery systems. Brief group therapy is the most notable example of how the confluence of these factors has influenced the practice of group psychotherapy.

One of the fringe benefits of the emergence of managed mental health care in the last decade has been the increased interest in and greater clinical experience with cost- and time-efficient models of psychotherapy. Short-term group therapies have been the major beneficiaries of this shift in emphasis spurred by concerns about the escalating economics of health care costs.

Brief group therapy is at the leading edge of the changes that are evolving in the practice of contemporary group psychotherapy. As such, it forms the basis for the first chapter in this section, the purpose of which is to study several applications of group therapy that have gained popularity and appear to be emblematic of the trends in clinical group work likely to persist into the next decade.

Short-term group therapy has been the subject of increased study, so the mechanisms underlying its efficacy have been delineated clearly. It is also a model that engages with the challenges of limited time and limited funding, provides a format for traditionally oriented therapists to expand rather than abandon their existing skills and grow professionally, and, in our opinion, represents the nucleus of group therapies of the future.

BASIC PRINCIPLES OF BRIEF GROUP THERAPY

Brief group therapy formats have followed the lead of their individual psychotherapeutic counterparts and subscribe to many of the same general principles. Consensus exists among leading exponents of the model (Budman, 1988; MacKenzie, 1990) that six elements are essential to brief group therapy: circumscribed treatment focus, active group leadership, establishment of group cohesion, fixed group time limits, contemporary focus, and careful patient selection.

Circumscribed Treatment Focus

Time constraints dictate that goals in short-term groups be focal and as specific as possible. Global, vague, or excessively ambitious treatment goals are not attainable in brief therapy groups. An example of a focal group goal is found in a cognitive therapy group designed to teach stress management skills and relaxation exercises to patients experiencing excessive anxiety symptoms.

Contrast this with the more amorphous goals of resolving depressive symptoms, changing personality structures, or resolving family problems. The latter examples are problematic in two ways. First, they may reflect a fuzziness in the thinking of the group leader, who has set goals that are either imprecise or too far reaching for a brief therapy experience. Second, if the group is paid for by a managed mental health organization, a treatment plan with vague goals is likely to be rejected. When conducting groups under the umbrella of managed care, it is best to describe group goals in terms of the functional impairments that group members demonstrate. With depressed patients, the global group goal of resolution of depressive symptoms translates into the focal goals of evaluation for antidepressant medication, social skills training to counter isolation, informing members about the nature of their condition, and use of a group experience to encourage open expression of depressive feelings.

Active Group Leadership

When the leader of a brief therapy group is active from the outset, therapeutic group norms are more likely to emerge quickly. Constructive leadership in brief groups includes setting a clear framework for the group, ensuring that positive group norms are instituted, maintaining a relevant group focus, and guarding against potential harmful trends in the group.

Leaders of short-term therapy groups need to be vigilant in keeping the group on target and avoiding the inevitable temptation for members to detour the group from its course owing to their anxieties about change. Budman (1992) coined the term "informed eclecticism" to describe a leadership style believed to be most readily adaptable to a brief therapy format. The sentiment conveyed in this orientation appreciates the value of both flexibility and firmness as essential qualities of the group therapist in the time-limited approach. Leaders who are active and are comfortable with the idea of combining elements of several group orientations into their brief therapy approach are those most likely to maximize the inherent resources of the short-term therapy group.

Establishment of Group Cohesion

Cohesion is not the frosting on the cake in group therapy; rather, it is the cake itself. In brief as well as long-term groups, establishment of group cohesiveness is an essential task. In brief groups, a higher premium is placed on the rapid emergence of group cohesion, since there is less overall treatment time available. Short-term group leaders emphasize the similarities among members from the first meeting in order to promote the acceleration of group cohesion.

The emphasis on similarities not only helps with the construction of early group cohesion but reinforces the commonality of goals for all group members. Cohesion can act as a safeguard against scapegoating in brief and open-ended groups. With an early sense of the security provided by group cohesion, the group can begin to address its therapeutic agenda more rapidly and comfortably.

Fixed Group Time Limits

Setting a finite limit on the number of sessions communicates a sense of therapeutic urgency. Fixed time limits help define the tasks of the group and the time frame available for their completion. A predetermined group format includes an estimate of the time needed to accomplish the group's goals. Time limits in short-term group therapy are determined in advance and are not open to revision during the course of the group.

Contemporary Focus

Therapists in brief therapy groups ordinarily strive to keep the group centered on present-day themes. The focal points can be intragroup phenomena or events in the current life circumstances of group members. With rare exceptions, forays into the past histories are rare unless the group model is a brief psychodynamic one on the order of the model espoused by Piper and colleagues (1992) in their work with short-term groups for people who have sustained a severe personal loss.

The underlying assumption for this is based largely on the fact that interactions among group members will demonstrate the "in-group" version of their problems. Rather than have the leader and members hear reports of historical events involving people they have never met, it seems a much more viable alternative to keep the spotlight on the intragroup transactions that replicate unresolved historical themes.

Careful Patient Selection

The issue of screening and evaluating prospective group members takes on added significance in groups with time constraints. The necessity of having homogeneity of group composition in short-term groups dictates careful attention to the selection of members who share common problems and personal characteristics. Maximizing similarities among members facilitates a more rapid induction into the group, an accelerated first phase of the group itself, and a greater probability of attaining group cohesiveness built around membership similarities.

CLINICAL POINTS OF EMPHASIS IN BRIEF THERAPY GROUPS

Two critical elements that are central to the success of time-limited groups are the notion of increased patient responsibility for change and the commitment to apply that which is learned in the group to real-life situations outside the group. Each member must have a clear and well-thought-out reason for being in a particular group. The leader of the brief therapy group has to convey the orientation that therapy is a joint venture, a major portion of which will rest on the shoulders of the patient. The leader can be explicit in defining how he or she will participate in a collaborative way with group members, indicating that this is not a substitute for individual action on the member's part.

In groups that are psychoeducational, cognitive, or behavioral in form, patients are required to apply knowledge gleaned from the group and to practice the specific techniques taught. From a practical standpoint, the leader makes specific out-of-session assignments that are reviewed in the subsequent group meeting. Relaxation training for patients with anxiety disorders, in vivo desensitization assignments for phobic patients, and homework tasks that help with assertiveness training for shy or passive patients are all concrete examples of work done by members outside of the brief group that reinforces the goals on the group agenda.

In addition to specific task assignments for group members, an underlying tenet of brief group therapy is that change is an ongoing process, only part of which takes place in formal sessions. Patients are oriented to the philosophy that change will occur over the course of their lifetime. The direction of change, rather than the degree of the change, is what is of central importance. Interruption of self-defeating patterns or self-destructive individual and interpersonal behavior starts a therapeutic trend in motion that will be reinforced in patients' future living patterns and in subsequent psychotherapy experiences they may undergo.

Members are encouraged to be active participants in setting their therapeutic goals in brief groups. The clinical questions then become "What is the purpose of this group at this point in time for you?" and "How can this be accomplished through membership in a short-term group?" When group members are taught to think about changes in their lives over a long period of time, it helps clarify for them what aspects of living the current group can best address.

One group member described a strong family history of depression and a battle with his own depression since adolescence. Now, in his 40s, he had finally been successfully treated with an antidepressant medication that removed the neurovegetative symptoms of his depression. His sleep improved, his attention span and powers of concentration increased, his mood was stable, his interest in sex returned, and his capacity to experience pleasure was restored.

His current problem was that he had lived the life of a chronically depressed person. He had no close friends, was underemployed, had the desire but lacked the ability to reach out to people to form relationships, and had lived with a severely distorted and undervalued image of himself (as a by-product of his depressive thought patterns) that he was afraid to expose to others for fear they would reject him. What he needed from a group was not treatment for his depressive symptomatology but an experience that would put him in regular, safe, and accepting contact with other people.

Placement in a short-term group for people who had been depressed and were now faced with the task of reentering life in a nondepressed state was more relevant to his current life circumstances. The group agenda was to teach social skills experientially through interactions with others in a group setting, to get realistic feedback from the leader and members that would upgrade his poor self-image, and to encourage engagement with life issues as opposed to the chronic avoidance pattern he had developed while suffering from a serious affective disorder.

A third, and very frequently neglected, aspect of brief therapy groups is the way in which leaders can capitalize on the heterogeneous elements present in the composition of the group. While the overwhelming emphasis in short-term therapy has been placed on patient similarities for purposes of accelerating group cohesiveness, there is added potential therapeutic value in employing aspects of the ways in which group members differ from one another. Members may be homogeneous in terms of problem set, gender, diagnosis, age, and other characteristics, but thinking of them exclusively in terms of their similarities is a convenience for the therapist, since it eases management of the initial phase of the group.

In actuality, all people differ from one another in many ways. For a group leader to ignore the differences among patients in a therapy group is equivalent to participating in a distortion of reality exercise for the sake of convenience. Acknowledging differences among group members helps create a baseline level of group tension that can be used to counter the tendency for complacency and can assist in motivating patients to work on their treatment issues. Heterogeneity also spurs interaction in groups, picking up the pace of the group and helping the group achieve a sense of balance between similarities and differences. Teaching people to differ openly but respectfully is another advantage of the use of group differences. Later in the life of a brief therapy group, when issues of individuality, separateness, and autonomy are being addressed, the therapeutic leverage for the therapist derives from the differences, rather than the similarities, among group participants.

While the focus on similarities is universally accepted as a core element of the brief group therapy approach, group leaders should not lose sight of the possibilities of simultaneous therapeutic use of the ways in which individual group members are unique.

LEADERSHIP CONSIDERATIONS IN BRIEF THERAPY GROUPS

Therapeutic Orientation

Brief group therapies run the gamut from psychodynamically oriented models to behavioral ones, with a variety of eclectic models in between that merge selected aspects of insight-oriented therapies and cognitive approaches. The leader of the brief group must select elements in a therapeutic plan that best suit the aims of the group. In order for this to occur, attitudinal as well as technical shifts are necessary. For many group therapists, this is the most difficult part of leading a brief therapy group.

If, as is the case with the majority of psychotherapists, the therapist's clinical orientation is to longer-term therapies, then becoming comfortable with brief therapy requires some reorientation. A primary assumption about brief groups that differs from the traditional model is that not all change has to take place within the confines of the therapy itself. In long-term groups, members leave the group only when their therapeutic goals have been reached. Short-term groups have a more narrow focus and try to set a process in motion that will lead to a greater sense of control and mastery on the part of group members. It is assumed that reinforcement of the changes initiated in brief groups will be complemented by factors outside the group sessions per se. Family involvement, the use of adjunctive community resources, and the social reinforcement resulting from the patients' desire to repeat new behaviors that bring satisfying interpersonal results all add to the therapeutic impact of short-term therapy groups. When viewed in this way, the pressure to "get it all done in one sitting" to which many long-term therapists are accustomed is greatly reduced.

Group therapists' definitions of what constitutes a brief therapy experience vary widely. In order to feel comfortable leading a short-term therapy group, the leader must have a clear concept of short- versus long-term group models. Brief therapy groups can be viewed as having a predetermined length. A therapeutic plan of 10-20 weekly sessions may seem like an impossibility to a therapist who is accustomed to an open-ended model of group therapy that often lasts for years. Traditional therapists can reassure themselves by reviewing some of the literature (MacKenzie, 1990; Budman et al., 1994) on short-term group therapy documenting the amount of change that takes place within the very early stages of brief groups.

One other pivotal leadership consideration is the therapist's opinion about the relative value of brief therapy in general. Those therapists who view brief therapies as adjunctive (as opposed to primary) therapies for patients run the risk of failing as leaders of short-term groups. Even more troublesome is the case of therapists who possess a bias against brief therapy, often expressed in derogatory labels such as "band-aid" therapy, "quick fix" therapy, or "superficial" therapy. If the therapist subscribes to such views, they will inevitably be communicated to the patients, and the group experience is headed for disaster.

When the therapist can shift to a focus on the benefits of brief groups, a sense of optimism and hope is conveyed to group members. Emphasizing the opportunities for new learning in the group, highlighting patients' strengths rather than their weaknesses, communicating a sense of enthusiasm to new members, and having an open attitude toward the simultaneous integration of several techniques correlate strongly with positive outcomes in brief group therapy.

The Therapeutic Alliance

The positive aspects of the relationship between therapist and patient constitute the core of the therapeutic alliance. This variable is critical to any psychotherapeutic endeavor. In brief therapy groups, the therapeutic alliance is a subject unto itself for two major reasons. First, as a result of time limitations, there is less opportunity to forge a working alliance over time. Second, there is a growing awareness of threats to the therapeutic alliance in brief groups conducted in managed care settings (Spitz, 1997; Tuttman, 1997; Zimet, 1997).

Strictly speaking, the initial patient-therapist contact is the inception of the therapeutic alliance. The emphasis earlier in this volume on the therapist's posture in the pregroup preparation and orientation of members was designed to hasten a positive working relationship in a short-term milieu. Building the therapeutic alliance does not start in the first session of brief group therapy but precedes it. Those group leaders who are sensitive to the fears and concerns of their prospective group patients can realistically clarify and demystify areas of worry for members and, in so doing, take a supportive stance that is maximally conducive to the establishment of an early therapeutic alliance with new patients.

In group treatment, confidentiality is at the core of the therapeutic relationship. Members need to feel safe and secure in the knowledge that whatever they reveal about themselves will be treated with respect and will not leave the confines of the group. This applies to the group leader as well. The influx of patients who have their therapy paid for through a system of managed care results in the group therapist being in a delicate position with respect to confidentiality.

The therapist has a dual obligation to the patient and to the third-party payer. A therapeutic "loyalty bind" occurs for most group leaders, who feel that confidentiality is vital to a positive therapeutic alliance. At the same time, the leader is asked to disclose information to managed care personnel, which makes the boundary between absolute confidentiality and legitimate requests for assessment of patient progress less distinct. The leader of a brief group under managed care must be careful to preserve the primary allegiance to the group member.

This may be handled by taking more time in the pregroup orientation period to focus specifically on confidentiality. Group therapists must inform their patients about the kinds of information they will be required to discuss with managed care companies, what will happen to this information, and how it may have any future consequences for the patient. In this way, the leader takes a stance demonstrating that the first order of concern is the patient's well-being. It also involves the patient in certain treatment decisions, assertively models taking a stand on the side of the group member, exercises a kind of fiduciary role with regard to the protection of patients in treatment, and helps in forging a strong and positive therapeutic alliance.

ISSUES OF DIAGNOSIS AND TIME-RELATED FACTORS IN BRIEF GROUP THERAPY

The prevailing patient populations for whom brief group therapies have been prescribed largely fall into the Axis I diagnostic categories of the American Psychiatric Association's *Diagnostic and Statistical Manual of Mental Disorders* (*DSM-IV*). Quite naturally, questions have been raised about the efficacy, or lack thereof, of brief group therapy experiences in the treatment of patients in other diagnostic categories. In response to these concerns, a body of group work is emerging that uses a brief group model with patients who have Axis II personality disorder diagnoses.

There is no way to adequately explore the question of diagnostic appropriateness for brief group therapies without reference to the issue of time, which is inextricably linked to diagnosis and treatment planning. What constitutes "brief" in the model of brief group psychotherapy? There are no data in the literature on brief group or individual psychotherapy supporting the premise that patients with personality disorders will be able to receive effective treatment in very short-term therapy formats. Conventional short-term group programs of up to 20 sessions are regarded as too brief to accomplish much of the therapeutic work necessary with patients having this diagnosis.

Historically, personality disorders, psychoses, and major affective disorders have been seen as contraindications to the use of brief group therapy. However, several practitioners of brief therapy (Budman et al., 1996; Linehan, 1993; Marziali & Monroe-Bloom, 1994) have specifically addressed issues of the relationship between psychiatric diagnosis and brief group therapy format. The significant clinical observations and promising preliminary results already emanating from these clinical studies may point the way to the future of the field of brief group therapy.

The following is a sampling of the emerging trends in brief group work with patients other than those at the high-functioning end of the diagnostic spectrum. New group models are being used for patients with personality disorders. These are formats that are aimed at specific target behaviors frequently associated with personality disorders and are seen as distinct "episodes" (Budman, 1996) of brief group therapy. These models involve different concepts of time limitations. One group format encourages the use of 6-month therapeutic contracts for patients that are reviewed close to the time of expiration and can be renewed, depending on the group member's clinical course, for a period of up to 18 months.

The dovetailing of diagnostic and temporal issues has been modified to provide a new interpretation of what is an appropriate and realistic time frame within which to work on the life issues of personality-disordered patients in groups. Time is extended, but in distinct modules. In this way, therapy usually lasts more than the conventional 10 to 20 sessions for patients with Axis I issues. The incremental time increase is offset by the added ability to work on themes that do not lend themselves to resolution merely because time is limited. What makes administrative or economic sense is not necessarily correlated with what makes good clinical sense.

The economics of managed care and coexisting concerns over the skyrocketing costs of keeping psychiatric patients in the hospital have led to a glut of patients flowing into outpatient settings for psychiatric treatment. Certainly, groups can accommodate many more people per unit of time than individual therapy formats. In many places, patients are referred for group therapy without regard to specificity in matching patients to groups that would offer them maximum benefit. This practice is appealing since it reduces staff time expenditures and is easier to keep within mental health care budgets. The problem is that merely shortening the time frame of therapy and seeing many patients at one sitting are not sufficient unto themselves to provide first-rate therapy for the bulk of patients.

A medical analogy would be giving flu shots to tuberculosis patients; the practice lends the illusion that the condition is being managed efficiently. Treating the surface manifestations of a problem without incorporating the factors leading to its recurrence is clinically imprudent and economically shortsighted.

Understanding that a diagnosis of a personality disorder can, by definition, be a lifetime proposition, it seems more sensible to view the condition over the long term and treat current symptoms that intrude into central areas of the patient's life. It is assumed in these new brief group therapy models that other therapies, not only brief group treatment, will be needed to manage the course of a personality disorder over the patient's lifetime. The same case can be made for patients with major affective disorders and some forms of psychosis.

What may be developing is a model of brief group psychotherapy based in large measure on the presenting problems of patients and/or their psychiatric diagnosis. This system would include three potential categories of group treatment: (a) *short-term group therapy* (less than 20 sessions) of an eclectic nature, designed to treat patients with Axis I diagnoses (Type 1); (b) *intermediate group therapy* (up to 18 months) for patients with milder personality disorders (Type 2); and (c) *maintenance group therapy* (no specific limit over time) for patients with severe personality disorders, psychoses, and chronic affective disorders (Type 3).

The eclectic approach in short-term (Type 1) groups would consist of a combination of informational, cognitive, behavioral, and psychodynamic interventions and the assignment of out-of-session tasks. The patient populations most suitable for Type 1 groups are people with anxiety disorders; phobic symptoms; crisis situations; reactive problems such as a depressive reaction to job loss, ending of a love relationship, or death of a significant person; adult life cycle problems; and other conditions in the neurotic range of issues.

Intermediate groups (Type 2) are based loosely on the group prototype described by Budman et al. (1996). Type 2 groups focus on symptoms and behaviors and match members with similar specific functional impairments. The leadership style is active and is geared to establishing a group climate of security and safety, with clear boundaries, limits on inappropriate behavior, a sense of consistency over time, and a judicious use of mild confrontation of members. Most of the group focus is in the "here and now," with the use of skills training, group exercises, psychotropic medication, interpretation of group processes, summaries of sessions, and reexamination of treatment goals over the course of the group's existence (with an option to review and renew a therapeutic contract every 6 months).

Addressing problems with regulation of affect, reducing self-defeating and self-destructive behavior, using the reality testing properties of the group to correct distorted perceptions of interpersonal interactions, teaching the appropriate modes of expression of anger, modeling the creation and maintenance of relationships with others, and providing alternative strategies for dealing with authority figures and peers are but a smattering of the focal points of intermediate groups.

Most of the appropriate candidates for Type 2 groups are those diagnosed as having personality disorders. Within the range of personality disorders, individuals with schizotypal, paranoid, or schizoid disorders are excluded from group membership. Again, as in all brief therapy groups, functional impairment and similarity of symptoms, rather than strict diagnostic labeling, guide Type 2 group composition.

Type 3 groups are not, strictly speaking, brief treatment experiences. They are included in a discussion of "brief" therapy because clinicians know empirically that there a substantial pool of people will enter and leave many group experiences over the course of their lives. Most of these patients have severe, recurrent psychiatric illness characterized by exacerbations and remissions. During periods of acute flare-up, active treatment intervention is necessary. Hospitalization, medication, and psychotherapy are common components of a treatment plan for patients with serious psychiatric conditions. Very often, the psychotherapeutic component of the plan includes some form of group therapy. Whether inpatient ward meetings, day hospital support groups, or ongoing outpatient medication monitoring and social skills enhancement groups, groups of variable time frames play a central role in the treatment and rehabilitation of chronically mentally ill patients.

Although group treatment of the chronically impaired patient is described in more detail later (Chapter 11), it is fitting to outline some of the broad characteristics of Type 3 groups in this section. The most desirable leadership style is one that avoids extremes of passivity or activity. Group therapists are role models for members and, in that capacity, can educate through their actions. Support, structure,

The economic advantages to third-party payers of using brief group methods are apparent. At this point in time, however, implementation of group therapy in systems of managed care lags far behind incorporation of other treatment modalities. Several factors have contributed to this delay.

1. *Referral problems:* Most clinicians still subscribe to, or are more familiar with, individual forms of intervention for psychological problems. As a result, brief individual psychotherapies and the use of psychotropic medications are the rule. In addition, the evaluation process is often initiated by clinicians who are less aware of the broad utility of short-term groups and hence do not think in terms of group therapy or recommend it as a primary form of treatment.

2. *Systemic problems:* Even when a patient is deemed to be an appropriate candidate for brief group therapy, the managed care organization that approves or disapproves the treatment plan is usually ill equipped to track the progress of a group and its members. Information systems are individually oriented and have not yet been adapted to incorporate important data relevant to therapy in the group setting. While such systems are being developed, they are still in their infancy.

3. *Economic factors:* The mental health care financing field is in such a dramatic stage of flux that the turnover in organizations and policies owing to mergers and acquisitions of companies complicates the picture. A sense of discontinuity is present in treatment results and plans, such as those designed to work group therapy into the system.

4. *Staffing deficiencies:* Very few managed care organizations have a staff position designated for a coordinator of group therapy services. The absence of such a person leaves a conspicuous gap in the process of mainstreaming group services into the overall program.

5. *Education and training:* The absence of a group program coordinator also leaves a gap in the training of case evaluators who make judgments about the form and frequency of psychiatric treatment. Some organizations have recognized this shortcoming and have contracted with outside specialists to conduct brief, intensive training courses in group psychotherapy for permanent staff members. Despite these efforts, many people in key decision-making positions, both on an individual case basis and on an organizational level, are not familiar with group therapy in general and brief group therapy in particular.

The net effect of the confluence of the factors just noted is that there currently exists a large discrepancy between the theoretical appreciation of short-term group therapy and its operationalization into clinically relevant forms under systems of managed care. As the virtues of brief group therapy become better understood, it is reasonable to assume that short-term group therapies will become integrated into newer health care delivery systems.

encouragement, working with patient strengths or successes, having a clear plan of treatment, and using interventions that are concrete, practical, and teachable are most welcome in these groups. Leaders of Type 3 groups are cautioned to avoid delusional material, steer the group away from analysis of transference, and resist using interpretation of unconscious material.

Ideally, groups should be specifically geared to meet the needs of their members. Type 3 groups that exemplify this principle are drop-in groups for outpatients who attend when they feel they are getting into psychological trouble, crisis groups wherein stabilization and deciding whether or not to hospitalize the patient are the focus, and medication groups that monitor individual symptoms and interpersonal function of patients. These are planned and organized short-term group experiences.

Type 3 groups need to be differentiated from de facto brief group experiences in which patients come and go according to their level of comfort or discomfort. Patients who make "cameo appearances" in groups and those who titrate their group attendance against their current level of anxiety by staying in group for brief periods are not in planned, intermittent, maintenance group therapy for chronic patients. The effectiveness of brief group therapy for seriously disturbed psychiatric patients is related to their participation in scheduled, structured, and symptom-oriented therapy groups led by knowledgeable group therapists who are accepting of patterns of irregular attendance. Popping in and out of a group does not meet the criteria for useful short-term group experiences for patients who require a lifelong course of psychological treatment.

Brief group psychotherapy is on the cutting edge of the study of contemporary applications of group treatment. The appeal of the brief group model, when properly employed, resides in the enhanced ability for clinicians to engage in focal and definitive therapy involving problems that interfere with people's successful adaptation to their life circumstances. Given the current and future economic trends in mental health and substance abuse treatment, it seems clear that brief group therapy will play a critical role in the treatment of psychiatric patients in all diagnostic categories.

8

Group Approaches to the Treatment of Substance Abuse

Group experiences play an integral part in the treatment of problems related to substance abuse. Groups are unparalleled in their value in terms of the flexibility they afford in addressing the issues involved in the life of someone who is addicted to drugs and/or alcohol. This chapter delineates the therapeutic decisions faced by leaders of groups composed exclusively of substance-abusing patients.

The most popular group frameworks applied to the problem of substance abuse are self-help and psychotherapy. Table 8.1 illustrates some of the similarities and differences between self-help groups and psychotherapy groups in treating problems of addiction. Contemporary self-help groups incorporate elements of religious, philosophic, or encounter group experiences in a large-group format. Interpersonal networking and supportive and educational functions form the matrix of many self-help group designs.

Price (1978) defined self-help groups as "voluntary, small group structures for mutual aid and the accomplishment of a special purpose. They are usually formed by peers who come together for mutual assistance in satisfying a common need, overcoming a common handicap or life-disrupting problem, and bringing about desired social...or personal change" (p. 6). Self-help groups can be classified in many ways. Levy (1979) conceives self-help groups as being of four major types: (a) behavioral control or conduct reorganization groups, (b) stress-coping and support groups, (c) survival-oriented groups, and (d) personal growth and self-actualization groups. The substance abuse self-help model falls predominantly into the first two categories. Such self-help groups consist of members who share a common drug problem that interferes with the successful conduct of their lives. Group membership focuses almost exclusively on the drug problem and avoids addressing non-drug-related issues in order to bring the addiction under control and prevent relapse into drug and/or alcohol abuse.

All substance abuse self-help groups subscribe to universally accepted group goals emanating from the membership. In the same sense that goals are group goals, action is also group related. Individuals undertake change on their own but do so in a manner consonant with the ideals and prohibitions of the group. High degrees of altruism and support typify self-help group experiences. Positive value is placed on fellowship, mutuality, and a spirit of cooperation among group members. The power base of the group comes from the membership itself, and little or no reliance is placed on outside influences or organizations.

Group psychotherapy applied to a substance-abusing population is a newer form of intervention that blends elements of the self-help group and the psychotherapy

Table 8.1. Group interventions for problems related to substance abuse

	Self-help group	Psychotherapy group
Size	Large (size often unlimited)	Small (8–15 members)
Leadership	Peer leader or recovered substance abuser; leadership is earned status over time; implicit hierarchical leadership structure	Mental health professional; self-appointed leadership; formal hierarchical leadership structure
Participation	Voluntary	Voluntary and involuntary
Group government	Self-governing	Leader governed
Content	Environmental factors, no examination of group interaction; emphasis on similarities among members; "here and now" focus	Examination of intragroup behavior and extragroup factors; emphasis on differences among members over time; "here and now" focus plus historical focus
Screening interview	None	Always
Group processes	Universalization, empathy, affective sharing, self-disclosure (public statement of problem), mutual affirmation, morale building, catharsis, immediate positive feedback, high degree of persuasiveness	Cohesion, mutual identification, education, catharsis, use of group pressure re. abstinence and retention of group membership
Outside socialization	Encouraged strongly; construction of social network actively sought	Cautious re. extragroup contact; intermember networking optional
Group goals	Positive goal setting; behaviorally immediate problem; focus on the "group as a whole"	Ambitious goals: oriented plus individual personality issues; individual as well as group focus and similarities among members
Leader activity	Educator/role model, catalyst for therapeutic group experience; less member-to-leader distance	Responsible for learning; more member-to-leader distance
Use of psychodynamic techniques	No	Yes
Confidentiality	Anonymity preserved	Strongly emphasized
Sponsorship program	Yes (usually same sex)	None
Deselection	Members may leave group at their own choosing; members may avoid self-disclosure or discussion of any subject	Predetermined minimal term of group membership; avoidance of discussion seen as "resistance"

(continued)

Table 8.1. (Continued)

	Self-help group	Psychotherapy group
Involvement in other therapies	Yes	Yes—eclectic models; no—psychodynamic models
Time factors	Unlimited group participation possible over years	Often time-limited group experiences
Frequency of meetings	Active encouragement of daily participation	Meets less frequently (often once or twice weekly)

group to meet the unique needs of the drug-dependent person. The specific clinical questions posed by composing groups that are homogeneous in terms of the problem of substance abuse form the basis of the discussion to follow.

GOALS OF PSYCHOTHERAPY GROUPS FOR SUBSTANCE ABUSE

There is strong consensus among treatment programs with diverse theoretical orientations that the highest initial priority in substance abuse treatment is to get the addiction under control. The first goal in any successful therapeutic effort is to design a plan for achieving safe and rapid abstinence from *all* mind- and mood-altering substances.

An initial decision must be made regarding the ability to manage the detoxification phase on an outpatient or inpatient basis. The type of addiction determines this choice. Mixed addictions (e.g., alcohol and heroin) carry a high risk for withdrawal syndromes in the course of detoxification. These conditions are best managed in the hospital setting. Exclusive addiction to cocaine or marijuana permits outpatient management of the initial phase of treatment. Detoxification ordinarily precedes entry into a therapy group.

Once detoxification has been accomplished, the central treatment goal becomes that of helping the substance-abusing patient achieve a sense of initial stabilization and emotional equilibrium. When, as part of the detoxification phase, substance abusers cut their ties to the drug-using subculture, they are often left without an interpersonal network. Rapid placement in a psychotherapy group, combined with attendance at 12-step meetings, counters the feeling of isolation common to people early in recovery.

Early entry into a group experience provides a drug-free network of peers; counters excessive feelings of loneliness, alienation, and loss; and functions as an interpersonal anchor during the predictably difficult phase of initial abstinence. Disabling emotional states, including anxiety, panic, and depression, commonly characterize the immediate psychological sequelae of detoxification. Group participation aids in restoring emotional balance through peer support, advice giving, and the sense of acceptance that comes from being part of a therapeutic group. Com-

BASIC PRINCIPLE 8

Whenever a person is attending more than one type of group, make sure that the form, purpose, and timing of each experience are clearly explained to and understood by the patient. Many important issues are highlighted at the intersection between the self-help group and the psychotherapy group. Ideally, these groups are used simultaneously, and each reinforces the goals of the other. While the overarching goal of all substance abuse groups is to attain and maintain sobriety, the routes to that end are varied.

When a substance-abusing person is encouraged to attend 12-step meetings, it is not always a suggestion that meets with enthusiasm. In fact, many people who attend AA meetings, for example, feel confused, conflicted, or put off by the experience. For some, this is clearly nothing more than a variation on the theme of resistance to giving up drugs and alcohol couched as a discontent with the self-help model. Others, however, may have legitimate concerns that require attention, understanding, and clarification.

One prominent example of an interface issue is visible in the role of interpersonal feedback in recovery groups. One alcoholic young man returned from an AA meeting and described his frustration with the lack of interaction in the meeting. Since he had been in group therapy in the past, he put a high value on feedback from other group members, a factor he felt was absent in the 12-step model.

It proved helpful to explain to him that rather than see this as a deficiency of the self-help model, it was more accurate to make a distinction between the concept of "sharing" and that of "feedback." Sharing is a major precept of Alcoholics Anonymous and involves the relating of life experiences to the group. It is not designed to be a catalyst for group interactions such as confrontations among members.

Interpersonal feedback in the form of interaction among group members and a group leader is part of the psychotherapy group model and differs from the 12-step philosophy. It is not the case that one is superior to the other; rather, they serve different purposes for people in recovery. For the patient just described, a combination of the support elements that accrue from sharing in AA meetings and the interactional elements of traditional group therapies proved to be most satisfactory. Once he was able to appreciate the distinctions between the two group formats, he availed himself of the benefits of both.

Similar issues that bring out the differences between self-help and psychotherapy groups for addiction include those related to contact among members outside of meetings, inclusion of spiritual/religious elements, focus on the present versus the past, sponsorship of recovering members, frequency of meetings, and use of medications for comorbid psychiatric conditions.

In addition to self-help groups for drug-abusing patients, coping and support self-help groups for families of substance abusers have grown dramatically in recent years. Based on the 12-step principles of Alcoholics Anonymous, adjunctive groups have developed to meet the needs of families, friends, and significant others involved in the lives of people who turn to excessive use of drugs and alcohol. Al-Anon, Adult Children of Alcoholics (ACOA), and Al-Ateen are examples of groups that play a prominent role in the comprehensive treatment of substance abuse.

monalities among members not only form the basis for group cohesion and support but also facilitate the emergence of the shared life issues that form the themes at the core of a substance abuse group. Examples of recurrent group themes include fears of failure or success, appropriate expression of anger, competitive feelings, concerns about sexuality, problems with self-assertion, and the dilemma of how to find pleasure and excitement in life without resorting to drug or alcohol abuse.

Another central goal in substance abuse groups is the effort to teach self-monitoring techniques to group members. The educational and confrontational elements present in effective drug treatment groups contribute to the increased ability of members to prevent relapse by understanding those factors that place vulnerable individuals at risk to resume drug use.

Requiring a commitment to the group is another essential goal for members with substance abuse problems. Members are asked to agree to a therapeutic contract requiring that they attend a minimum of 10 to 12 sessions, and they consent to comply with urine testing for drugs on a random basis. Aside from providing a stable group nucleus, this initial group contract helps group members and leaders understand the current level of motivation for change on the part of new members. In this way, denial defenses, so prominent among people who abuse substances, can be identified, assessed, and challenged when necessary.

Development of problem-solving skills and new, drug-free methods of coping with life issues is an ongoing dimension of all substance abuse groups. As part of the group norm of engaging with reality, members help one another with pragmatic issues as well as emotional and psychological problems. Group members with longer term sobriety help new members make plans to return to work, repay accumulated debts, and develop ways of engaging with family and friends who have been affected as a by-product of chronic substance abuse.

Attitudinal shifts and lifestyle changes are critical for the genesis and maintenance of abstinence and for relapse prevention. Group membership provides enormous opportunities for learning how to delay needs for immediate satisfaction, to deromanticize the recollection of former drug and alcohol use, and to avoid the "people, places, and things" that facilitated overuse of substances.

CLINICAL ORIENTATION OF SUBSTANCE ABUSE GROUPS

The leader of a group of substance-abusing patients will do well to begin the group with an emphasis on support, encouragement, and the affiliative elements present in the members. The peer and leadership vectors of the group provide the group's initial binding forces. As the desire for acceptance among group members increases and relationships in the group deepen with time, the leader can use these needs to help members move toward the establishment of therapeutic group norms. In substance abuse groups, group support, while desirable, is not unconditional. Members and leaders do not condone lying, irregular attendance, poor motivation for change, sabotaging behaviors, or frequent lapses back into drug use. All such postures are detrimental to the group effort and run counter to the goals of the group.

Little tolerance for these counterproductive attitudes and actions will be found among members of a functioning substance abuse group. As a result, high degrees of confrontation are present in many group sessions. Group therapists have to be careful to monitor and direct peer confrontation in ways that are not destructive. Instances of "character assassination" and scapegoating of other members are to be avoided at all costs. Instead, a gentle or "caring confrontation" (Rachman &

Raboult, 1985) that blends confrontation with concern allows for the maintenance of a workable group climate and avoids the purging of less popular or frightening members from the group.

Experiential learning forms a cornerstone of substance abuse groups. Learning through group participation occurs on several levels simultaneously. On the affective plane, members are taught how to recognize and accurately label what they are feeling. The cumulative effect of years of drug and alcohol use interferes with a member's ability to experience and clearly identify his or her inner emotional state at any point in time. Group aims to teach substance-abusing patients how to regulate and express important feelings appropriately. On a cognitive level, members are helped to deal with the fears and unrealistic expectations that have contributed to a pattern of drug abuse. Behaviorally, the group models constructive alternatives to the self-defeating behaviors that emerged form these irrational belief systems. Psychodynamically, learning in the group includes the acquisition of personal insight into the genetic, motivational, familial, and environmental factors that foster drug and alcohol abuse.

Insight-oriented drug abuse groups value place a premium on self-awareness and structure group treatment in a way that promotes the attainment of insight for group members. Groups of this design use the interpretation of in-group and historical material, analysis of transference and resistance, and other psychoanalytically derived techniques. The aim is to expand self-understanding in group members, which in turn will facilitate changes in their drug-oriented behavioral patterns.

Psychotherapy groups are good venues for members to deal with intense affective states. Anger, depression, and the feelings evoked by the prospect of being in an intimate relationship with another person are three distinct forms of emotion lending themselves to examination in small-group experiences. In eclectically designed psychodynamic group formats, the leader can incorporate behavioral techniques that mobilize strong affect, which can then be channeled into constructive forms of expression. Role-playing, aspects of psychodrama, behavior rehearsal, and communication skills training are vehicles for helping substance- abusing patients become conversant and comfortable with their full range of emotions.

Although substance abuse is the focus of this chapter, many patients in actual clinical practice have coexisting psychiatric problems. The dually diagnosed substance abuser is often a person with a drug or drinking problem and a mood disorder, most commonly some form of depression. Both aspects of the patient's condition require attention if recovery is to take place. Since depression and its manifestations are so prevalent among people who drink and use drugs excessively, the capacity of groups for support and lifting morale makes them an ideal setting to engage comorbid conditions. Two of Yalom's "curative factors," universalization and countering hopelessness, come into play in groups in which the addicted member is also depressed. In addition, feelings of alienation and negative self-images can be repaired through active group work. Substance-abusing members can upgrade their self-deprecating view of themselves as "junkies" to a more affirmative attitude of an alcoholic or drug abuser in recovery. Interaction and healthy identification with other group members interrupt the pessimistic preoccupations and morbid introspection commonly seen in depressed substance abusers.

In essence, membership in a psychotherapeutically oriented recovery group provides a new and alternative peer network that is not contingent upon the use of drugs or alcohol. Groups bridge the initial gap between active drug use and abstinence. Continued group participation reinforces the recovery process and builds strengths for long-term rehabilitation and improved functional capacity.

STAGES OF SUBSTANCE ABUSE GROUPS

Leaders have to be aware of the stage of development in all groups in order to make timely therapeutic interventions. Substance abuse requires care and attention to the evaluation, diagnostic, and patient orientation portion that predates group entry. The developmental stages or phases of a substance abuse or recovery group are not markedly different from those observed in other groups with the exception that members almost invariably enter the group in some form of drug- and/or alcohol-related crisis. Consequently, the initial stage of a substance abuse group can be viewed as consisting of two parts: crisis management and stabilization.

The immediate stimulus for many addicts who seek professional help is an experience of loss in their personal or professional lives. Breakup of a romantic relationship, job loss, and loss of control wherein drug use escalates to the point of requiring possible hospitalization are a few recognizable crisis states requiring immediate attention.

Once the presenting crisis has been addressed and detoxification has been completed, the patient is emotionally stable enough to enter into the next phase, during which induction into the group takes place. The significance of the induction phase for substance abusers is that it is the period during which group dropout is most likely. Owing to the newness of their sobriety, many members are faced with difficult emotions that have been camouflaged historically by escape into drug use. Flight from the group and the temptation to resume a drug-governed existence are reduced when group cohesion is established. This is the rationale for the earlier emphasis on support and similarities in the group. In most instances, the positive factors present in groups offset the tendency to flee from painful emotional states and help members stay in treatment and remain sober.

The induction phase of substance abuse groups is characterized by concerns about establishing trust, fears of unacceptability, and jockeying for a comfortable position in the group. Group cohesion develops as a result of the interaction and support elements present in the induction stage, and the group progresses to the working group phase. Greater personal disclosure, less defensiveness, and higher levels of affect emerge during the working stage. In psychotherapy groups for addiction, it is the working stage where accumulated insights are translated into action in the safety of the group session.

Eventually, participation concludes with transition out of the group. Salient issues encountered during this stage include a review of past accomplishments, dealing with feelings of separation from and loss of the group, and plans for aftercare and relapse prevention strategies. The therapist's awareness of the stages of group development in substance abuse groups provides a unique channel for rapid differentiation between normal and hazardous developmental sequences in psychotherapy groups.

CLINICAL MANAGEMENT DECISIONS

Leaders of substance abuse groups are charged with the task of considering varied dimensions of the group experience in order to tailor it to the specific needs of a substance-abusing patient population. The decisions that influence clinical management can be conceptualized as those centering around leadership factors and those clustering in the domain of membership concerns. Most leadership decisions focus on the structure, "ground rules," and leadership stance considered most appropriate when working with people who abuse drugs and alcohol. Some of the core decisions to be made by the leader are discussed in the sections to follow.

Solo Leadership Versus Co-Leadership

The workload of the leader who functions alone can be formidable in a substance abuse group. It is incumbent upon the leader to be supportive and confrontational at the same time. There are many problems of living that involve the family of the substance abuser and require attention on the part of the group leader. Extragroup issues, including legal problems, debt, housing, and employment, are important in conducting a group composed of substance abusers.

These factors, coupled with the empirical observation that staff burnout is high among those who work exclusively with problems of substance abuse, have led to a trend to use more than one leader in these groups. Team leadership is advantageous in that it allows for the sharing of leadership tasks in the group. The presence of more than one leader increases the options for identification, interaction, and the exploration of intragroup relationships. As a result, the leader's therapeutic load is lightened, and the pace of the group can be accelerated by the presence of two leaders as objects of psychological investment by members.

When cotherapy is used, leaders must be clear about their respective roles if they are to function collaboratively. Co-leaders who integrate their realistic differences concerning professional discipline, gender, and theoretical orientation provide the group with an excellent role models for collaborative functioning in adult relationships.

A form of cotherapy that is uniquely the province of substance abuse groups involves the use of a recovered alcoholic or drug addict as part of the therapy team. The recovered user occupies a position midway between that of a leader and a member. These individuals' memberlike qualities, including their firsthand experiences with drugs and alcohol, add a dimension to the group that cannot be supplied by the professional mental health staff. In order to be considered for this "elder statesperson" role in the group, former substance abusers must have a documented history of at least 2 years of sobriety. They must also consent to urine screening during the course of group therapy. The professional staff and recovered counselors meet immediately following each group session to discuss group events and the peer counselor's reactions to them. The postgroup discussion is designed to plan a course for future sessions and to ensure that the dynamics of the group do not pose a threat to the sobriety of the counselors themselves.

Group Climate

The construction of a therapeutic climate that is maximally conducive to positive change is a key leadership concern. Leaders contribute to the creation of a constructive group atmosphere by supplying a group structure and setting limits for members. While this can be said of any psychotherapy group, it takes on added meaning in substance abuse groups since so many members come from families in which limits were not set and interpersonal and intergenerational boundaries were not successfully delineated.

Group Rules

Firmness and fairness are the components of a therapeutic stance in substance abuse groups. The norm of total abstinence from all drugs and alcohol is an example of a standard group rule. This rule is in the interest of all members and is presented by the leader as a nonnegotiable condition for group membership. Failure to implement a tight therapeutic framework for substance abusers in groups runs the risk of encouraging avoidable discussions about limited or recreational drug and alcohol use. The setting of a total abstinence guideline from the outset helps keep the group on track and circumvents detours that are merely disguised resistances to the drug-free model.

Open Versus Closed Group Membership

In all groups, the leader must decide which membership model, open or closed, best suits the needs of the group. In substance abuse groups, the question is whether it is more advantageous to start with a core group and add members over time, as individuals either recover or drop out, or to start and finish the group with the original members. In our view, the benefits of the open group model outweigh those of the fixed membership model.

Adding members over the course of time allows the group to retain a population of sufficient size. If the group size is approximately 8 members for therapists who work alone and 12–15 for co-led groups, there may be a problem with rapid patient turnover in substance abuse groups. The addictive properties of the drugs themselves, the legal problems (e.g., arrest and incarceration) that accompany illegal drug use or drug sales, and the tendency of substance-abusing group members to use flight and avoidance as defense mechanisms contribute to a potentially unstable group membership. For these reasons, keeping the group open to inclusion of new members allows for a minimum of 7 or 8 members at each meeting.

When a new member is added to an established group, there is an inevitable pause in the flow of established group patterns. New members of substance abuse groups are less far advanced in the recovery process than their charter member counterparts. The addition of a new member frequently makes established members anxious. Seeing someone who is just beginning the recovery process serves as a graphic reminder to members with longer term sobriety of their own earlier struggles to give up drug use. In this respect, new members serve a catalytic function in groups, simultaneously testing the resolve of established members and providing a focal point for the altruistic needs of members who are eager to be helpful to neophytes sincere about their desire to stop using drugs and alcohol.

The introduction of new members mobilizes group themes of competition that are valuable items for discussion. The act of including new members models openness to new experiences and flexibility on the part of the group leader. This posture serves as an alternative role model to counter the tendency of many group members to think and act in rigid ways. Relatively little is required from the standpoint of group management when adding new members. The two considerations for the leader are optimal timing and how to help new members make a smooth transition into the group. Members should not be added to groups in which there is an individual or group crisis that must first be resolved, and they should not be added soon after the departure of a group member if the group has not had time to deal with the issues stimulated by the loss of that member.

Family Involvement

The comprehensive clinical evaluation of every substance-abusing patient should include an appreciation of the patient's family circumstances. Families are a concern for leaders of substance abuse groups in terms of both the positive contributions they can make to successful treatment and their potential for undermining the therapeutic alliance and the overall therapeutic effort.

The use of an initial family interview is invaluable in treatment planning. Since many substance abuse patients are not reliable historians owing either to lapses in their memory of past events or their habit of engaging in manipulative behavior that interprets and distorts experience, direct observation of the patient "in action" with his or her family supplies vital information for treatment planning and group placement. Not only is the family an excellent source of historical material, but the view that it affords the therapist of the patient interacting in the small group context of the family yields behavioral data referable to timing and type of group therapy.

Families can often be enlisted in the service of recruiting resistant drug and alcohol abusers into sorely needed treatment. Guided family interventions mobilize powerful intrafamilial forces that push the ambivalent family member into the first phase of a drug rehabilitation program, a core component of which is a psychotherapy group.

Use of Psychotropic Medication

One area of potential controversy in substance abuse treatment centers around the use of therapeutically prescribed medications to treat psychologically disabling symptoms. Judicious use of specific medications for depression, bipolar disorder, or schizophrenia or as an adjunct to the detoxification and withdrawal process is never presented as a solution to the drug problem itself. Medication is used on a brief basis whenever possible, and medication-related issues are discussed openly in group sessions.

Medication can be a source of legitimate concern for many substance abusers who subscribe to a strict 12-step philosophy of total abstinence from all drugs. Using a drug to treat a drug problem often seems paradoxical to members who are new to sobriety. This same line of reasoning is also misused by members who are fearful of taking medication when they try to undermine the leader by using his or her recommendation for medication as a basis for questioning the leader's overall judgment and competence. A clear distinction must be made between a patient's genuine concern about medication (which can be managed by education and reassurance) and use of the medication issue to create a therapeutic roadblock by resistant group members who want to shift the group focus onto the leader and deflect it from themselves.

A strong effort should be made to differentiate between drugs with abuse potential and those designed to treat a psychological symptom or condition. Themes related to medication can be present in virtually every session of a group whose members' major adaptation to life has been through the use of chemical substances to relieve emotional distress. Members are encouraged to express their feelings about medication, including the fear that it is merely a substitution of one "crutch" for another and the possible confusion between being totally drug free and yet able to take selected medications.

Other Therapies

Groups are commonly part of a more comprehensive treatment plan. While they offer many advantages and the scope of psychotherapy groups is broad, there are still limitations to what can be accomplished. Consequently, the treatment of substance abuse problems usually involves several types of therapeutic interventions simultaneously. Concurrent use of group therapy and AA meetings, couples therapy, family therapy, or individual psychotherapy is common.

When group therapy is the hub of the treatment wheel, it becomes the responsibility of the group leader to coordinate all treatment efforts to ensure that they reinforce one another. Observations made about the patient's behavior in the group are useful in determining what needs have to be met through experiences other than the psychotherapy group. The most common combination of interventions is weekly or twice- weekly group therapy and daily 12-step self-help meetings. In this way, group members can be in contact with some form of rehabilitative experience on a daily basis.

Hospitalization

Despite the fact that drug monitoring via urine testing is built into the group model, there are still instances in which a group member will require an inpatient stay. Hospitalization of group members is considered when there is a pattern of repeated relapses or "slips" that are unresponsive to management in the group alone. Habitual drug use violates the basic principles of the group and calls into question the viability of the group alone as the primary treatment for the patient with a chronic pattern of relapse.

Other indications for a hospital stay include repeated outpatient treatment failures, familial and/or social circumstances highly reinforcing of continued drug use, and the possibility of a severe withdrawal state. Groups can be instrumental in helping members realize when they need to be hospitalized. Group support extends to include an open invitation for the hospitalized member to rejoin the group upon discharge from the hospital and to attend meetings while on an inpatient service. Hospitalization of a member who has an escalating pattern of drug abuse serves to defuse a tense time in the life of the group. It spares the member in question, and the group, from the additional stress of being the recipient of the collective group anger born out of futile attempts to reach the member who is in a downward drug spiral.

Peer Networking

Once group cohesion is firmly in place, it may be advisable to construct a telephone network among members. Patients can exchange phone numbers and agree that they will call a fellow group member as an alternative to "getting high" when they feel a craving for drugs or alcohol. These extramural contacts are discussed openly in the subsequent group session, and their significance is explored. This can provide a rich level of information about the relationships that develop during the course of group therapy and serve as an extra layer of protection against the urges to lapse back into drug use.

It has proven effective for the leader of a substance abuse group to adopt a stance that values honesty and access to information about group members above the prohibition or sanctioning of behavior. Once the leader has set the group ground rules and established a therapeutic contract, there is less of a need to assume a rigid posture toward individuals in the group. Contacts outside the group are best viewed as behavioral information concerning the nature, extent, and purpose of the interaction. If the leader is excessively prescriptive, he or she runs the risk of being seen as too authoritarian or as a critical parent. When leaders are experienced in this way, members often edit what they bring back to the group for fear of punitive consequences.

The leader who can work collaboratively with a group member in helping him or her understand the significance of contacts outside of the group is in a better position to use information that comes from outside the group and translate it into a form in which members may promote their rehabilitation. The "district attorney" model of substance abuse group leadership, in which members are constantly "grilled" about their actions outside of the group, usually evokes secrecy and silence in response. Relating to group members as adults who can take charge of their behavior is not only more respectful, but it strengthens individual responsibility for behavior change and allows the therapist to join the patient in supporting healthy efforts to understand himself or herself.

Age Factors

Age is often a consideration in composing substance abuse groups. The adolescent substance abuse group encompasses many of the ideas underlying the use of age-specific group treatment models for substance abusers at different stages of the life cycle. Group homogeneity based on age allows the group to most closely approximate the external life circumstances of members. In adolescent groups, the advantages of restricting the group to adolescents include the following:

1. Peer group experiences are central to the experience of every adolescent. An adolescent group provides a therapeutic arena in which to work on this critical issue.
2. Groups help in consolidating the normal developmental process of ego and identity formation in young men and women.
3. Teenagers are often more receptive to a therapeutic plan that includes their peers. While many may shy away from all attempts at therapeutic intervention, group experiences are regularly viewed by adolescents as less unappealing than others. Their school and social experiences are naturally occurring group experiences, and hence they have some precedent for being in a group of contemporaries.
4. The social aspects of the group overlap with the age-related social concerns of the adolescent.
5. Groups allow for experimentation with interpersonal transactions and can be used as a safe place to try out new, drug-free ways of relating to others.

Gender Issues

The issue of homogeneous group composition can come into play when considering group experiences for people in the early stages of recovery. Virtually everyone who has had a drug problem has also had a problem maintaining an intimate relationship with someone of the opposite sex. Mixed (male and female) groups pose the threat of mobilizing social and sexual anxieties that can be overwhelming to an individual not far removed from his or her most recent drinking or drug-taking episode. In order to concentrate more intensively on attaining a stable sense of sobriety, it may be advisable to place some substance abusers with high levels of relationship anxiety in a same-gender group.

Although they constitute an artificial arrangement with respect to the lives members lead outside the group, same-sex groups remove the extra layer of stress that comes from having to interact with opposite-sex members and thereby permit members who would otherwise drop out of the group to be retained. Another advantage is that vulnerable group members are shielded from exposure to deprecatory attitudes about men and women expressed by members with these unresolved issues.

A representative clinical example occurred in a men's cocaine group, where the majority of members reported that the bulk of their experience with women was through relationships with prostitutes or other women who were addicts. The prevailing sentiment was that ''most women are coke whores,'' a skewed and stereotypical opinion that was not only factually untrue but would be undermining for women, particularly those in the early phase of recovery.

Most of the men in this group exhibited profound discomfort in the presence of women, were excessively concerned about being sexually inadequate, and possessed strong competitive feelings for positions of favor in the group such that they said they would have no qualms about being hostile to any woman entering the group. In such instances, the group leader must consider the initial protective value of same-sex groups. Later in therapy, when longer term sobriety has been attained and members are dealing with relationship themes, is a better time to switch people into mixed groups of men and women.

Confidentiality

Confidentiality is a sine qua non of all psychotherapy groups. It deserves special mention in addiction groups since substance abusers in the same group come from all walks of life. Different people are unified by their use of a common substance. As a result, group members are exposed to people they might not meet in the ordinary course of their lives. Celebrities and well-known business, community, and political figures are regular members of drug and alcohol recovery groups. Members must be cautioned to preserve the anonymity of others in the group, no matter how tempting it might be to disclose the identity of a famous group member. In addiction groups, breaches of confidentiality are discussed as part of the therapeutic contract and are grounds for dismissal.

Administrative Group Issues

Issues related to attendance, promptness, calling in if members will be absent, payment of fees, and other topics necessary for optimal group function are discussed with each member and with the entire group when it initially convenes. In outpatient substance abuse groups, a fee arrangement can be made in which members whose motivation is questionable pay for sessions in advance. This "motivation money" model attaches a financial penalty to members who miss sessions. Advance group payment and random urine testing are two prime examples of the incorporation of contingency-contracting aspects of behavioral therapies that complement the psychodynamic elements in group therapy for substance-abusing patients.

In summary, groups occupy a position of prominence in the field of substance abuse. The broad applicability of diverse group formats has led to an interest in expanding conventional group models to meet the challenges presented by the increasing numbers of people seeking help for drug- and alcohol-related problems. Although the field is still growing and new techniques are constantly evolving, there is an established body of data attesting to the fact that groups will continue to play a central role in the treatment of substance-abusing patients and their families.

9

Group Psychotherapy With Couples and Families

There is a natural overlap between experiences in groups and those in families. The therapeutic parallel is the intersection between group and family therapies. Once thought of as two distinct disciplines, group and family techniques are now intertwined in the clinical practice of specialized psychotherapy groups. Groups composed of couples and groups consisting of several families are the two most common examples. The clinical issues that are unique to couples and multifamily groups form the basis of this chapter.

GENERAL PRINCIPLES

Generally speaking, families and groups are similar in that both are small interactional, interpersonal systems. For therapeutic purposes, the differences between family systems and psychotherapy groups determine the choice, timing, and form of intervention most appropriate to the problems to be addressed in treatment. Families have a preexisting history, established patterns of interaction of which the therapist is not a part, and a surplus of emotion that often propels them to seek professional help. Groups are new entities that do not have a history that predates the therapist, their interactional patterns will be formed throughout group participation, and there is no historical preloading of emotion since members have not met prior to the group's inception. Consequently, the initial therapeutic tasks are different in group and family therapy.

Most initial efforts with couples and families are designed to stabilize the family system, determine a point of entry into the existing family structure, and take charge of the therapy in order to resolve the current crisis. Emotions are likely to have escalated, so emotional containment and reduction or avoidance of strong affect are indicated. The opposite is the case in group psychotherapy.

Early interventions in groups are designed to stimulate affect so that new relationships can be built among members and between members and the therapist. The group therapist uses his or her influence to establish adaptive patterns of verbal and emotional interchange among the membership. Group leaders have power and authority from the outset. In contrast, the therapist in a family session has to search for an opening in the system in order to gain a therapeutic foothold.

Group therapy with couples and families faces the challenge of combining basic elements from different fields to create a new format providing unique opportunities for the resolution of acute and chronic relationship problems. Several steps are necessary if the full potential of multifamily and couples groups is to be realized. The process begins with the initial contact with a family, couple, or group.

THE INITIAL INTERVIEW

The first session with a couple or family serves both diagnostic and therapeutic purposes. The goals of the first interview are as follows:

1. To accumulate significant present and past information relevant to an understanding of family dynamics.
2. To observe the family or couple in action to see the spontaneous operation of their system and to clarify relationship structures and patterns.
3. To look for ways to engage *all* family members in the treatment process.
4. To formulate a problem that singles no individual out and can be translated into the basis for an initial therapeutic contract.
5. To identify and think about plans for managing early resistances.
6. To determine whether a group therapy experience is the most appropriate setting in which to address the family's or couple's problems.

The initial family or couple interview includes many components directly related to determination of whether or not a group experience would be the treatment of choice at this time. Standard individual interviews for group suitability lack many dimensions present when the therapist sees a couple or family. In the same way that individual therapists are taught to remember that when they see an individual, they are also seeing part of a family, the converse applies when seeing the whole family. An interview of a couple or a family is, in essence, an interview of a small group. Information relative to the roles and functions of individual family members is the added source of information to seek in an initial contact.

Many times, the data gleaned from an initial family session translate directly into a group treatment focus or treatment goals. Some of the specific areas of inquiry in assessing families or couples for possible group placement are described in the sections to follow.

Communication Patterns

One of the most common complaints voiced by couples and families is a problem in communicating with another person. "Communication problems" is a catchall phrase that often reflects the only level on which a family can acknowledge that they are having difficulties. More often than not, what is expressed as a breakdown of communication is merely the surface manifestation of more serious marital and family problems.

There are instances where the actual way in which people talk to each other is maladaptive and can be changed through a therapy experience. Escalating blame patterns where each person views the other as having the problem and attacks those characteristics that are unacceptable in the partner are a common entry posture for couples who seek therapy for relationship problems. These couples increase in the frequency of their complaints and the decibel level of their conversations, which invariably end without conflict resolution. Couples with escalating blame or rage patterns often talk from a "you" stance and need to be taught to begin their communication with alternative opening statements such as "I think" or "I feel that." In so doing there is room for dialogue, since the person opening the conversation takes responsibility for his or her thoughts and feelings, which can then be incorporated as a new element in the conversation.

"You" statements are basically thinly disguised accusations against which the recipient of the blame can only defend, counterattack, or withdraw. By introducing an individual, or "I," component, one can discuss either the observations made by the one initiating the communication or the behavior that is bothersome. Communication then becomes dialogue rather than a one-directional assault on a partner. For example, a man who was attending a business dinner failed to call his wife at a prearranged time. When he came home, his wife said, "You are totally selfish and irresponsible. You never keep your promises. Were you with another woman? You can't be trusted, and it is not possible to be married to someone like you who has no ability to be loyal."

An alternative would have been the following: "I don't understand why you didn't call when you were supposed to. I was worried that something might have happened to you or that you might not have been where you said you were. Please tell me what happened earlier this evening." Here the wife's concern, her unspoken assumptions, and her legitimate uncertainty can be addressed along with the husband's behavior.

Couples who demonstrate these specific forms of dysfunctional communication can be placed in communication skills training groups in which the emphasis is on clear, direct, and honest communication with concern for the impact of comments on one's partner. Couples can benefit from seeing alternative, more constructive communication modeled by other couples in the group and by the group leaders. Problem-solving capacities are increased, and relationship issues can be explored in a safer climate.

Methods of Managing Intense Affect

A norm in healthy family relationships is the capacity to express a full range of emotions. Managing anger effectively is a common problem that propels couples and families into psychological therapies. Family members invariably enter therapy with the conviction that the problem that needs to be solved resides in someone other than themselves. Complaints by parents such as "If only our child would stop using drugs" are familiar to family therapists as sincere but inaccurate descriptions.

These conceptualizations locate the trouble as residing in one person and ignore the contribution of other family members in the genesis and maintenance of dysfunctional family patterns. When symptoms are viewed as individual phenomena, the family presents with a model of an "identified patient" who needs to be "fixed" through therapy. The job of the clinician in the initial assessment of a family is to shift the emphasis from identified patient to identified problem.

BASIC PRINCIPLE 9

Set group norms as early as possible in order to ensure constructive use of group sessions. In a couples group, define the norms for effective communication at the start of the first meeting.

Couples who seek therapy for relationship problems can benefit from some structure or ground rules that increase the chance of promoting effective communication and problem solving. This is often painfully clear when couples describe or demonstrate how they handle conflict. Many times, the statements made by partners invite counterattack or withdrawal but not dialogue. The couples group therapist needs to offer a model for how partners can differ respectfully and nontraumatically. The rules for "fair fighting" in relationships are a prime example of this principle in action.

The first group session begins with an orientation that includes a statement about the group standards. As part of this orientation, the group leader(s) should be specific in defining appropriate and inappropriate modes of expression of anger in relationships. A basic set of "dos and don'ts" includes the following:

1. Take personal responsibility for your thoughts and feelings. Start with a statement about yourself such as "I think it was unfair of you not to include me in making the plans for our vacation."
2. When making a critical comment about your partner, be prepared to cite examples that allow the group to understand what it is that you are objecting to. This is group therapy, not a courtroom. Examples are illustrations meant to clarify the situation for the group, not "convict" the partner.
3. Confine your comments to behavior. Never attack the character of your partner. Ad hominum accusations such as "You are not capable of honesty"; "You're irresponsible"; "Not only are you a terrible wife, you're also a lousy mother"; and "I hate you" never lead to productive exchanges between spouses.
4. Keep the focus in the present. Avoid using a litany of past injustices to fortify the case against your partner. "You always disappoint me," "You never pay the taxes on time," and "I can't rely on you to keep a job" are common examples of using the past as ammunition in relationship fights. Confining the focus to the "here and now" interrupts this process.
5. Never attack your partner's original family. Statements such as "You're exactly like your lazy father" are gratuitous and provocative and interfere with good communication.
6. Avoid comparisons. On occasion a person will single out another group member over her or his partner as an example of someone with a preferred behavior pattern (e.g., "You see how sensitive she is to him. Why can't you ever act like that?"). This diminishes the partner in the eyes of the others and sets up unnecessarily competitive themes in the group. Reinforcing desirable behavior works better. Statements such as "I really appreciated your support when my mother was sick" reward the behavior one would like to see more often.
7. Never threaten to leave the relationship. One form of emotional blackmail is the threat of abandonment. Couples frequently raise the ante to the point where one makes a direct statement of intent to divorce one's partner. Not only is this inflammatory to the partner, but it raises the level of threat in the group by amplifying similar anxieties in other members. The initial group orientation and the statement of group rules should be emphatic in requiring that all couples agree that they will make no threats to leave during the course of their therapy.

   Dissolution of the relationship can be discussed as an open issue in the group but never in response to a threat made by one partner. For example, it is perfectly acceptable

(continued)

BASIC PRINCIPLE 9 (continued)

for group members to state that they are seriously unhappy and are questioning the viability of their relationship. This tone is less incendiary and allows the group to address the relevance of such issues in their own relationships.

8. Do not try to enlist the group leaders in support of an attack or criticism of your partner. The temptation is great in groups to use the perceived power of the leaders to give weight and authority to a complaint lodged against a partner. The leaders of couples groups should make it clear from the outset that they will not engage in collusive alliances with one partner against another.

In so doing, the entire family system is viewed as maintaining the current family homeostasis, and their participation is necessary to resolve the presenting problem. Scapegoating of a psychologically symptomatic family member, excessive worry about one person in the family, and guilt in regard to being the cause of the problem are typical emotional reactions that result from not viewing the family as a system. Redefinition of the problem as one that involves all family members prevents an unfair focus on any single person or on symptoms rather than the context in which they occur.

The couple parallel of this situation is frequently seen in initial complaints such as "If only he could control his temper," "She has problems with intimacy," and "How can you be in an open relationship with someone who always attacks you?" Here, too, the emphasis has to be on the reciprocal nature of interactions in couples. *Both* partners are involved in perpetuating the problems at hand. An understanding of the role of each sets the stage for introduction of a therapeutic contract that is more balanced. The alcoholic marriage is a familiar example of this process. The nonaddicted partner presents himself or herself as asymptomatic and willing to come along to help treat the partner's problems. A treatment contract that fails to note the spouse's enabling, codependent, or masochistic behavior ignores the interactive nature of relationships.

Questions such as "How has this been a problem for the *family* or for the *two* of you (with couples)?" subtly shift the emphasis from individual to interpersonal issues. Intense affect generated by the former is reduced, and families/couples are in a better position to achieve understanding and resolution of problems engendering intense affective responses.

Function of Symptoms in the Family System

Once a systems-oriented perspective is taken with a family, it is easier to understand the importance of symptom creation and maintenance in the context of marriage and family life. The nature and timing of the presenting complaint in terms of the developmental stage of the family yield significant information about the way in which psychological problems play a role in the family. Anxieties about separation in families are prime examples of this principle in clinical work.

Transition times in relationships and in family life are potential risk points for the emergence of problems generated by the family's or couple's difficulty in moving to the next stage in the life cycle. When the time comes for adolescent or young adult children to leave home, there is an inevitable realignment in the homeostasis of the family. Parents may experience a loss of focus after many years of life being governed by the needs of their children. Children who are biologically children but are chronologically young adults have their own anxieties about living on their own. Going to college, taking a first job, and forming a relationship with someone outside the family are three arenas in which separation issues surface.

Families who get "stuck" and are struggling with the move to the next appropriate adult stage often come in for psychological help. In most cases, someone in the family is psychologically symptomatic in a way that is reflective of the conflicts underlying the present family dilemma. Symptoms can be viewed as detours or distractions that allow the family to avoid dealing with the more troublesome or complicated underlying issues.

Consider a family in which the mother and father have significant marital problems. The child who is on the brink of leaving the home may be fearful to leave because of concerns about what effect it will have in terms of further stress to the parents' marriage. The emergence of symptoms in the late adolescent gives the parents a unifying focus around their shared concerns as parents of their child. It is accomplished, however, at the expense of the teenager's developing autonomy. The normal separation process is stalled, the marital problems are obscured, and the child, undoubtedly fearing the worst, sacrificially offers himself or herself up as the symptom carrier in lieu of the real family conflict being exposed.

Family therapy, multiple family group therapy, and couples groups are all venues in which the symptom can be addressed in the context in which it was formed—the family's origin or the couple's relationship. If alternative models of successful separation are needed and peer support will help the child separate and the parents "let go," then placement in a homogeneously composed multifamily group can be very useful.

When the problem is redefined and parental marital conflict is acknowledged, couples therapy or placement in a couples group can play a key role in problem resolution. Couples therapy strengthens individuals' identity as adults and as a marital unit and concretizes the importance of reinforcing the boundary lines between the generations in a family. Thus, information emanating from a first encounter with a family or couple can be immediately operationalized into a treatment plan involving some combination of group and family therapy that will accelerate progress in therapy and provide the most familylike treatment conditions for reproducing the specific issues with which the family is wrestling.

Families of Origin

In the case of families that are experiencing problems, several generations of family history are invaluable sources of information about what may be contributing to the current conflict and what form of therapeutic intervention stands the best chance of offering a resolution. In evaluating couples, the therapist needs to explore the features of each partner's family of origin in order to place the present relationship problems in their proper historical context. Unlike the initial interview in individual therapy, the relevant family history has more to do with patterns experienced by each spouse that are intruding negatively into the interaction in the marriage.

Themes that include what the spouses learned from being a member of their original families about closeness and distance, power and control, gender issues, the expression of emotions, resolving relationship conflict, parenting, and collaboration and competition are but a few of the residual family issues that are frequently replayed in contemporary relationships. Understanding the family residue for each partner helps humanize many of the objectionable behaviors one partner feels are being unfairly directed at him or her and demonstrates how it can actually be impersonal when someone automatically reproduces old family patterns with a new partner.

Family history can be obtained through conventional history taking for a therapist who is accustomed to the traditional initial interview that focuses on the family as a whole. Another popular way to obtain family histories in a systematized fashion is to use McGoldrick and Gerson's (1985) genogram method. Starting with grandparents and progressing through subsequent generations, the therapist looks for past history elements that have a direct bearing on the family's current dilemma. The result of this effort is a three-generational picture of important events in the life of the family. Milestones such as births and deaths, divorce, serious mental illness (including hospitalizations and suicide), relocation, remarriages, secrets, traditions, alliances, and separation issues are some of the significant highlights of the family history.

A genogram illustrates the patterns being transmitted through successive generations of a family. An awareness of these patterns from the outset makes it easier for the therapist and family to arrive an initial treatment agenda. Consideration of the possibility of a group treatment intervention can be entertained at this point.

Assessment of Strengths

It is relatively easy to get an idea of the problems in a family in the first session. What is more difficult is to evaluate the individual, couple, and family assets present in the system. Strengths form the basis for the tools people will use to repair damage. It is striking how often couples and families are perplexed when asked to enumerate their positive attributes. This does not mean that these qualities are absent. More often, it reflects the fact that people in dysfunctional relationships are in defensive postures with respect to others in the family. When individuals are called upon in sessions to talk about other family members as allies or sources of support, there are often long silences.

Information referable to strengths in a couple can be obtained by taking the focus away from the "here and now" and adding a historical perspective. This allows couples to retain their defenses and to "save face" by speaking of better feelings at an earlier time in the marriage. Even when spouses are unable to relinquish their present self-protective stances, they readily respond to inquiries about their past. Questions such as "What attracted you about him/her that caused you to choose one another?" and "What were things like earlier in your relationship prior to the onset of the current problem?" elicit information about the original motive for the relationship, what positive qualities were present earlier but are now underrepresented or absent, and how partners handled stressful situations in the past in ways that might be useful in resolving their present complaints.

The process of thinking in positive terms softens the negative emotional intensity between partners and paves the way for setting a more collaborative therapeutic course. Couples who are having problems with each other often speak of the other partner in positive terms in areas outside the dyadic relationship. Comments such as "He's a devoted father" or "She is very accomplished and talented in her work" suggest that there may be more assets to work with in therapy than initially noted. The therapist has to be active in pursuing the exploration of strengths in a couple since they are not currently thinking about their partner in those terms. Failure to understand the assets in a relationship runs the serious risk of underestimating a couple's chances for change and may lend an unnecessarily pessimistic tone to the start of the therapeutic process.

Power and Control Issues

A range of potential trouble spots for families and couples derive from issues that relate in some fashion to difficulties in attaining a sense of equal distribution of power and control in family systems. In couples, these themes play themselves out around sex, the management of money, the division of labor in the relationship, the defense mechanisms used to control the level of closeness or distance in the relationship, the ways in which couples fight, and the conceptualization of who needs to change through therapy.

In families, power and control issues can be observed in the ability or inability of parents to set appropriate limits on the behavior of their children. Child-centered families with inadequate limits placed on young children are a common example of this phenomenon. Families in which children have too much power and control and those that are too restrictive of adolescent or older children who need to separate and develop an appropriate sense of individual autonomy are clinical patterns that often prompt a family's interest in family or group psychotherapy.

Abuses of power are seen at both subtle and profound levels in family life. Sexual and physical abuse of children are extreme illustrations of the misuse of parental power. Less dramatic, but no less problematic, are more insidious day-to-day attempts by family members to gain control at the expense of the well-being of another family member. Splits along age, gender, ethnic, religious, socioeconomic, and substance use lines are substrates on which one person tries to induce a sense of superiority over another. Marriages are common battlefield sites on which these interpersonal power struggles are enacted. The initial interview must include a component examining marital and family life along the axis of power and control. These may be the central issues for which treatment is necessary. Group therapy is viewed as particularly useful in cases in which abuses of power are the chief complaint. The ability to find other role models in the group and the group's capacity to apply pressure for change are two major reasons for considering a group approach when dealing with problems related to misuse of power in families.

Previous Relationship History

In much the same way as the therapist explores the family of origin, the past relationships of couples represent an important area to assess in an initial interview. Individuals who repeatedly seek the same type of unsatisfying relationship with people over time are not likely to fare very well. Those who seek to be ''reparented'' through their present partner are in for disappointment unless the partner has a reciprocal need to be a caretaker. People who choose partners they think will be most (compliant/submissive pattern) or least (rebellious pattern) acceptable to their parents are also at high risk for relationship problems. Despite repeated experiences in similar relationships, many people who enter therapy are surprisingly unaware of their repetitive, unsuccessful choices of partners.

The original motivation for the relationship and the relationship's interactional patterns are both vital to an understanding of what is contributing to the difficulties and to finding a rewarding match between partners. Once this is clearly understood, it is relatively simple to decide upon a therapeutic intervention that focuses on changing maladaptive patterns.

Extramarital relationships are frequent occurrences that form part of the relationship history of a couple. A provision has to be made to obtain information early in the evaluation or therapeutic phase about the timing and form of these relationships in order to appreciate their role in terms of the marriage. The therapist who inquires directly should not assume that he or she will be told the truth but should still pursue the topic of affairs as a way of modeling the fact that this is an area for ongoing therapy and one that will not be handled by entering into a collusive arrangement of secrecy.

A nonjudgmental stance that views extramarital affairs in the context of the primary relationship is one that will provide the most useful information for treatment purposes. For example, looking at an affair as an example of triangulation of a third party into a relationship where one partner is threatened by the prospect of intimacy with the spouse is a more clinically relevant notion than becoming caught up in the sexual or moralistic aspects of extramarital relations.

Prior Therapy Experiences

In instances in which the family or couple has had previous psychotherapy, it is essential to understand the impact of prior treatment efforts. Negative therapeutic experiences in which family members felt singled out or blamed for problems in the family fall in the category of past experiences that require repair work if current interventions are to succeed. The therapist has to backtrack in order to help explain how a new group or family therapy experience will be different from previous ones.

On the other hand, when people have had positive experiences in previous therapies, it is important to determine what aspects they regarded as most useful to them. Active feedback from the therapist, peer support from group members, psychoeducational learning, and crisis intervention are elements that people with successful prior therapy experiences report with regularity. These positive components of previous therapies point the direction for the outline of the present treatment plan.

Other Factors

Although it is beyond the scope of this book to dwell on the initial evaluation in any greater depth, there are a few areas of exploration worthy of mention before leaving the topic. A complete assessment for family or couples group therapy also takes into account a review of sexual problems in couples, an assessment of parenting skills in families with children, an estimate of the length of time the family discord has been present, what precipitates crisis situations, the couple's or family's ability to experience relaxation and restorative states as a unit, and the level of motivation of each potential participant in the therapy.

INDICATIONS FOR COUPLES OR FAMILY GROUP THERAPIES

Once the initial evaluation stage has been completed, the central focus of treatment is the decision about whether or not a group experience is indicated. In order to facilitate this process, a therapist's appreciation of several common clinical situations that point strongly to placement in a group for the resolution of family or marital discord is essential.

Examples of indications for couples group therapy include the following:

1. When dysfunctional relationship patterns are chronic, rigid, and ego syntonic.
2. When a stable marital homeostasis has not been reached.
3. When couples are socially isolated and require exposure to alternative ways of interacting.
4. When a couple comes in with a specific request to be in a group.
5. When support and stabilization are necessary during periods of relationship crisis.
6. When newly married couples and young couples have misconceptions about marriage, role definitions, sexual issues, and status concerns.
7. When couples are geographically relocated for work purposes and lose their peer network in the process.
8. When one or both members of the couple are in recovery from drug and/or alcohol addiction.
9. When couples require specific skills training models such as communication skills training or parenting skills acquisition.

A brief list of indications for multiple family group therapy would encompass the following:

1. When there is serious mental illness in a family member. (Groups that are vehicles for the transmission of accurate information about diagnosis and treatment of schizophrenia, manic-depressive illness, panic states, and obsessive-compulsive disorder may be useful in such situations.)
2. When social stigma is high in families with a mentally or medically ill, retarded, or drug-addicted member.

3. When parent-child problems are the chief complaint and parents would benefit from observing a range of parenting styles.
4. When psychotherapies other than group-based approaches have not been successful.
5. When there is a need for stabilization during periods of family crisis, particularly those surrounding threats of suicide or divorce or physical abuse of a child or spouse.
6. When separation and divorce have changed the family structure and have had a destabilizing effect.
7. When a family has difficulty performing basic family functions, including child rearing, maintenance of generational boundaries, adherence to sex-linked roles, and enculturation of offspring.
8. When a member of the family is hospitalized or has been recently discharged.
9. When young adults are engaged in efforts aimed at separation from the family of origin.
10. When individual therapy is not likely to be effective. (Example of this type are found with individuals who use their sessions primarily to discuss family issues, people who are not psychologically minded or insight oriented, and in circumstances in which it is clear that changes in one family member will result in overwhelming stress or symptom formation in other members of the family.)

The preceding lists of indications for interventions provide an overview of clinical presentations that stand a good chance of deriving benefit from either a couples or multiple family group. While far from exhaustive, these indications are a cross section of some commonly occurring circumstances that suggest group placement. When a couple or family has been evaluated and is deemed suitable for a group experience, the next phase in treatment is initiation of participation in the group itself. Whether they are entering a newly formed group or joining a preexisting group, the process of preparation and orientation of incoming members is similar for couples and families.

COUPLES GROUP THERAPY

Verbal interviews and psychological testing of couples constitute the diagnostic phase of treatment. Relationship-oriented diagnostic aids survey selected areas of couple functioning and provide an adjunct to the initial interview. The results of these tests serve as a rough guide for anticipating in-group behavior and setting realistic group goals. The more popular areas of diagnostic testing of couples study interactional patterns and conflict resolution capacity, marital integration, communication and consensus in relationships, responses to hypothetical conflict situations, role perception, altruism, and empathy.

In spite of innovations in evaluation and testing in recent years, it is still not possible to predict with assurance how a given set of partners will participate in the group. The gap between pregroup screening and entry into the group is bridged by attention to the patient preparation format described earlier in this volume (see Chapter 4).

Design of the Group

Couples groups can be short or long term in design. Both types of groups consist of three to six couples with a solo leader or opposite-sex cotherapy team leaders. Most groups meet weekly for sessions ranging from 1 to 2 hours in length. The leader's clinical orientation will determine whether group variations (e.g., weekend workshops, time-extended sessions) will be a part of the group's design.

Time-limited couples groups are more task oriented in nature and focus on symptom resolution, crisis intervention, and acquisition of specific skills. Time-unlimited groups are more ambitious and strive to alter both individual and relationship patterns.

Group composition is central to the success of couples group therapy. Participants, although not necessarily married, must be involved in a committed relationship. Groups composed of gay and lesbian couples are homogeneously composed so that all members are of the same sex. As in non-couples groups, the leader tries to reach a balance between the similarities and differences among couples in the group. This increases the opportunities for identification among members and for role modeling of alternate coping styles in relationships.

The optimum group has members homogeneous enough to trust one another and be able to relate to each other easily while at the same time being diverse enough to interact with one another, confront each other, and create interpersonal tension so that the group does not become so comfortable that members become complacent. Some exponents of couples groups advocate more specificity in group composition. Groups matched in terms of age and adult developmental stage, length of relationship, couples with or without children, and duration of relationship disharmony are examples of greater refinement of composition criteria for couples groups.

Group Dynamics

In addition to the generic list of curative factors (Yalom, 1985) described earlier in this volume, there are interesting dynamics unique to the couples group experience. Interactional patterns are reproduced in the group, thereby providing a glimpse into the spontaneous function of the dyadic relationship. The presence of other couples dramatically increases opportunities for feedback from those who observe a couple enacting their problems in the group. It also helps the group leader in modifying dysfunctional relationship patterns by providing confrontation of couples by peers. Peer confrontation is generally less threatening than confrontation by the leader(s). As a result, couples are exposed to valuable reflections about their relationships in a therapeutic atmosphere in which excessive authority anxiety is reduced. This facilitates interpersonal learning and fosters the development of group cohesion.

When several couples exhibit similar patterns, it serves to realistically counter negativism emanating from feelings of isolation, uniqueness, and alienation. Identification processes are strengthened, and group support can be mobilized to help alter maladaptive behavior. It is important at this stage of a couples group to have couples who are at different points along a spectrum of coping with similar issues. In this way, there is enough common ground to promote trust and empathy while providing couples with a range of alternative coping mechanisms to afford concrete options for change. Variety in this aspect of group composition helps avert the problem of static or unproductive group sessions that can occur when groups are composed too homogeneously.

Family feelings are reactivated in groups. The inherent potential that psychotherapy groups have to stimulate feelings generated in the original families of each partner figures prominently in the power and impact of a couples group experience. Mobilization of family feelings when the therapeutic goal is to resolve current family-related issues increases the options for experiential learning among group members.

Couples groups capitalize on family reenactment in several ways. The new-group atmosphere stimulates old family feelings in a safe and controlled setting. This anachronistic reaction ushers in a period of psychological ''updating'' allowing the group member to more clearly separate past family experiences from interchanges with his or her current partner. Cohesive couples groups can serve as nurturing vehicles for members of couples whose primary family experience has been one of deprivation, detachment, or divorce. The couples group itself becomes a corrective emotional experience in a familylike setting.

A supportive and spontaneous group climate fosters the expression of strong positive affect in the membership. Although intense emotion of all kinds finds expression in couples work, the leader's emphasis on the acceptance and trust present in the group helps develop intense positive feelings among participants. This state of good feeling usually stands in sharp contrast to the experience in the primary families of couples who seek psychotherapeutic assistance.

Couples groups are excellent modalities for resolution of lingering issues from the original family. Incomplete separation from the family is a prime example of how couples groups can be helpful in the resolution of family issues. The group serves as a transitional life experience demonstrating the use of relationships with contemporaries as a source of emotional satisfaction formerly sought only from members of one's original family. Couples are encouraged to develop the idea of meeting some of their essential needs through more age-appropriate relationships characterized by the kind of adult interdependency present in the group. Many couples reap the benefits of this dimension of the group and learn to incorporate these principles into their relationship as resources for managing marital problems.

Reality testing and education form the cornerstones of many couples groups. Consensual feedback is part and parcel of all couples groups and serves as a counterforce to the irrationality and destructive tendencies present in the group. Reality testing in couples groups usually occurs in two major areas: communication distortions and personal neurotic distortions. Accurate interpersonal feedback can be extremely useful in highlighting defense mechanisms used by members of the group to interfere with constructive relationship building.

The group focus is on unrealistic expectations partners have about each other and about their specific patterns of communication. Habits of mutual blaming, double binding, escalating rage, and the like are subject to group scrutiny. At times, specialized group techniques are used to examine perceptions of group members. Adversarial behaviors, attack postures, and other deterrents to successful couple communication are identified, labeled, and rechanneled into more useful forms of dialogue.

One unique dynamic in couples groups relates to discussions of divorce or dissolution of the relationship. Even though the language of divorce is present in the everyday fights of many couples, the impact of facing the end of the relationship is intensified when it occurs in the context of a group. It is not possible to use denial defenses to ignore the real prospect that the relationship may be terminating. The group, as a social microcosm, has the effect of allowing spouses to experience the interpersonal consequences of a decision to end their relationship. Group themes such as division of mutual friendships, doubts about one's ability to function as a single person, and feelings of loss and depression are mobilized when couples contemplate the reality of divorce in the group. The result of such an experience is often a reexamination by couples of the assets and liabilities in their relationship.

A by-product of feedback in a couples group is the emergence of shared group themes that subsequently become focal points for theme-oriented group sessions. Areas of consensus dealt with in many couples groups include leadership and role definition in the relationship, sexual attitudes and behavior, management of money, intrusions of extended family into the marriage, goal conflicts, and the balance between work and family life.

Transference issues are readily apparent in couples groups. For groups with a psychodynamic orientation, connections between past and present experiences are legion. In addition to the expected horizontal (member-to-member) and vertical (member-to-leader) transferences and the therapist's countertransference, partner-to-partner transference emerges in bold relief in couples groups. It is this latter dimension that is unique to couples groups and provides a visible example of transference in action. The increased intervention in relationships at the intrarelationship transference level is where much of the therapeutic work of couples group transpires.

Finally, the enhanced opportunities for role modeling in couples groups mentioned earlier contribute to the appeal of these groups when relationship problems are a primary complaint. Role modeling occurs through the styles represented by couples in the group and through the role of the leader(s). Through a process of identification and imitative behavior, group members can test out new ways of behaving as they see them represented in the other relationships in the group. Co-leaders, in particular, can demonstrate the desirable aspects of relationship function between adults through their ongoing interaction over the course of the group. This takes the form of modeling open communication, expressing feelings with concern for the impact on the recipient, mutual respect, positive regard, negotiation of differences, alternation of leadership positions, and other aspects of healthy relationship functioning.

Technical Problems

The most common problems of concern in couples group therapy are those that relate primarily to leadership issues. Highest on the list of potential leadership problems is the issue of countertransference. Work with families is notorious for inducing strong personal responses in the therapist. Couples groups are no exception and, in fact, may be more evocative for the leader because of the presence of many families. The group leader's unique blind spots are tapped in a continuing way.

The couples group therapist must be aware of the workings of his or her family of origin and present-day family, since feelings in regard to family will be activated during group sessions. It is also critical for leaders to explore their feelings on a host of subjects likely to be aroused by the group process. The therapist's personal view of divorce is a cardinal area in which countertransferential pitfalls can arise. Anxiety in the leader associated with the prospect of divorce must be examined in light of the therapist's religious, social, and family value systems. The group leader's view of divorce as a "failure" is an example of a countertransferential issue that may intrude into the conduct of the clinical work.

When cotherapists lead the group, caution must be observed to ensure that the relationship model provided is egalitarian. Cotherapy works best when both leaders are aware of their respective strengths and limitations and use them collaboratively. Sibling issues often reverberate in cotherapy relationships and can result in co-leaders departing from their cooperative stance only to find themselves embroiled in a competitive struggle for favor of the group members.

Co-leaders have to take care not to let anxious group members turn the group focus from their relationships onto the leaders' relationship. When co-leaders choose to work together because they respect one another and recognize the contribution each can make to the group, the chance of members splitting the leadership team is dramatically reduced. In order to reach this plateau, cotherapists need to resolve issues related to their realistic differences as people and as therapists. Since it is critical in couples group work for the therapist "couple" to model constructive relationship interchanges, the leaders must come to terms with their differences in terms of gender, professional discipline, marital status, level of experience in working with couples, personality, temperament, and theoretical orientation.

Inadequate or underactive leadership, alone or in cotherapy, is usually indicative of excessive anxiety in the group therapist. Failure to set appropriate limits for the group and abdication of one or more leadership prerogatives signal a leader who is not in charge of the group. Some of the problems often ensuing from poor leadership are breaches of confidentiality, subgroup formation, and disruptive contact among members outside the group. Other problems to which the leader has to be alert are a tendency for members to pressure others to stay together because of fears about separation and divorce, efforts to resist change and maintain the status quo in relationships, and manipulative attempts to gain support of other group members to fortify one's belief that one's partner is the cause of relationship troubles.

Couples groups have wide applicability for a variety of clinical problems. Currently, couples groups include management of issues related to alcoholism and drug abuse, sexual dysfunction, remarriage following divorce, HIV diagnoses, adoption, kidney dialysis, bipolar disorder, serious medical illness in the family, and behavior problems in children. Recent research and emerging trends suggest that couples groups hold still greater promise in meeting the increasing demands for therapeutic interventions in marital and family life.

MULTIFAMILY GROUP THERAPY

Many of the benefits of the couples group model apply equally to the management of family problems in the group setting. Before leaving the subject of the group and family therapy interface, a few comments on multiple-family group therapy are in order.

The rationale for seeing several families in the same group was expressed succinctly by Tucker and Maxmen (1975) in their description of the inherent benefits of such a group format. These principles are as valid today as they were more than 20 years ago. Tucker and Maxmen selected 11 factors that contributed to clinical enthusiasm for the increased use of these group models. In summary, multiple-family groups (MFGs) were seen as offering families a reduced sense of isolation, increasing opportunities for socialization and support, transmitting information through educational components, encouraging appropriate expression of affect, assisting in the learning of problem-solving techniques, developing a sense of therapeutic competence in family members, providing a realistic basis for hopefulness, destigmatizing mental illness, promoting interfamily learning by seeing other families in operation, facilitating the course of group therapy by having the entire family present, and representing a source of data for families and clinical research.

The overall goal of an MFG is to provide a supportive, family-centered milieu in which families will come to a better understanding of their own attitudes, beliefs, and behavior by sharing an ongoing relationship with other families in the group. Families are selected for the group, and they must agree to have all members of the family or all those living in the household come to group sessions. Families who cannot make this commitment are screened out and placed in other forms of therapy. Some MFGs have an age cutoff for younger children so that the continuity of the group is not disturbed by the need to take care of young children during therapy time. On the other pole of the composition spectrum are groups that include all family members regardless of age. The premise is that it is essential to see as true a picture of family life in the group as possible. Editing out family members skews this picture and may confuse or delay the treatment plan. If parents are unable to control their children, they are demonstrating some of their issues for the group and the leaders to see.

MFGs for chemically dependent family members and their relatives serve as a prototype for describing some of the essential aspects of all multifamily groups. MFGs rely heavily on educational elements to realize their goals. Families with chemically dependent members are rapidly oriented to a view of substance abuse that acknowledges the central role of family factors in recovery and relapse. Family, as well as individual, denial defenses are confronted in multiple-family group sessions. Dysfunctional family patterns of enmeshment, coercion, scapegoating, detouring other family emotional conflict through the focus on the addict in the family, enabling behaviors, and inflexibility are uncovered and explicated as behaviors that reinforce addiction.

Family groups consist minimally of three families and are led by at least two staff members. In very large MFGs, there are often more than two leaders, each having a designated role. Because of the large size of the group, the leaders have many therapeutic options at their disposal. Initially, families can identify with each other in recognizing the impact of living with a drug-dependent member. Frequently, as is the case in single-parent families, members of multiple-family groups help "fill in" much-needed support gaps for substance abusers and their families.

Cross-family learning is dramatic in these groups. Participants are able to recognize, in members of other families in the group, the very things they vigorously deny in their own family. As a result, intermember and family-to-family levels of the group become prominent channels for both support and confrontation. This adds therapeutic leverage to the task of attempting to change established patterns in drug-abusing family systems.

The multiple-family group also serves as a resource for its membership. Families are made aware of and encouraged to join support groups based on the principles of Al-Anon. The emphasis on addiction as a "family affair" helps mobilize important family members who would otherwise resist efforts to be involved in the therapeutic process. The group aims to counter feelings of demoralization and despair that are offshoots of family life with an addicted member who has gone through many cycles of relapse and recovery.

Multiple-family groups attempt to define maladaptive coping mechanisms that lead to perpetuation of addiction-prone behavior. A strong effort is made to involve the family in the resolution of interpersonal tensions. Family participation is reframed as essential to recovery rather than as the cause of the addiction. The leaders try to demonstrate how normal family needs have taken a back seat to the addiction, which usually governs the life of the family. Exclusive family focus on addiction, psychopathology, and illness is useful only in the early stages of recovery. In the ongoing work of MFGs for addiction, families are taught the importance of striving for a balance between the needs of the addicted member and those of other family members.

Group participation models flexibility and creativity in addressing addiction-related family problems. Each family in the group stands an excellent chance of broadening their problem-solving and social repertoire. In the process, solutions or behaviors that would not have occurred to one family can be adopted by another and applied to their similar struggles. Participation in a family group serves a social function and offsets the sense of isolation experienced by many families who have a substance-abusing member in their ranks.

MFGs lend their support to the consolidation of adaptive behaviors in all members of the group. Long-term sobriety is seen as a triumph for the entire family. Both the individual group members and the families in the group experience their ability to contribute to one another's success. The therapeutic factors of altruism, identification, and peer support are present in all stages of the MFG. Open communication in the group about issues that formerly engendered feelings of shame in families reduces inhibition in members about being judged harshly by others. A spirit of community prevails in well-functioning MFGs. Problems are identified, and members cooperate in trying to find practical solutions to them. "Shame and blame" are replaced by honest efforts to understand the basis for problems of addiction and the impact on the family.

Multifamily groups and couples groups are illustrations of the good "marriage" between group and family therapies. When psychotherapy is treated not as an adversarial issue (i.e., which form of therapy is superior to another) but as a joint venture, the therapy, like the relationships it aims to treat, will flourish.

10

Group Therapy With Medically Ill Patients

The increasing interest in and research on the psychological problems encountered by patients with serious physical illnesses have given rise to a significant body of work tailored to meet the unique needs of these patients and their families. One clear result of this trend has been the formation of psychotherapeutic group experiences for medically ill patients.

GENERAL PRINCIPLES OF MEDICAL ILLNESS GROUPS

Medical illness groups have at least two overall purposes: to help members comply with medical and surgical treatment plans and to define and treat psychological factors that contribute etiologically to, or are by-products of, serious physical illness. Stress reduction, education, and lifestyle management skills form the mainstay of many of these groups.

The array of conditions and types of patients for which groups have been designed is impressive. A partial list includes groups for patients with coronary artery disease, HIV infection, multiple sclerosis, psoriasis, irritable bowel syndrome, Type A behavior, asthma, hypertension, cancer, epilepsy, renal dialysis, diabetes, organ transplantation, chronic pain, and arthritis. Groups have also been formed for postoperative amputees, children with cerebral palsy or other neurological conditions, and family members and caregivers involved with the sick patient. Despite the outwardly disparate nature of these groups, they share many common goals.

The overwhelming majority of groups for somatic conditions are composed homogeneously in that all members have experienced the same illness. This homogeneity both facilitates entry into the group and forms the building blocks for group cohesion based on shared life circumstances. Common group themes can be used to engage patients who commonly resist defining themselves as needing psychological help. Groups become an acceptable alternative for medically ill patients who might decline or drop out of individual psychotherapy.

Groups of this type strive to help patients live more realistically and comfortably with their diseases. The peer and staff support elements of these groups are important influences toward this end. Feelings of isolation from the "healthy" world, negative self-image issues (e.g., disfigurement or physical decline), and fears about the future are attenuated through the group's focus on maintaining and rebuilding the damaged self-esteem of members. A health care staff sensitive to the emotional vulnerabilities of patients with life-compromising or life-threatening conditions is an essential component of these groups.

One focal point of group discussions is the impact of debilitating illness or chronic disease on both individuals and families. Most groups make an organized attempt to enlist families, caregivers, and social support systems in the overall treatment program. Encouragement of clear and open communication among patients, families, and the health care team is an intrinsic part of these group models. Coordination of medical and psychological treatment interventions and integration of social support efforts are part of the treatment plan in groups composed of medically ill members.

Multidisciplinary leadership is a common model in this group format. In work with arthritis patients, for example, the leadership of the group might consist of a representative from the mental health field along with someone from internal medicine or physical medicine. The advantages that accrue from interdisciplinary team leadership include a higher degree of expertise about the primary medical condition and continuity of leadership during periods in which one leader must be absent. Comprehensive patient care is simplified by having all of the disciplines involved in care present at group sessions. This leadership model works most efficiently when each leader has a clearly defined and noncompetitive role in the group.

Group work with cardiac patients has led to some generally agreed upon components in groups defined by shared physical illness. Core elements are identification of risk factors and an educational component involving changes in lifestyle and in habits that tend to exacerbate the illness. Whenever possible, early intervention is highly valued. Spouses, significant others, and caregivers should have a role in the therapy program both to assist the index patient and to reduce caregiver burden and the tendency toward "burnout" in those intimately connected with the patient.

Therapists in these groups need not be physicians but should be staff members who are informed about the physical manifestations of the illness and the psychological risk factors leading to exacerbation of the illness. Groups are seen as desirable because many people who become ill are poorly suited to intensive, insight-oriented long-term individual psychotherapy and would do better in a therapeutic milieu emphasizing support, education, and cognitive/behavioral interventions.

In terms of monitoring the rehabilitative phase of illnesses such as coronary artery disease, hypertension, and stroke, groups are used to measure the affective state of members. Therapeutic interventions are aimed at reducing dysphoric affects while providing a constructive counseling setting that delineates the shifts necessary to create and maintain a more adaptive lifestyle. Prevention or reduction of relapse becomes a central goal of medical illness groups consisting of patients in the recovery stage of the primary illness.

Many programs appreciate the value of brief, adjunctive groups that are focal in theme, time limited, task oriented, and largely behavioral in nature. These groups address destructive habits modifiable through the acquisition of alternative coping strategies contained in relaxation training, hypnosis, and cognitive reorientation of patterns that lead to excessive anxiety and negative thinking. The adjunctive group helps coronary-prone patients stop smoking, give up alcohol, control their weight, practice principles of sound nutrition and exercise, and make sensible plans for the resumption of activities such as work, sex, and recreation.

Medical illness groups are a prime place to see developments in technically eclectic group leadership in action. Psychodynamic, educational, psychopharmacological, cognitive, behavioral, and brief therapies are all regularly blended into treatment models specifically addressing the emotional needs of patients with a given medical condition.

UNIQUE TREATMENT CONSIDERATIONS
IN MEDICAL ILLNESS GROUPS

Therapists who lead illness-focused groups are confronted with many clinical decisions related to the unique composition of these groups. To highlight specific issues, the following sections examine some of the more common choices or dilemmas therapists can anticipate in these groups. In order to link principles with clinical practice, each decision point is illustrated by an application with a specific medical condition. Since large amounts of clinical research have centered around AIDS treatment in recent years, the HIV group model is the predominant condition used to show the application of key aspects of group work with medical illness.

Initial Patient Evaluation

In addition to generic evaluations of patient suitability for group therapy, the therapist has to evaluate several parameters when working with physically ill patients. The degree of impairment caused by the disease may interfere with the patient's ability to participate in a group. Patients who have experienced cognitive changes as a result of organic brain involvement may be too impaired to address their issues in a group framework. Similarly, patients whose physical mobility is limited need to have arrangements made with caregivers to accompany them to group and for transportation to and from the facility where the group is held. Unless this is addressed, many medically ill patients will exhibit irregular group attendance and will gain less from group membership. Since the primary illness and its natural clinical course often dictate involuntary breaks in the continuity of treatment owing to hospitalization or exacerbation of the condition, it is particularly important to ensure that members attend group meetings as regularly as their condition permits.

Appraisal of level of depression and risk of suicide is a critical part of the initial evaluation of a patient with a life-threatening illness. The initial panic that seizes the patient at the point of realization that he or she may not recover from the illness is a high-risk time in terms of depression and suicidal ideation. In assessing suicide risk in HIV/AIDS patients, the clinician reviews premorbid risk factors such as age, gender, family history of depression or suicide, socioeconomic factors, history of prior suicide attempts, substance abuse, relationship status, preexisting psychopathology, and attitude toward suicide.

In addition, one must include an evaluation of the patient's current stage on the HIV/AIDS continuum. Frost (1996) described a three-stage model including a first phase ushered in by learning of the initial diagnosis of the condition, a second phase of being in relatively good health, and a final stage of being chronically ill. An awareness of the patient's stage along the health and illness spectrum relates directly to an appreciation of her or his level of dysphoria and preoccupation with self-destructive thoughts.

Rudnick (1991) enumerated a list of areas that can be used in the initial evaluation of the HIV/AIDS patient or easily adapted to apply to patients with other medical illnesses. This schema involves examination of the anxiety and fear level of the patient and how the patient manages intense affect. Some patients, such as those with coronary-prone (Type A) personality traits, can benefit from the dilution of anger that takes place in most medical illness groups. Self-esteem and identity issues are always affected by serious medical illness and are evaluated for the possibility of working with the patient's damaged self-image in ongoing outpatient groups.

The patient's interpersonal functioning, both in the family and with others in the work and social networks, must be included in any initial evaluation for group therapy. A medically ill patient can experience a reduction in his or her interpersonal field due, in part, to the fears engendered in others by virtue of their awareness of the patient's altered health status. Unwarranted fears of contagion (e.g., as in cases of HIV/AIDS), a sense of being overwhelmed by the prospect of losing the sick person, and feelings of powerless and of one's own mortality generated by contact with a severely ill person cause many to flee from contact with the patient.

Interactions with systems in the outside world represent another often-neglected aspect of the initial evaluation of a medically ill patient. In addition to the financial burden of illness, important legal, employment, disability, and insurance issues contribute to the stress level of any person afflicted with a major medical condition. These factors influence the treatment options and goals for each prospective group member and need to be fully understood before a specific group is recommended.

Finally, innovative techniques for global evaluation of patients admitted to hospitals are developing in conjunction with increased experience in working with HIV/AIDS patients. Worth and Halman (1994) recommend an evaluation technique known as "running the HIV marathon." This is a quick way of gaining an overview of the stress factors and coping mechanisms in the patient's life using the metaphor of the stages involved in preparing for and running a long-distance race. This model defines four areas to be addressed: training, personal team, "pit stops," and corporate support. In traditional psychological language, these four dimensions translate into (a) a picture of the patient's strengths and responses to previous adversity, (b) the people in the patient's support network, (c) what the patient can do to have a respite from HIV/AIDS, and (d) the patient's resources for health care and for financing his or her treatment. Directions for initial psychotherapeutic planning derive from the information gained from this simple, bedside survey of the life circumstances of every HIV/AIDS patient.

Selection of a Group Modality

The phase of the illness often determines the type of group that would be most beneficial for a patient newly diagnosed with a medical problem. One initial consideration is whether the illness is potentially life threatening. In conditions such

as cancer, the needs of patients with more advanced disease may differ significantly from the needs of those with a treatable form of the illness. Cancer patients
with metastatic lesions at the time of initial diagnosis have a sense or panic and
urgency about their fate. Crisis intervention, immediate family involvement, and
understanding of the treatment options and prognosis are the first line of concern
for many therapists. Once these factors are addressed, a second-stage plan can be
made for the ongoing management of the case. Group therapy can be used for
either stage in the process.

The setting also determines the choice of intervention and whether or not the
patient's condition or treatment permits group participation. Patients in the hospital
may be undergoing medical diagnostic and treatment procedures that will preclude
regular attendance at group sessions. This, coupled with the trend of shortened
hospital stays, reduces the time available for patients to attend group therapy. As
a consequence, inpatient groups have more patient turnover, less continuity from
session to session, and a feeling for the therapist of trying to treat a patient who
is a "moving target." In the time available for group treatment, the emphasis
is on obtaining a psychosocial history, educating the patient about his/her illness,
understanding the immediate precipitating events that caused the current admission,
encouraging compliance with medical treatment plans, arranging for outpatient
medical and psychiatric follow-up, and exploring the familial, interpersonal, and
financial circumstances of the hospitalized patient.

Outpatient groups have the luxury of more time to construct a treatment protocol
that will effectively address the emotional concomitants of physical illness. While
many of the same goals just enumerated for inpatients apply equally to those
outside of the hospital, the ongoing nature of the outpatient experience permits the
pursuit of additional therapeutic themes. Psychodynamic issues can be explored in
outpatient groups, and psychological diagnoses of depression, suicidality, anxiety
and panic disorders, and organic mental states can be evaluated for change over
the course of outpatient medical and psychological therapies.

Major Group Types for Treating Medically Ill Patients

The most popular group interventions are those that are supportive, cogni-
tive/behavioral, and psychodynamic in nature. The shorter the group time frame,
the more the group will fall into one of the first two group types. Support groups
make use of the group's ability to provide social support during times of crisis.
The role of the support group leader is to encourage members to share problems,
describe their feelings about being ill, voice their fears and how they are handling
them, and learn from others in the group who have had to contend with similar
problems. Theme-centered sessions are commonly used in medical illness groups.
In HIV/AIDS groups, new treatments for the disease, work-related issues, physical
symptoms, and death and dying are representative subjects around which support
group experiences are built.

Cognitive/behavioral groups (CBT groups) teach methods for more effectively
managing the anxiety and depression that accompany medical illness. Each group
session has a specific focus. Usually, the focus consists of describing and demonstrating the use of a cognitive or behavioral method that members are instructed to

practice at home in the time between sessions. CBT groups also allow for members to ask questions about the technique being taught, but the discussion is practically focused in areas such as how the members can make the best use of the method in their lives outside the group. Group meetings comprise a wide variety of behavioral techniques, including behavior rehearsal, desensitization for phobic complaints, behavioral contracting, relaxation training, meditation, and role-playing.

These groups also involve an educational component addressing the significance of the serological status of group members, issues related to safe sexual practices, and the varied course the condition may take over time. Out-of-session homework is a regular fixture in CBT groups for patients who are medically ill. Along with the value of homework assignments in reinforcing mastery of a specific cognitive or behavioral technique, such tasks serve the dual purpose of giving patients a constructive focus for their time spent outside of sessions. In this way, the tendency toward obsessional thinking about the illness so common among patients who are physically compromised is interrupted on a regular basis.

Psychodynamic approaches are applied when the context of the treatment allows for a longer term group experience. Such groups aim to engage shared underlying conflicts and concerns of group members. Prominent in the psychodynamic group approach is a focus on themes of shame, loss, guilt, anger, abandonment, betrayal, diminished self-image, fear, attitudes toward illness, social stigma, unresolved issues stemming from the family of origin, and existential issues ushered in by the illness. Psychodynamic groups are more flexible when the members are medically ill patients. Advice giving, education, and support are all regular modifications of strict psychodynamic approaches that make them more suited to the problems emanating from the unique position of patients who are physically and psychologically symptomatic. Leadership is more active, self-disclosing, and emotionally available to members of these groups.

Independent of the theoretical orientation of a specific group, all medical illness groups share common overall goals. Rudnick (1991) has categorized the focal points of psychotherapy for HIV/AIDS patients into a system that has enormous value for clinicians new to this kind of group work. Treatment goals are divided into subgroups that involve the patient, the illness per se, the family, interactions with the outside world, and the therapist. Education of the patient, recognition and acceptance of deficits, behavioral modification, attaining compliance with medical or surgical treatment, and teaching problem-solving skills are some of the patient-centered goals. The illness itself generates a sense of anxiety and intensifies affect. Group intervention is effective in containing the extremes of emotion stimulated by a disease. Goals include increasing the tolerance for anxiety and understanding the positive use of emotions as signals of psychological distress that can alert people to danger and hence help them adapt rapidly to the source of their concern.

Family goals also include an organized educational and orientation component, inclusion of family and significant others in treatment planning, understanding the alteration of family roles that occurs with a medical illness, countering excessive use of denial defenses, and addressing issues related to the burden of illness on the caregivers in the family. Interpersonal goals extend beyond the group and include a view of the interaction of the patient with the outside world. Health insurance, legal, disability, employment, and patient advocacy issues are all examples of the intersection between the patient's world and elements in the outside world that have a direct bearing on the quality of his or her treatment.

An analysis of treatment goals includes the role of the group therapist. Active recognition and management of feelings evoked in the group leader are essential to the success of the group. Countertransference themes of many kinds are factors in goal setting and in the ongoing conduct of the group. These issues are of such critical import that they are discussed as a separate category later in this chapter.

Group Themes

Whether or not a group is designed to have theme-oriented sessions, certain predictable issues emerge in medical illness groups. An awareness of these themes provides the leader invaluable information concerning the points of urgency in the group, the stage of development of the group, and the planning of timely treatment interventions. One can safely assume that group members who are newly diagnosed will have a high level of fear associated with their illness. Fear can be an initial bonding force in groups of this nature. Peer and therapist support help reduce fears to manageable levels. In illnesses such as cancer and HIV/AIDS, the strongest fears often center around recurrence or worsening of the disease.

Dependency themes are exacerbated in those who are medically ill. Group members need to be able to rely on their peers in the group for appropriate support during trying times. Reliance on the group leader is frequently intense. Members invest their hopes in the leader, on whom they depend for guidance, information, nurturing, and comfort. In one group for HIV patients, a member tearfully described how virtually all members of his family and many in his circle of friends had "turned their backs" on him once they learned of his diagnosis. He felt he had "nowhere to go" with his emotional pain. The leader and members were moved by his poignant story and closed ranks in support of him. In subsequent group meetings, he reported how meaningful the acceptance and warmth of the group were to him in helping offset his feelings of isolation and despair.

Body-image themes are aspects of patients' self-concepts that are altered by serious illness. The feeling of no longer being "whole" is a common expression of this phenomenon. Patients who have significant weight loss or loss of hair following chemotherapy and radiation, those who have had radical surgery, and those who can no longer physically do what they were once able to do all experience a revision in their self-image. A major portion of this revised self-image results from the altered perception of their body image. Participation in group therapy allows these members to realize that their acceptability is not contingent upon their state of health. In the same way that unconditional positive regard for patients has been the hallmark of psychoanalysis, the group parallel is unconditional inclusion and acceptance of people regardless of their state of health or illness.

Guilt feelings are prevalent in group of patients with a medical illness. In a group for post-myocardial infarction patients, one member castigated himself severely for not sticking to his diet, continuing to smoke three packs of cigarettes a day, and avoiding exercise whenever he could. He believed he was "the cause" of his heart attack and felt remorseful. Some of what he said was true, and the group helped him in sorting out those things over which he had control (e.g., diet, exercise, and smoking) and those not of his own doing (e.g., a genetic predisposition to heart disease).

Similar kinds of guilt feelings are seen in HIV/AIDS patients, in whom recriminations about past sexual behavior may dominate in terms of thoughts. Although guilt feelings can occupy a large portion of many people's thinking time, they need not have a deleterious effect on self-worth. The group leader must make a concerted effort to steer members away from sessions sidetracked by a litany of self-flagellation. A more constructive way to use this material is to encourage the group to take a present and future perspective. In this way, past experience becomes the basis for behavior change. Cardiac patients who neglected themselves in the past are encouraged to use past experiences as an incentive to improve their present habits and lifestyle and thereby speed up their recovery and lower the probability of a second heart attack.

Universal feelings associated with the impact of a debilitating medical illness can be used as themes for group sessions. The leader who senses that the membership is concerned about a particular issue does well to identify this issue and formalize it as the focus of the group session (e.g., ''Today we are going to discuss the feeling of isolation many of you have discussed recently''). Other topics that lend themselves to theme-centered group meetings are medication side effects, the doctor-patient relationship, new advances in treatment of the condition, religious attitudes toward illness and death, acceptance of illness, how to regain a modicum of control over life changes, and discussions about the overall quality of life when one is ill.

Death of a Group Member

A reality of life-threatening illness is that members of the group may die at some point during the course of group therapy. The impact of this experience is profound. Even though death is discussed as a regular part of many medical illness groups, the actual event breaks through whatever remaining denial defenses exist in the members. Patients commonly panic when they realize that not only is death a possibility, but they can envision their own demise. The feeling that ''I'm next'' is an expression of this sentiment.

In groups in which there are members who are likely to die, there is a dynamic tension in the group between involvement with and distance from others. When an actual death takes place, most members retreat back to a distant interpersonal position as a self-protective measure. Psychological regressions occur with regularity, and fears abound in the group. This is a critical juncture for the leader to take active control of the sessions and structure the group experience in such a way that the death of a member is dealt with constructively.

The leader has to encourage a bereavement component of the meetings in order to help members make a successful adaptation to loss. In the bereavement process, members may reveal important issues that shed light on the problems they are having in coping with aspects of death and dying. In groups such as HIV/AIDS groups, mourning is an integral part of the ongoing sessions predating the death of a group member. Since so many people afflicted with HIV/AIDS have already experienced deaths in their social networks, the awareness of death is heightened in these groups. The phenomenon of having a fellow group member die slowly or suddenly only amplifies these preexisting themes.

Practically speaking, the therapist should make it clear that attending the funeral of a group member is voluntary but entirely appropriate in a medical illness group. It is absolutely not an acting out of a resistance through contact outside the group. Many groups feel comforted by going as a group to funerals, making condolence calls, or taking part in other rituals surrounding an individual's death. Leaders are encouraged to follow suit if they feel it is consonant with the work of the group.

The sentiment in many groups, following the loss of a member through death, is a renewed emphasis on living rather than dying. The demoralization that accompanies the tragedy of seeing a group member die can be addressed, in part, by a sense of tempered optimism encouraging members to live each day to the fullest. Since a certain amount of denial is necessary to adopt this perspective, the therapist must determine how much denial is useful to the group.

The matter of the use and misuse of denial is an issue for leaders of all medical illness groups. The death of a member places this subject in bold relief. In essence, the leader's commitment to being realistic does not permit a stance that joins in a negation of the possibility of death among the members. At the same time, hopefulness is often the only emotion that sustains patients through times of extreme tribulation. To extinguish hope would be inhumane. As an alternative, the leader can raise the issue of the therapeutic value of selective use of denial. This not only counters denial in the group but endorses engagement with difficult feelings intensified by illness in a direct manner. The hope is that a sense of emotional mastery or empowerment will result from the novel experience of open interaction in regard to a supercharged topic.

Many death-related emotions are present in group members. It usually makes sense to establish group cohesion and then encourage the in-group expression of fears surrounding death and dying. In one HIV/AIDS group, a member who was withdrawn following the death of another member was encouraged to express himself rather than keep feelings hidden. What the death of the group member evoked for him was not so much the fear of dying but the process of dying and, specifically, the fear of dying alone. Most group members had also worried about this possibility but were similarly disinclined to speak openly about it for fear of embarrassment in the group. The group rallied around this member, praised him for having the "guts" to raise the issue, and reassured him that they would be available to him if the occasion arose where he needed them. The group established a telephone support network and a "buddy system" wherein each member contacted another prior to a group meeting to see if any assistance was required in getting to the meeting; this practice was a tangible sign of the group members' willingness to support one another.

Extragroup Contact

Planned contacts among group members in a medical illness group are part of the treatment design. Since feelings of isolation are so prominent among the medically ill, groups try to extend their therapeutic influence beyond the walls of the group therapy meeting. In order to accomplish this, a variety of extramural contacts among members are suggested to the group. The buddy system and telephone networks are but two of a broad range of options available to medically ill patients outside of the group. Concurrent attendance at self-help groups such as cancer support groups provides additional emotional bolstering for members of a therapy group. Visiting a sick member in the hospital or holding the group session in the patient's room lends continuity to the group experience and keeps the hospitalized patient anchored to the world outside of the hospital. Accompanying other members to doctor's appointments or medical therapy sessions is another useful employment of contact among members that takes place between group sessions.

In groups of medically ill patients, those interactions occurring outside of the group are not interpreted in terms of their psychodynamic meaning. To do so inhibits the process of members approaching each other in the spirit of cooperation and altruism. These contacts are regarded as adaptive extensions of the goals of the primary therapy group.

Family Involvement

It has been emphasized often that the family of the medically ill patient needs to be enlisted as a resource in treatment planning. The families themselves have needs resulting from having a member with a serious illness. Couples and family support groups on the model of Cancer Care are two means by which the fears of families and the burden of being the caregiver to a gravely ill person can be addressed.

Illness brings about a shift in the dynamics of the family system. This is seen dramatically with HIV/AIDS patients who become ill and may have to rely on their original families for the first time in many years. Such a situation is initially awkward for all concerned, particularly if the family has been estranged as a result of disapproval of the lifestyle of addiction or homosexuality that led to contracting the illness. The patient may have lost his or her partner to the same illness and may be alone again at the time of diagnosis. When the patient reaches a more debilitated state in which he or she can no longer function independently, family members are often viewed as the most likely candidates to take over the patient's care.

Some families are ambivalent, at best, about assuming this role. In like fashion, the patient who has long been emancipated from the family regards this as a throwback to earlier, more emotionally conflicted times. A course of brief family therapy may be indicated (in conjunction with group therapy) in order to resolve the complex family feelings triggered by the HIV/AIDS patient's need for care. Other issues, including a family's irrational fears of contagion through physical contact with the patient, helping the family negotiate the intricacies and red tape of the health care system, and validating the economic and emotional stress placed on family members as a by-product of medical illness, are focal points of family intervention as well.

COUNTERTRANSFERENCE IN MEDICAL ILLNESS GROUPS

The intensity and variety of feelings projected onto a group leader are considerable. When the variable of a serious medical illness is added to this equation, the pressures on the group leader become significantly increased. In response to the charged emotional climate of the medical illness group, feelings are induced in

BASIC PRINCIPLE 10

When a significant medical problem affects a member of the group, consider the needs of both the group and the individual in determining whether a mixed group or a homogeneous medical illness group would be most beneficial to all concerned.

One situation that often occurs but has not been adequately addressed in the literature is that in which a member of a non-medical illness group has a preexisting condition or develops a serious medical problem during the course of the group. The key treatment decisions for the group leader revolve around whether the medical state of the member will permit continued group participation, how the group members will handle the information, what this will mean in terms of the original focus of the group, and how much group time should be devoted to the medically ill member.

The nature of the illness, its current stage, and the prognosis of the condition often dictate whether or not a member will be able to attend regularly enough to have a meaningful role in the group. Since groups are designed to help people deal with unforeseen life problems, a strong effort should be made to retain the sick member if at all possible. When the member remains in the group but is clearly quite ill, the reaction of the group is frequently one of fear. The group leader has to monitor the temptation of group members to maladaptively cope with their fears by distancing themselves from the ill member or attempting to scapegoat the member in the hopes of driving her or him out of the group. Neither response is beneficial for the medically ill member or the group.

In a weekly adult outpatient group for people with Axis I (*DSM-IV*) diagnoses of dysthymia and/or anxiety disorders, a relatively new member announced that she would miss the next session because she had to go in for "some tests to find out why this swelling in my neck doesn't go away." Upon her return to the group in 2 weeks, she began the meeting by dramatically announcing "I have cancer!" The group was somewhat forewarned by her earlier statements about going in for tests, but the impact of her revelation was intense nonetheless.

The group was torn between wanting to know more and wanting to ignore her plight. The leader asked her to be more forthcoming and to provide some details about what she was told of the nature of her condition. It became apparent that while, strictly speaking, she had lymphoma, a form of cancer of the lymph nodes, she was also informed that it was the "mildest form of cancer" and that it was probably not life threatening. She would require a course of medical treatment, but it would not intrude on her ability to attend group sessions on a regular basis.

The reaction in the group was quite mixed. Several members voiced disapproval of the way in which she presented her information, feeling that it was unnecessarily alarming. Others were able to see beyond the surface and suggested to her that her need to embellish her symptoms was an indirect request for the attention and support of the group and a result of her fears of being abandoned by them. Once these feelings were aired, the group felt it was beneficial to deal with the anxiety-laden material introduced by one of their peers. The recently diagnosed member described a feeling of inclusion and acceptance resulting from her being more direct in discussing fears about her altered status in the group.

Health and illness issues are a part of every group experience. Even in groups that are not specifically designed to be illness-focused experiences, themes of illness in a member or in those close to someone in the group insinuate themselves. The leader can use some of the same general principles that apply to homogeneous medical illness groups to devise a strategy for managing the illness-related issues that come up in the lives of members of heterogeneous groups.

the group leader that have to be understood in order for the therapist to function effectively.

The ideal relationship between a sick patient and the therapist has been described as a "caring partnership" (Cadwell, 1997). In order to achieve and maintain this ideal state, the therapist must negotiate complex personal feelings evoked in the course of working with a terminally ill patient. Patients who have a life-threatening condition experience intense emotions of all kinds. Many of the most troubling feeling states relate to the prospect of death and dying. The "five D's" of emotions engendered by extreme illness are disappointment, demoralization, denial, depression, and despair. All of these powerful feelings contribute to reactions in therapists who work with this patient population. The transitory and ongoing emotional states of the therapist in response to this difficult work are broadly defined as countertransference responses. Countertransference can be positive as well as negative, but the latter form creates problems for the therapist and hence is the primary focus of this discussion. Some of the most common countertransference reactions are discussed in the sections to follow.

Anger

The therapist's feeling of futility in the face of a progressive medical illness is an issue that can have a negative impact in psychotherapy. Help-rejecting behavior and incessant description of physical symptoms are two common points of irritation for leaders of medical illness groups. The leader has to make a determination regarding the basis for the oppositional stance of the patient. Is it a product of the illness and, as such, involuntary, or is it volitional and in need of confrontation, as one would do in a conventional psychotherapy group? The blurring of the distinction between the two often leaves the group leader temporarily immobilized and feeling powerless. In response, leaders may become angry with the patient, allow the group to scapegoat this individual, or threaten to remove the patient from the group. These are all examples of the dangers of misdirected therapist emotion in groups.

To further complicate the scenario, when a therapist has overreacted to a patient, there is an accompanying sense of guilt. When the patient in question is also terminally ill, the remorse on the therapist's part can be profound. Therapists aware of their own psychodynamic issues stirred by the group can either avert these reactions or engage in a therapeutic "repair" (if they note a countertransferential blind spot in an exchange with a group member).

Depression

Although not unique to medical illness groups, the feelings of depression that arise in the leader of a group can be problematic. If the leader feels defeated, then the tendency is to lapse into a leadership role that is too passive. A group climate of despair predisposes the possibility of the therapist becoming caught up in the prevailing sense of negativity and fear that threatens to dominate the group.

In spite of an inner sense of depression, group leaders, in their in-group posture, must strive to keep hope and optimism alive. Through a focus on patient strengths, good prognostic developments in a patient's course, and advances in treatment, the trend toward demoralization can be appreciably offset. Needless to say, if the therapist feels that work with dying patients is resulting in a personal state that goes beyond the confines of countertransference, then personal therapy, supervision, and peer consultation with colleagues may be indicated.

Therapist Burnout

Closely allied to the feelings of depression just noted, many staff members who work with chronically ill patients are at risk of becoming "burned out." Although the endpoint is a negative psychological state, the route to getting there is often born out of positive feelings for the patient. Therapists who genuinely care about the fate of their patients are vulnerable to the indirect trauma that comes from working with those who are seriously or terminally ill. The line between a healthy identification with the patient and overidentification is not always easy to discern. As a consequence, interpersonal boundaries between patient and therapist become blurred, and the stage is set for potential problems.

When therapist and patient personal traits such as age, gender, religion, and family background are similar, the likelihood of overidentification of the therapist with the patient is higher. Therapists who live vicariously through their patients also inherit the pains of their patients. The emotional load very often becomes overwhelming, and the therapist no longer feels interested in or capable of leading the group.

Leaders of medical illness groups can prevent burnout by taking care of themselves as well as their patients. Brief breaks from therapy in the form of short vacations, staff debriefing meetings to allow for expression of the therapist's emotions, participation in support groups for colleagues doing similar work, and working with a cotherapist to share the emotional load of the group are all efforts that a leader can make to help his or her own cause.

Magical Thinking

The therapist's version of denial often takes the form of a belief that the illness can be cured or conquered. Group leaders and group members can let their dreams outweigh the reality of their circumstances and collude in a belief that the therapist can be helpful, in a way that no one else can, in eradicating the disease. The narcissistic needs or grandiose feelings of the therapist are flattered by the notion that he or she possesses special talents that will be uniquely useful to the patient. The patient's denial articulates with this dimension of the therapist's personality to create a set of unattainable treatment goals.

The group leader needs to have a realistic sense of his or her assets and liabilities in order to strike a healthy balance between appropriate involvement and therapeutic distance. Being too supportive at the expense of the truth is well meaning but ultimately disappointing to patients. Leaders who make promises they cannot deliver are setting their patients up for an eventual fall. Realistic hope and optimism are the desired group norm. This allows the leader sufficient latitude for the expression of his or her desire to be helpful without transgressing the boundary between therapist and patient.

Vulnerability to Loss

The personal side of the group leader's life is specifically tapped in the area of his or her own experiences with illness and death when working in the milieu of the chronic illness group. Significant personal losses of family members, colleagues, and contemporaries are reactivated in leading a group of people whom the leader will eventually lose through death.

An example of this vulnerability occurred in an HIV/AIDS group following the death of a member who was the same age as the therapist. More important, the therapist had a brother who had died of AIDS. As part of the therapist's adaptation to his own loss, he decided to lead an HIV/AIDS group so that he could make a contribution to the treatment of the illness and keep the memory of his brother alive. Not surprisingly, the death of the group member he felt was "most like my brother" caused an acute state of upset in the leader. Upon personal reflection and consultation with a valued colleague, he was able to see what, to others outside the group, was an obvious connection between the patient and his late brother. To the therapist, however, the linkage was not as apparent, since he bore the emotional charge of being in regular contact with the patient through twice-weekly group sessions.

The double impact of loss, both of the group member in the here and now and the family member in the past, gives rise to the vulnerability theme described in this vignette. One way for group leaders to manage their emotional responses is to realize when a group event has evoked a larger than normal reaction in them. The leader's intensity of emotion points the direction to the source of the emotional overlay occurring in response to current events in the group. The therapist's sensitivity in terms of personal loss is an extremely common and normal reaction to the death of a group member.

On occasion, therapists who have identified the origins of their overreaction can share some of this with the group members. The caveat here is that the leader not use the group for resolution of his or her own problems but, instead, see a therapeutic purpose in modeling the value of sharing self-awareness, being introspective, and behaving as an authentic ally in relationships. A therapist's judicious use of conscious, voluntary self-disclosure to make a specific point in treatment is appropriate and welcome in many medical illness groups.

Personal Values of the Therapist

Not only the professional posture of the therapist but the person of the therapist is involved in the transactions that occur in medical illness groups. A host of personal values and beliefs are mobilized for therapists who lead groups of critically ill patients. The HIV/AIDS group illustrates this concept regularly.

Two primary modes of acquisition of HIV are unsafe sexual practices and intravenous drug use. Even though therapists are trained to be aware of their biases and to act in an appropriate professional manner, there are still many private feelings and personal judgments involved in work with HIV/AIDS patients in groups. The therapist's personal beliefs about drug addiction, homosexuality, suicide, and monogamy are just a few representative examples of this phenomenon. The therapist's religious, cultural, moral, and ethical values are constantly tested in working with this patient population. For some group leaders, these issues override their emotional threshold and infiltrate the group. Whenever possible, group leaders have to keep tabs on their own personal conflicts, which become amplified in group work. Both in advance of leading a medical illness group and during the ongoing group process, the leader must be vigilant in his or her self-monitoring in order to ensure that the "person" of the therapist works only as a positive force in the group experience.

Those who have experience leading medical illness groups suggest several survival strategies, in addition to those mentioned earlier, for successful tenure as a group leader. In the same way that therapists encourage patients not to be harsh with themselves, they, too, must practice what they preach. Group leaders need to understand that many of the strong emotions they feel in the course of leading groups of seriously ill patients are well within the normal range of responses. It is not only necessary but desirable to punctuate the work experience with outside activities that help differentiate the personal from the professional lives of group therapists. Common sense dictates guilt-free expressions of the pressures generated by this type of group work with colleagues as a way of keeping the pressure level on the therapist at a manageable point.

Limiting the number of medically ill patients one sees provides variety and balance in one's clinical work. Grief work and stress management skills are assets that help the group leader keep a healthy perspective in regard to his or her work with patients. Finally, the leader's well-being can be enhanced by applying the adage that, in order to have a long and productive career as a therapist, one needs an avid interest in the work itself, a full outside life, and a sense of humor to counter the pain and suffering that are ever present in medical illness groups.

Groups specifically constructed for medically ill patients are gaining favor in group circles. A great part of their appeal is the ability for patients and therapists alike to deal simultaneously with disease entities and their psychological manifestations. Many years later, the spirit of the medical illness group model originally expressed by Speigel and Yalom (1978) remains: to enable terminally ill patients "to plan and live through the remainder of their lives with an enhanced sense of meaning and dignity."

11

Group Therapy With the Chronic Psychiatric Patient

Chronic mental illness poses an ongoing concern for patients, their families, and members of the mental health care community. A range of psychiatric conditions, including schizophrenia, manic-depressive illness, organic mental conditions, substance abuse, and other states of mood and/or thinking disorders, can require attention over the course of a person's life span. Since its inception, group therapy has played a dominant role as part of the comprehensive care of the chronically ill psychiatric patient.

OVERVIEW

Groups address many of the central issues in managing patients with severe psychiatric impairments. From crisis control to diagnostic evaluation and as a primary form of psychosocial therapy, the group milieu offers enormous flexibility in creating a foundation for a comprehensive treatment program for the chronic patient. Inpatient, transitional, and outpatient groups constitute the group resources available to the clinician. The choice of group options is primarily related to the patient's diagnosis and to the stage of severity of the primary psychiatric problem.

Using this paradigm, groups for chronically ill psychiatric patients can be conceptualized as acute, transitional, and maintenance or aftercare in nature. Patients with acute first episodes of a condition or with an exacerbation of a long-standing problem are primarily hospital based. Inpatient group therapies encompass quiet-activity groups; art, poetry, and dance programs; occupational therapy; discussion groups; and community meetings. Transition groups refer to the transition from hospital-based treatment to outpatient and community-based programs. This process begins with discharge planning in the hospital. Patients who are about to leave the hospital participate in groups addressing the real-life issues that face them upon discharge. Discharge planning groups, social skills training groups, family groups, job-focused behavioral groups, and medication groups are all representative of groups for people in the process of leaving the hospital.

Groups in the outpatient setting are designed to prevent a relapse that would require readmission to the hospital and to help participants develop rewarding social, familial, and vocational lives. There are countless outpatient groups for chronic psychiatric patients, but the variability among outpatient group models is not as diverse as it might appear. In general, all such groups aim to reduce social isolation, monitor the effect of medication (as measured by the patient's level of interpersonal functioning), aid in reality testing, provide social support, reduce the stigma associated with being mentally ill, and transmit accurate, up-to-date information about the primary condition.

Outpatient groups are usually homogeneous in that the members share the same illness. Leadership is active, especially in terms of establishing a therapeutic structure around which the group can consolidate. Psychotropic medication is almost always involved, whether or not the group is a medication group per se. Occasionally, groups are composed homogeneously in regard to factors other than the primary diagnosis. Young adult groups, geriatric groups, dual diagnosis groups, and multiple-family or couples groups are common outpatient models currently in use.

With the possible exception of psychodynamically oriented psychotherapy groups for chronic patients, most groups are based on principles of supportive psychotherapy. Exploration of unconscious material, delusional themes, and affect related to

Table 11.1. Group therapy with psychotic and nonpsychotic patients

	Psychotic	Nonpsychotic
Composition	Homogeneous for level of function; poor ego strengths	Homogeneous—brief group therapy; heterogeneous—long-term therapy; able to learn from group feedback
Goals	Crisis intervention; stabilization; improved communication; social skills development	Improved self-perception; improved interpersonal function; resolution of personality problems
Educational elements	Central to the group model	Elective: yes—brief groups; no—psychodynamic groups
Therapeutic factors	Reality testing; identification; social support; bolster defenses	Cohesion; challenging defenses; use of transference and unconscious material
Cohesion	Desirable but difficult to attain	Mainstay of the group model; easier to attain quickly
Leader role	Active around structuring the group; avoids agressive and irrational themes	Spontaneous group interaction; leader in catalyst for group process
Confrontation	Strongly avoided	Actively encouraged
Interpretation	Only on occasion; limited to the "here and now"	Regularly used for in-group transactions and transferential issues
Medication	Almost always part of the group	May or may not be a group issue
Group focus	Present and future	"Here and now" plus historical focus
Socialization	Strongly encouraged	Generally discouraged
Time span	Brief and long-term models; open-ended "maintenance" group therapy	Brief—symptom focused; long term—personality and behavior change
Group participation	Involuntary and voluntary	Voluntary

anger and hostility is to be avoided. The emphasis is on patient strengths and the accumulation of small, incremental successes started in the group and extended to life outside the group. Problem solving, advice giving, and teaching of new coping strategies are hallmarks of outpatient groups for patients with chronic and debilitating mental illness.

Table 11.1 illustrates the similarities and differences between groups that include psychotic members and those that do not.

MAJOR GROUP TYPES FOR CHRONIC PSYCHIATRIC PATIENTS

Acute Patient Groups

When a crisis or relapse necessitates hospital treatment, the patient is considered to be in an acute phase of his or her illness. Invariably, the setting best equipped to handle problems at the acute stage is the inpatient psychiatric service of a hospital. Rapid evaluation and stabilization of the patient are the priorities in treatment. Opinion is divided as to whether groups can be useful at a point this early in the process when patients are disorganized, often disoriented, and impaired in other basic ways that would preclude their ability to function in or tolerate a group experience. Acutely psychotic patients, those whose potential for suicide or harm to others is not known, and people whose mental function is hampered by organic changes are ill suited for immediate group placement. They are better served by starting a treatment plan that assesses them diagnostically, prescribes appropriate neuroleptic medication, and helps them move out of the crisis mode.

Once a sense of initial stabilization has been achieved, acutely ill patients can be considered for group placement. Even patients with active thought disorders, hallucinations, and impaired views of reality can be placed in groups after their initial crisis is under modest control. Part of the purpose of early group placement is to assist in the process of establishing clear treatment goals for patients who are no longer in crisis. The locale of the group and the philosophy of the inpatient service toward group therapy can help or hinder the ability to accumulate, have available, and retain members of inpatient groups. On services that are not group oriented, these tasks are much more difficult.

In the best circumstances, the hospital staff appreciates the value of group therapy and cooperates in terms of not scheduling other staff or patient activities that overlap with group time. Even in this case, however, inpatient groups face several potential programmatic drawbacks. Yalom (1989) concisely outlined features of inpatient groups that can slow down or interfere with successful group work with acutely ill patients: brevity of hospital stay (resulting in either a patient tenure in the group that is too brief or rapid patient turnover); inadequate patient preparation prior to group entry; rotating staff, resulting in inconsistent group leadership; overdiversity in terms of psychopathology among group members, leading to difficulties in defining a common group focus; and intrusions of contacts outside of the group with staff and other group members, contradicting guidelines espoused in the group.

Given these possible generic restrictions, clinicians need to create inpatient group formats that are viable within the context in which they practice. Yalom (1983) advises thinking about each group session as a complete therapy in miniature. Acutely ill inpatients are encouraged to use every session as an opportunity to define a goal for themselves and implement the attainment of that goal in the same session. In so doing, patients can experience a small success each time they attend a group meeting.

Goals are modest and within the adaptive capacity of each group member. An isolated and withdrawn patient can strive to talk to two other group members during a meeting. The goal for the patient can be to interact enough to report back to the group at the end of the session, stating the names and one fact about the people he or she spoke with in the meeting. For others, a goal may be to formulate their own agenda for the meeting and, no matter how simple, to try to accomplish it. An agitated patient may create the agenda of being able to stay in the group for the full session without getting out of his or her seat and without leaving the room.

Another regular component of an inpatient stay is the community meeting. These are daily groups composed of all patients and staff. Issues raised are virtually unlimited, including discussion of events on the ward, hospital policy, complaints about food, medication questions, and patient-staff interactions. Since the meetings are open, patients at all levels of recovery attend the same session. Groups are led by a designated staff member, usually the unit chief or another permanent staff member, on a rotational basis. We prefer the model with the same leader for each session since this is less confusing to the more disturbed patients and provides a sense of object constancy for people who are impaired enough to require hospitalization.

With milieu therapy services, the ward meeting is used as a fish bowl to observe the operation of the hospital unit as reflected in the transactions in the group. When important incidents occur, the community meeting becomes the vehicle for processing the event and estimating the impact it has had on the patients. For example, a newly admitted 23-year-old schizophrenic woman attempted suicide in the shower room of the ward by trying to hang herself. A nurses aide discovered the patient in the act and interceded. Word of this episode immediately spread throughout the unit, and patients were visibly upset.

An emergency community meeting was called. During the meeting, several patients expressed their fear of being suicidal themselves and worried that they would impulsively do something self-destructive. One patient said she would never associate with anyone who tried to take her life, since this was not God's will and the person who did it was a sinner. Still another man claimed that he had special clairvoyant powers and could have predicted this event long before it happened if only the staff had taken him at his word. Many patients were silent, and it was unclear how the event touched them. The leader initiated a go-around in which each patient was required to comment on his or her reaction to the attempted suicide. In the process, patients were able to have their anxieties identified and allayed, express feelings triggered in them by the suicide attempt, and model dealing with the event as an open, rather than secretive of shameful, issue. For the staff, the community meeting offered an opportunity to see how patients were coping with the stress and to understand the alliances and support elements present among the patients.

Key themes regularly come up in therapeutic community meetings. Group leaders are well advised to understand some of these underlying themes that prompt the communication content of community meetings. Some of the more common themes outlined by Winer and Ornstein (1994) in their discussion of unconscious relationship themes in psychoanalytically oriented community meetings also apply to group therapies differing from their interpretive approach. Membership concerns about being exploited by staff, especially in inpatient settings where research protocols are being conducted; fears of neglect by caretakers and betrayal by staff and other patients; abandonment worries; problems involving competition with others; perceived inconsistency on the part of the hospital personnel; and themes of jealousy and envy form the emotional underpinnings for many group discussions.

The large community meeting assists in crisis avoidance and restoration of a state of equilibrium to the unit. The group milieu provides for the immediate processing of potentially traumatic events that occur with the inpatient service. Prevention of problems emerging from life on the ward helps keep the length of the hospital stay brief and averts the need for resorting exclusively to psychotropic medications as the solution to new problems.

Transitional Groups

At the point in recovery where patients have benefited from a coordinated inpatient treatment plan, they are ready to be involved in groups that prepare them for life outside the hospital. Transition groups literally deal with the transition from being an inpatient to being an outpatient. These groups can be held either on inpatient services or as part of partial hospitalization programs for patients who need a more gradual return to the community.

The goals of transitional groups extend beyond the global theme of leaving the hospital. They are conducted in a way that encourages members to experiment with and practice new behaviors that will be helpful to them in an ongoing manner. Members can be taught simple (e.g., making eye contact when speaking to someone) and complex (e.g., conversational and assertiveness behaviors) social skills. Transitional groups attempt to create a lessening of the chronic patient's feelings of alienation and low self-esteem. Gentle confrontation, avoidance of criticism, and encouragement of controlled release of tensions through words instead of actions characterize the essential emotional climate in these groups. Achievement of group goals is facilitated by working on an immediate-reward basis in the group and adopting a problem-solving approach that emphasizes participants' strengths and deemphasizes negative notions of psychopathology, illness, and impairment. Positively reframing the view of the patient as a person who is active in engaging with life issues is much more preferable than the fatalistic view holding that mental illness is a chronic, relapsing state destined to deteriorate over time.

Transitional groups encourage members to make connections and identifications with one another. Altering traits such as passivity, expectation of rejection, and expression of aggressive feelings is central to the work of the transitional group. Work and family adjustment are prominent themes in terms of the content of many group sessions. Practical advice, modeling of adaptive behavior, support, and encouragement are the prevailing modes of intervention. Psychodynamic interpretation of patient thinking or behavior is avoided, since this practice is at best unhelpful and at worst potentially dangerous to the severely ill psychiatric patient at this stage of recovery.

Transitional groups occupy a position midway between inpatient and outpatient groups and, as such, meet less frequently than the former and more frequently than the latter. Two or three meetings per week lasting 45 minutes to an hour each are standard in this format. Groups range from 8 to 12 members, and group leadership is often included in transition groups. Patients discuss administrative and managerial topics such as going out on pass from the hospital and having their hospital privileges increased. These issues are dealt with as they arise and are framed by the leader in a way that is most consistent with the goals for individual patients.

In one group, a patient with strong paranoid feelings complained that he was being persecuted in that his recent request for a weekend pass had been denied. He felt singled out by a particular staff member he believed was behind "the plot to keep me a prisoner in this hospital." The issue was first dealt with in the "here and now." The group was asked whether any other members had experienced troubles with this staff member. The group consensus was that most of their dealings with the nurse in question were uneventful or supportive. Their reactions stood in sharp contrast to those of the patient who had initiated the discussion. He was forced to do a "reality check" and consider why his opinion was at variance with the opinions of others in the group. Since the purpose of the group was to aid in the transition to life outside the hospital, the leader also chose to generalize the discussion to the theme of how this patient and others in the group handled situations in life when they felt they were being misunderstood or mistreated. The group leader attempted to combine present events with thematic content relevant to all group members and introduce the notion of looking ahead to spotting these kind of problems in the future.

Stone (1996) categorized the six functions of the leader in groups of chronically ill patients as identifying themes, managing boundaries, bonding members, managing affect, promoting problem solving, and handling metaphors. These leadership tasks apply primarily to transitional groups and to outpatient groups. Leaders of groups with psychotic patients must have a tolerance for ambiguity, an acceptance of a patient's inability to function at a higher level, and a long range view of where the treatment they are conducting fits into the immediate and long-term needs of the patient.

A primary goal of a transitional group experience is to get patients to like being in group therapy. Since groups will form a major part of their aftercare plan, it is critical for patients to have a positive initial group experience in the hospital. When this is accomplished, it is more likely that discharged patients will follow through with aftercare plans and not drop out of treatment during the transition from in-patient stay to community living arrangements.

Outpatient Groups for Chronic Psychiatric Patients

Chronic psychiatric patients who are well enough to live outside of the hospital are candidates for outpatient therapy groups. The fact that many people are discharged from hospitals is not synonymous with notion that they are without significant psychological and interpersonal impairments. Outpatient groups are designed to join patients on their clinical path and closely address their current psychological needs.

A system that applies this idea is the stage model for placement of patients in outpatient groups. A patient is evaluated to determine his or her location along the breakdown-recovery continuum. Groups are created that accept members at beginning, intermediate, and advanced stages of their clinical course. Patients are then matched to homogeneous groups corresponding to the level of functioning of the group members.

Much of the foundation for this approach is rooted in earlier work taking place at a time when the trend of deinstitutionalizing chronic psychiatric patients coincided with the development of longer acting, injectable neuroleptic drugs. Psychopharmacological advances permitted patients to be medicated for weeks at a time, thereby facilitating their maintenance outside of hospitals. Doubts about whether patients were taking their medications were removed, and patients who formerly required hospital monitoring were free to live in the community. The concept of the three-stage model of outpatient therapy groups for chronic patients operates in the following manner.

In Stage 1 (beginning) groups, patients assemble to have medication checks. Instead of patients coming in individually, they are given a common appointment time, and all come to a meeting at the same time. Individual patients are called out of the group to meet with the doctor who is managing their medication. In the interim, a staff member attempts to engage the patients in embryonic attempts at socialization. These groups are large in size and meet approximately once per month. Over time, patients get to see familiar faces, and many develop a sense of preaffiliation. The focus allows patients who are fearful of relating to others or who fear being in "therapy" an acceptable alternative way to be in the company of others.

The staff member in the beginners' group facilitates introductions of members to one another, points out similarities (e.g., which patients live near each other), and assiduously avoids any behaviors that might represent traditional psychotherapeutic interventions. These groups do not involve interpretation, confrontation, or singling out of any member. Within this orientation, some patients will go beyond preaffiliation and form a semblance of a relationship with other group members. These patients are then considered for advancement to the intermediate stage group.

Intermediate groups meet more frequently, usually on alternate weeks, and are smaller in size, consisting of about 10 to 12 members. Medication monitoring is conducted in conjunction with group sessions when the time comes for each patient to see the psychoharmacologist. Groups are co-led by a male-female cotherapy team, one member of which may be the person who prescribes medications. Interpersonal interactions among patients are observed as a measure of their stage of recovery, and goals are identified and updated. Regular attendance is encouraged, but missed sessions are common. Patients who feel an allegiance to the program, even though their attendance may be spotty, do the best in these groups over time.

The focus in the intermediate group is on education, advice giving, reinforcing patient similarities, and symptom description. A typical intermediate group discussion is one that centers on medication. In one group, a patient diagnosed as having schizoaffective-type schizophrenia complained about the side effects of the medication prescribed for him. He began by reciting his symptoms of lack of motivation, drowsiness, reduced concentration, muscle stiffness, and mood fluctuations. Virtually everyone in the group was able to identify with his plight, and many cited examples of their own in which medication had been problematic. There were two constructive outcomes of this discussion. First, the patient's complaints were taken at face value and his medication was reviewed by the doctor, resulting in a small but significant dosage change. Second, the patient felt good about being "heard" by the group and the staff. At the same time, he provided the group with a theme around which they could coalesce. He felt less isolated and was better able to understand why this particular group was chosen for him. This sentiment was echoed by most of the other group members.

As in beginning groups, some members of intermediate groups demonstrate, through their in-group behavior, that they may be ready to move on to a group with more ambitious goals. The advanced stage group comes closest to approximating an outpatient group experience for nonpsychotic patients. Groups of this nature may be led alone or in cotherapy, and they usually consist of fewer than 10 members. The frequency of meetings is increased to once per week, although the duration of each session is rarely more than 1 hour. The content of advanced groups invites discussion of family issues, identification of stressors associated with relapse, assignment of homework outside of sessions, plans for addressing residual symptomatology, and themes common to all group members, including living with the stigma of mental illness.

The advanced group focus is on the "here and now," and the leader keeps the conversation concrete and centered, making sure that patients understand what has been said before moving on to new topics. Kanas (1995) has underscored the importance of the therapist's ability to be patient and to have a willingness to repeat points that may not be clear. Whether because of the side effects of medication or because of their primary psychiatric state, patients often are unable to process information in the group in a timely manner. A central role of the leader in these groups is to steer conversations away from subjects that threaten the adjustment of group members. It is critical that the therapist reiterate the essential role of confidentiality, especially since these groups usually include members with a strong paranoid component to their illness. The group climate must be supportive and safe. When this atmosphere is present, group dropout is less likely, and members' expectations of interpersonal contact shift over time from a fearful mind-set to anticipation of acceptance and cohesion in the group.

Social support should not be mistaken as superficiality. Many advanced group sessions are indistinguishable from outpatient group therapy with higher functioning patients. The literature on outcomes in group therapies for schizophrenia shows that a group is a critical adjunct to medication in the treatment of patients. Specifically, 70% of studies demonstrate that group treatment is superior to no group treatment and that interactive groups based in the "here and now" are more effective than insight-oriented approaches (Kanas, 1995).

BASIC PRINCIPLE 11

Give careful thought to the timing of medication management, and be aware of the nonmedication issues attached to this process. Medication management forms an integral part of the treatment of patients with severe psychiatric disorders. There are important issues linked to the prescribing of psychotropic medications when group therapy is part of the treatment. Some of these issues include whether or not the group leader is also the person managing the medication, the timing of reviews of group members' symptoms and progress, whether to write prescriptions in or out of sessions, and how much of the group focus should be devoted to discussion of medications and medication-related themes.

Very often, the group therapist is not the psychopharmacologist for the patients in the group. In such instances, the same general principles that apply to combined therapy (group therapy along with one or more other simultaneous interventions) are in force. The group therapist needs to obtain the patient's permission to communicate with the person prescribing the medication so that maximum coordination of therapy is achieved. The dialogue between the two clinicians is invaluable since it affords the group leader with a realistic set of expectations for what changes to anticipate in the patient's clinical picture. In the other direction, the person managing the medication gains information on the patient's level of functioning from the interpersonal perspective of the group leader. This channel of information, which is less accessible in the individual medication session, is central to an assessment of the patient's current psychological state.

When the group leader is also the person who manages patients' medication, each group session affords an opportunity to observe patients in action. This interactional information is factored into an appraisal of which medication is most appropriate and whether changes in drugs or dosage are necessary.

Some difference of opinion exists regarding the optimal timing for introducing the medication aspect of the group meeting. Psychodynamically oriented therapists use medication and the emotional issues mobilized by medication management as venues for exploration in groups of higher functioning chronic patients. Medication provides entree into themes of caretaking and nurturing, dependency, vertical transference (transference from member to leader), competition, fantasy, unresolved family conflicts, and others.

Leaders with this orientation want to integrate medication issues into the life of the group and prefer to deal with medication at the start of each session. The rationale for choosing this sequence resides in the fact that reactions to how the therapist handles issues involving medication decisions are observable in all group members. Also, when medicine is prescribed at the outset, spillover from themes for which medication is a stimulus is available for exploration and clarification in the remainder of the group session.

An illustration of this premise is found in the following vignette. A psychiatrist was leading an outpatient group homogeneously composed of patients with schizophrenia. After all patients were evaluated and medication adjustments were made, one paranoid member became uncharacteristically silent and looked sullen. When the leader inquired about the change in his demeanor, the patient angrily said, "You never take me first. It's always someone else. I always suspected that you didn't like me and this proves it." Obviously, more than mere pharmacological issues were at play, even though medication was the focal point for the patient's feelings. Those who espouse medicating at the beginning of sessions want to allow for attention to important feelings, such as those just noted, in the group session that follows.

The case for medicating patients outside of the group or at the end of group sessions has more to do with administrative and managerial motives. Many therapists find it more convenient and time efficient to end each session with a review of progress and to write prescriptions at that time. This approach keeps the group session relatively free of symptom description and medication issues (e.g., delineation of details about unpleasant drug side effects). It also establishes a closing ritual for each session, a practice reassuring to many seriously impaired group members.

(continued)

BASIC PRINCIPLE 11 (continued)

Whenever patients are medicated by someone other than the group leader, the leader needs to solicit information related to medication that may be relevant to changes in the treatment plan. Both progress and setbacks are noteworthy in this regard. Negative feelings about the drugs being prescribed or the person doing the prescribing are often easier to discuss in the group session when the physician is not present. These discontents directly affect patient compliance, and the group leader has to be alert to their existence. Such issues are discussed both in the group and by the group leader with the prescribing doctor outside of group sessions.

GROUP MODELS FOR CHRONIC PSYCHIATRIC PROBLEMS

In brief, the point of difficulty for a person with a chronic psychiatric problem may vary considerably, even within the same diagnostic spectrum. Work, family, medication, finances, and personal relationships are common areas of concern for the person struggling with adaptation to life outside of a hospital. At times, place-ment in an adjunctive group with a specialized focus may facilitate the overall management of a particular person's life.

Groups for Patients With Bipolar Disorder

An interesting body of group work has been carried out with groups composed exclusively of patients with manic-depressive illness. Here, as with the treatment of schizophrenia spectrum disorders, the group therapy component is aimed more at the social and interpersonal consequences of having a major affective disorder. Lithium and other pharmacological agents are used to treat the primary symptoms of the condition.

The goals of groups with bipolar patients are twofold: (a) to allow patients to be more knowledgeable about their condition so that they can take an active role in shaping their adjustment to it and (b) to deal with those symptoms that cannot be resolved solely by taking appropriate medications. One prototypical group program for bipolar patients is the life goals program described by Bauer and McBride (1996). This is a two-stage structured group therapy model that begins, in the first stage, with an emphasis on using groups to enhance illness management skills. This is accomplished through the use of a structured, five-session psychoeducational phase with the specific group agenda of getting patients to think about their illness and how it has adversely affected their lives. Group discussion generates general topics that are recorded in a journal or workbook so that members can work on their particular problems related to being manic-depressive in the time between group meetings.

Phase 2 is less psychoeducational and more behavioral in nature. Group mem-bers are encouraged to examine their life goals in an attempt to understand how their psychological condition has interfered with the attainment of those goals. Once realistic life goals are delineated, the bulk of the second phase is devoted to constructing and implementing plans for their realization. Tangible tasks such as getting a driver's license, pursuing a hobby, and developing a relationship are examples of Phase 2 goals. Cognitive and behavioral strategies are coupled with peer support from the group to help members persevere in attaining goals that are achievable despite the fact that they are anxiety provoking.

Improvement of the quality of life for patients and families in which bipolar disorder is present is the central goal in most group approaches. Other popular group formats for this condition are couples and family groups. In couples groups, the nonbipolar partner can feel validated by others in the group who experience the same storminess in their relationships with a partner who has a severe mood disorder. Terms such as "intermittent incompatibility" often emerge from leaders of couples group who try to help both partners understand that the mercurial nature of the primary illness is likely to cause predictable fluctuations in the homeostasis of the relationship. Practical matters, such as how to help the partner who is grandiose, what to do when a partner uncontrollably overspends, how to plan for protecting oneself from attack when a partner is entering a manic phase of the illness, and how to assess suicidal potential, are integral parts of couples groups.

Family groups follow along similar lines and are conducted in the same manner as the multiple-family groups described in Chapter 9. Family support and identification, along with practical suggestions for coping with the problems associated with major mood disorders, are core elements of family support groups. Education about the genetics of the illness, mood-stabilizing medications and their side effects, the importance of maintaining regular sleep patterns, and avoidance of drugs, alcohol, caffeine, and over-the-counter medications that contain stimulants is provided to families in the group. Support and education in groups decrease the chances of the bipolar patient becoming an overwhelming burden to his or her family.

Self-Help Groups and Community-Based Programs

Friends, families, and significant others involved with a person who is mentally ill have made organized efforts to help one another cope with this shared life circumstance. Patients themselves have also become active on their own behalf by forming self-help groups, many of which are similar to the model found in Alcoholics Anonymous. Recovery Incorporated is representative of a self-help group for patients who have experienced severe psychiatric illness. Support and patient advocacy are essential goals of the group. These are leaderless groups that disseminate factual information about psychiatric disorders and advise the membership on how to negotiate the complex and often prejudicial aspects of the mental health care service delivery system.

Community-based programs such as group homes, halfway houses, and residential treatment centers include both formal and informal group contact as part of their design. Structured psychoeducational groups and learning through living with others experiences form the basis for many programs. These experiences, while technically not considered group psychotherapy, are indeed therapeutic and take place through the medium of socialization and interaction in groups. Adjunctive family groups are also regular components of community-based outpatient programs.

In essence, the group therapies for chronic psychiatric conditions replicate the experience of psychosocial treatment in general insofar as groups help mainly with the alleviation of negative symptoms and improvements in interpersonal competence. Groups do not presume to eradicate the primary condition. A focus on medication, education, socialization, vocation, and psychological integration is the constellation of the benefits chronically ill patients can derive from ongoing participation as members of groups.

12

Future Directions in Group Psychotherapy

The contemporary practice of group psychotherapy described in this book attests to the creative ways in which clinicians with varied points of view have come to appreciate and apply novel group approaches to mental health issues. At the present time, many domains of group work are under way and appear to hold promise for the future of the field. A partial listing of these areas would include the following: groups for patients with Axis II personality disorder diagnoses, particularly borderline patients (Marziali & Munroe-Bloom, 1994); eating disorders groups (Moreno, 1994); men's groups (Andronico, 1996); women's groups (deChant, 1996); groups for adult survivors of childhood sexual, physical, and emotional abuse (Webb & Leehan, 1996); geriatric groups (Erwin, 1996); and more specific groups (Seligman & Marshak, 1990) for phobias, posttraumatic stress disorder, head injury, pain control, and children with emotional and medical problems.

Managed care has had, and is likely to continue to have, an important impact on the practice patterns of group therapists. Short-term models that have arisen in response to cost-containment concerns are flourishing not as a panacea but as another way of adapting groups to meet the economic challenges of the times. While managed care has sparked interest in group therapies, it has also raised issues of great concern to group therapists. Preservation of confidentiality, the need to pathologize patients in order to obtain ongoing insurance benefits, the widespread potential for dissemination of sensitive patient material through computer-based health care recording systems, and other ethical dilemmas are having a deleterious impact on the therapeutic alliance in group therapy (Spitz, 1997).

It is also likely that training of group therapists will undergo changes in the near future. What skills will the group therapist need to add to the existing therapeutic armamentarium in order to maximize the benefits of group therapy under managed care? How will current training programs be updated to keep pace with emerging trends in health care delivery? The settings in which clinically relevant training takes place are likely to expand beyond the classroom and hospital to new sites that are by-products of the managed care movement. Employee assistance programs (EAPs) in corporate settings, managed care clinics, primary care satellite locations, consultation-liaison services, and multispecialty interdisciplinary practitioner groups may all be new sites of learning for the group therapist. The core curriculum of any group training program is likely to contain a greater emphasis on the use of brief group therapies with psychiatric and medically ill patient populations.

Education about group therapy will not be restricted solely to the practitioner. Public information dissemination will reduce confusion among consumers of mental health services as to what constitutes reliable group therapy versus misuse of such therapy for economic expediency. Quality control and public accountability of group therapists will become stronger. Organizations such as the National Registry of Certified Group Psychotherapists, a credentialing arm of the American Group Psychotherapy Association, will help consumers and payers know which clinicians have specific training in group psychotherapy in addition to their skills as generalists. An informed public can serve as a system of checks and balances against the excesses of a managed care system concerned more with profits than with good care for patients.

As Hellerstein (1996) noted, in order not only to survive as therapists but to flourish, mental health professionals in the era of managed care must be willing to "redefine [themselves] professionally without abandoning professional standards" (p. 1). The form this will take may vary. In the best of cases, group therapists will move more toward therapeutic technical orientations that incorporate the findings of recent research into clinical practice. Psychodynamic principles do not have to be abandoned. In a manner much like the development of family therapy, group therapists will flower if they use their awareness of individual and group dynamics to form the basis for timely group interventions, only a portion of which will involve conventional use of psychoanalytically derived techniques.

The inclusion of tasks outside of group sessions that tap relevant individual dynamics will expedite the therapeutic process. By operationalizing psychodynamic theory into active clinical form, the group leader can marry the best of the old and the best of the new. This process is likely to be stimulating rather than inhibiting for the clinician.

Groups will continue to play an increasingly visible role in the overall treatment of many conditions. "Subcontracting" models of treatment where several approaches are used simultaneously or sequentially, as is the case with schizophrenia and other chronic mental illnesses, personality disorders, and substance abuse, are gaining clinical favor. The advantages of groups in being both time and cost efficient and lightening the stress load for therapists will most certainly be appealing to practitioners in a wide variety of treatment settings.

Finally, as group therapy nears its centennial, clinicians are clearer about what has stood the test of time and what in the group field has fallen by the wayside. The trend toward more rigorous study of outcomes in group therapy, patient-therapist and patient-group matching, and greater experience with the application of groups to address new treatment challenges has resulted in a better understanding of how groups work and a greater feeling of confidence in the usefulness of groups on the part of practitioners. New developments in the field will undoubtedly add to this base and expand the existing body of knowledge about the flexibility that group therapy offers and the kinds of clinical skills that well-trained group therapists are particularly adept at providing.

References

Ackerman, N. W. (1958). *The psychodynamics of family life*. New York: Basic Books.

Adler, A. (1956). *Individual psychology of Alfred Adler: A systematic presentation in selections from his writings* (H. L. Ansbacher & H. H. Ansbacher, Eds.). New York: Basic Books.

American Psychiatric Association. (1994). *Diagnostic and statistical manual of mental disorders* (4th ed.). Washington, DC: Author.

Bauer, M. S., & McBride, L. (1996). *Structured group psychotherapy for bipolar disorder*. New York: Springer.

Budman, S. H. (1992). Models of brief individual and group psychotherapy. In J. L. Feldman & R. J. Fitzpatrick (Eds.), *Managed mental health care* (pp. 231–248). Washington, DC: American Psychiatric Press.

Budman, S. H., Cooley, S., Demby, A., Koppenaal, G., Koslof, J., & Powers, T. (1996). A model of time-effective group psychotherapy for patients with personality disorders: The clinical model. *International Journal of Group Psychotherapy, 46*, 329–355.

Budman, S. H., & Gurman, A. S. (1988). *Theory and practice of brief therapy*. New York: Guilford Press.

Budman, S. H., Simeone, P. G., Reilly, R., & Demby, A. (1994). Progress in short-term and time-limited group psychotherapy: Evidence and implications. In A. Fuhriman & G. Burlingame (Eds.), *Handbook of group psychotherapy* (pp. 319–339). New York: Wiley.

Burrow, T. (1927). *The social basis of consciousness*. New York: Harcourt, Brace & World.

Cadwell, S. A. (1997). Transference and countertransference. In M. F. O'Connor (Ed.), *Treating the psychological consequences of HIV* (pp. 1–32). San Francisco: Jossey-Bass.

Dreikurs, R. (1959). Early experiments with group psychotherapy. *American Journal of Psychotherapy, 13*, 882–891.

Freud, S. (1921). Group psychology and the analysis of the ego. In *Standard edition of the complete psychological works of Sigmund Freud* (Vol. 18). London: Hogarth Press.

Frost, J. C. (1993). Group psychotherapy with HIV-positive and AIDS patients. In A. Alonso & H. I. Swiller (Eds.), *Group therapy in clinical practice* (pp. 255–270). Washington, DC: American Psychiatric Press.

Grinberg, L., Sor, D., & Tabak-Bianchedi, E. (1977). *Introduction to the work of Bion*. New York: Jason Aronson.

Kanas, N. (1995). Group psychotherapy. In S. Vinogradov (Ed.), *Treating schizophrenia* (pp. 279–295). San Francisco: Jossey-Bass.

Lazell, E. W. (1921). The group treatment of dementia praecox. *Psychoanalytic Review, 8*, 168.

Levy, L. H. (1979). Processes and activities in groups. In M. A. Lieberman & L. D. Borman (Eds.), *Self-help groups for coping with crisis* (pp. 234–271). San Francisco: Jossey-Bass.

Lewin, T. (1996, May 22). Questions of privacy roil arena of psychotherapy. *New York Times.*

Lieberman, M. L., Yalom, I. D., & Miles, M. B. (1973). *Encounter groups: First facts.* New York: Basic Books.

Linehan, M. M. (1993). *Cognitive behavioral treatment of borderline patients.* New York: Guilford Press.

MacKenzie, K. R. (1990). *Introduction to time-limited group psychotherapy.* Washington, DC: American Psychiatric Press.

Marsh, L. C. (1931). Group treatment by the psychological equivalent of the revival. *Mental Hygiene, 15,* 328–349.

Marziali, E., & Monroe-Blum, H. (1994). *Interpersonal group psychotherapy for borderline personality disorder.* New York: Basic Books.

Masnik, R., Bucci, L., Isenberg, D., & Normand, W. (1974). "Coffee and . . . '': A way to treat the untreatable. *American Journal of Psychiatry, 128,* 164–167.

McGoldrick, M., & Gerson, R. (1985). *Genograms in family assessment.* New York: Norton.

Moreno, J. L. (1953). *Who shall survive?* New York: Beacon House.

Moreno, J. L. (1994). Group treatment for eating disorders. In A. Fuhriman & G. M. Burlingame (Eds.), *Handbook of group psychotherapy: An empirical and clinical synthesis* (pp. 416–457). New York: Wiley.

Perls, F. (1969). *Gestalt therapy verbatim.* Lafayette, CA: Real People Press.

Piper, W. E., Debanne, E. G., Bienvenu, J. P., & Garant, J. (1982). A study of group pre-training for group psychotherapy. *International Journal of Group Psychotherapy, 32,* 309–325.

Piper, W. E., & McCallum, M. (1994). Selection of patients for group interventions. In H. Bernard & K. R. MacKenzie (Eds.), *Basics of group psychotherapy.* New York: Guilford Press.

Piper, W. E., McCallum, M., & Azim, H. F. A. (1992). *Adaptation to loss through short-term group psychotherapy.* New York: Guilford Press.

Pratt, J. H. (1907). The class method of treating consumption in the homes of the poor. *Journal of the American Medical Association, 49,* 755–759.

Price, A. L. (1978, September/October). Self-help groups: Trouble on the frontier. *Current Concepts in Psychiatry,* pp. 6–14.

Rachman, A. W., & Raboult, R. R. (1985). The clinical practice of group psychotherapy with adolescent substance abusers. In T. E. Bratter & C. G. Forrest (Eds.), *Alcoholism and substance abuse: Strategies for clinical intervention.* New York: Free Press.

Rudnick, F. D. (1991, March). *Psychiatric treatment of frontal lobe syndromes.* Program presented at the conference on "The Frontal Lobes: Theoretical and Clinical Perspectives," Toronto, Ontario, Canada.

Schilder, P. (1936). The analysis of ideologies as a psychotherapeutic method, especially in group treatment. *American Journal of Psychiatry, 93,* 601.

Slavson, S. R. (1943). *A textbook in analytic group psychotherapy.* New York: International Universities Press.

Spiegel, D., & Yalom, I. D. (1978). A support group for dying patients. *International Journal of Group Psychotherapy, 2,* 233–245.

Spitz, H. I. (1984). Contemporary trends in group psychotherapy: A literature survey. *Hospital and Community Psychiatry, 35,* 132–142.

Spitz, H. I. (1996). *Group psychotherapy and managed mental health care: A clinical guide for providers.* New York: Brunner/Mazel.

Spitz, H. I. (1997). The effect of managed mental health care on group psychotherapy: Treatment, training and therapist morale issues. *International Journal of Group Psychotherapy, 47,* 23–30.

Spitz, H. I., & Rosecan, J. S. (Eds.). (1987). *Cocaine abuse: New directions in treatment and research.* New York: Brunner/Mazel. Stone, W. N. (1996). *Group psychotherapy for people with chronic mental illness.* New York: Guilford Press.

Tucker, G. J., & Maxmen, J. S. (1975). Multiple family group therapy in a psychiatric hospital. *Journal of Psychoanalysis in Groups, 27,* 34–39.

Wender, L. (1940). Group psychotherapy: A study of its application. *Psychiatric Quarterly, 14,* 708.

Winer, J. A., & Ornstein, E. (1994). Relational themes in community meeting. *International Journal of Group Psychotherapy, 44,* 313–332.

Wolf, A., & Schwartz, E. K. (1962). *Psychoanalysis in groups.* New York: Grune & Stratton.

Woth, J. L., & Halman, M. H. (1994). HIV/AIDS. In *Textbook of consultation-liaison psychiatry* (pp. 858–859). Washington, DC: American Psychiatric Press.

Yalom, I. D. (1975). *The theory and practice of group psychotherapy.* New York: Basic Books.

Yalom, I. D. (1983). *Inpatient group psychotherapy.* New York: Basic Books.

Yalom, I. D. (1985). *The theory and practice of group psychotherapy* (3rd ed.). New York: Basic Books.

Yalom, I. D., & Vinogradov, S. (1989). *A concise guide to group psychotherapy.* Washington, DC: American Psychiatric Press.

Index

AA (*see* Alcoholics Anonymous)

Absences, from group, 46–47, 50, 62

Abstinence, as group rule, in substance abuse groups, 101

Abuse, of power/control, in family life, 114

Ackerman, Nathan, and family therapy origins, 6

Acute patient groups, for chronic psychiatric patients, 141, 143–145

Addiction (*see* Detoxification phase, of substance abuse group; Substance abuse groups)

Addition, of group members, 45–46

Address, forms of, used in group, 58–61

Adjunctive groups, for medical illness groups, 126

Adler, Alfred, and group therapy origins, 4, 6

Adolescents
group therapy with, origins of, 5
(*See also* Family group therapy)
in substance abuse groups, 104–105

Affect, mobilization of, 4, 26–27
in couples/families therapy, 107, 109–111, 119
in substance abuse groups, 98

Age factors
in multifamily group therapy, 122
in substance abuse groups, 104–105

AIDS (*see* HIV/AIDS patients)

Alcoholics Anonymous, 11, 37, 96

Alcoholism (*see* Substance abuse groups)

Altruism, sense of, in groups, 21–22, 37

American Group Psychotherapy Association, 5, 154

American Psychiatric Association, diagnostic system of, 32, 87

Anger
management of, and couples therapy, 109–111
of therapist, in medical illness group, 136

Argumentative group members, 65–66

Assessment, for prospective group members, 29

Attendance, rules about, in group, 46–47, 50, 62, 97, 106

Basic Principle
1, 14
2, 23
3, 31
4, 33
5, 52
6, 56–57
7, 60–61
8, 96
9, 110–111
10, 135
11, 149–150

Behavior therapy groups, 10, 16t
homework given in, 67, 84
length of, 45
for medically ill patients, 129–130

Bereavement, after death of group member, 132–133

Bereavement groups, 45

Billing procedures, discussed in pregroup orientation, 47–48

Bion, Wilfred, and group-centered analytic therapy, 10

Bipolar disorder patients, group therapy with, 150–151

Body image theme, of medically ill patients, 131

Borderline personality disorder
in prospective group members, 32, 42
and use of splitting, 48, 60

Brief group psychotherapy, 17–18, 44–45, 81–91
basic principles of, 81–83
clinical points of emphasis in, 83–85
development stages in, 73–75
group cohesion in, 25
and homogeneity of group members, 15
inclusion criteria for, 34
initial session of, 62–63, 67
leader's opinion about, 86
leader's role in, 54, 85–87
and managed mental health care, 7, 81, 88, 153
termination of, 75–77, 76t

"Buddy system," outside of group, 49, 133

Burnout, of therapist, in medical illness groups, 137

Burrow, Trigant, and group therapy origins, 4

Cancer patients (*See also* Medically ill patients, group therapy with)
  crisis intervention for, 129
"Caring confrontation," in substance abuse groups, 97–98
Challenging/testing, of leader, by group members, 64–66
Change, patient responsibility for, in brief therapy groups, 83–84
"Cheerleader" therapy, vs. realistic hopefulness, 20
Children
  group therapy with, origins of, 5
    (*See also* Family group therapy)
  and power/control issues, in families, 114
Chronic psychiatric patients, 89–90
  and end-of-session summary, 68
  and group attendance rules, 47
  and group cohesion, 25
  group models for, 150–152
  with acute patient groups, 141, 143–145
  overview of therapy, 141–143
  group types for, 143–148
  socialization groups and, 22
Climate, of substance abuse group, 101
Closed membership groups, 17, 101
"Coffee" groups, development of, 58
Cognitive therapy groups, 10, 16t
  homework given in, 67, 84
  length of, 45
  for medically ill patients, 129–130
Cohesion (*see* Group cohesion)
Co-leadership, 18, 60–61
  in couples groups, 120–121
  developmental stages of, 60–61
  and forms of address, 59
  in substance abuse groups, 100–101
"Combat fatigue," and group therapy origins, 5
Combined therapy (individual/group), 13
Commonalities, among group members (*see* Group cohesion; Homogeneity, of group members; Universality, feeling of, in groups)
Communication patterns
  in cohesive couples groups, 26
  between couples/families, 108–111

Community meeting, for psychiatric patients, 144–145
Community mental health movement, and group therapy, ix, 5–6, 151–152
Comorbidity, with substance abuse, 98
Composition, of groups (*see* Group composition)
Confidentiality, 50
  and managed mental health care, 50, 87
  in substance abuse groups, 106
  and therapeutic alliance, 87
Confrontational group experiences, 12
  in couples group therapy, 118
  in substance abuse groups, 97–98
Confrontational group members, 65–66
Construction (*see* Group construction)
Control, issues of, in couples/families, 114
Cotherapy, 18, 60–61
  of couples groups, 120–121
  developmental stages of, 60–61
  and forms of address, 59
  in substance abuse groups, 100–101
Countertransference, 23, 75
  in couples therapy, 121
  with medically ill patients, 131, 134–139
Couples therapy groups, 11, 117–122
  and assessment of strengths, 113–114
  communication rules in, 110–111
  design of, 118
  dynamics of, 118–120
  general principles of, 107–108
  group cohesion in, 25–26
  indications for, 116
  initial interview for, 108–116
  and power/control issues, 114
Crisis creation, in groups, 59
Crisis groups, 12, 90
Crisis management, in substance abuse groups, 99
"Curative factors," in groups, 7, 19, 27, 98

Death, of medical-illness group member, 132–133
"Default" model, of patient selection, 34
Deinstitutionalization, and group therapy, ix, 5–6, 147
Denial, use/misuse of, in medical illness groups, 133, 137
Dependence vs. independence, as group theme, 64, 131

Depression
    and brief therapy group goals, 82, 84
    comorbid with substance abuse, 98
    and futility, patient's sense of, 20
    in HIV/AIDS patients, 127
    and pregroup orientation, 42
    in therapist, 136–137
Destigmatization, sense of, in groups, 21,
    37
Detoxification phase, of substance abuse
    group, 95
    (*See also* Total abstinence)
Developmental stages
    of cotherapy, 60–61
    of families, 111–112
    of psychotherapy groups, 71–77
        clinical significance of, 74–75
    of substance abuse groups, 99–100
Diagnosis
    and brief group therapy, 87–91
    and couples group therapy, 117
    of prospective group members, 32–33
    and room arrangement, 57
Diagnostic and Statistical Manual of Mental
    Disorders (DSM-IV), 32, 87
Didactic model, of group therapy, 20
    origins of, 4
Disease (*see* Medically ill patients, group
    therapy with)
Dissolution of relationship, discussed in
    couples therapy, 110, 120
Divorce
    discussed in couples therapy, 110, 120
    group leader's opinion of, 121
Dreikuers, Rudolph, and group therapy
    origins, 4, 6
Drop-in groups, for outpatients, 90
Drug abuse (*see* Substance abuse groups)
Drugs (*see* Psychotropic medications;
    Substance abuse groups)
DSM-IV, 32, 87

Eating, during group sessions, 57–58
Eclecticism, technical, 7, 14, 82, 85, 127
Education
    about groups, 153–154
    through groups, 19–20, 119, 126, 130
Education history, of prospective group
    member, 30
Emotional catharsis (*see* Affect, mobilization
    of)

Employee assistance programs (EAPs),
    153
Employment history, of prospective group
    member, 30–31
Encounter groups, origins of, 6
Ending, of initial session, 67–69
Evaluation
    for couples therapy, 117–118
    for medical illness group, 127–128
    of prospective group members, 29–31, 83
    pregroup orientation as, 40, 43, 49
Exclusion criteria, vs. inclusion criteria, for
    group membership, 34
Existential group therapy, 13
Extragroup contact/socialization, 22–24
    discussed in pregroup orientation, 49
    and medical illness groups, 133–134
    and substance abuse groups, 24, 49, 104
Extramarital relationships, and couples/
    families therapy, 115

False reassurance, vs. realistic hopefulness,
    20
Family
    of medically ill patients, 130, 134
    as source of patient motivation, 38
    and substance abuse group, 102
Family group therapy, 11, 38, 122–124
    and assessment of strengths, 113–114
    general principles of, 107–108
    indications for, 116–117
    initial interview for, 108–116
    origins of, 5–6
    and power/control issues, 114
Family interview, for substance abuse
    patients, 102
Family issues/dynamics, use of in groups
    and fee arrangements, 48
    origins of, 4
    and terms of address, 59–61
Family of origin, 22, 112–113
    and couples therapy, 119
    of group leader, 121
    and substance abuse patients, 36, 102
Fears, of group members
    in first session, 55
    in medical illness groups, 128, 131
Fees
    discussed in pregroup orientation, 47–48
    for substance abuse groups, as
        motivation, 106

First group meeting (*see* Initial group
    session)
First-name basis, group leader on, 58–61
Fixed membership groups, 17, 45–46
Food, during group sessions, 57–58
Formats, of group psychotherapy, 9–13
Freud, Sigmund, and group therapy origins, 4
Friendships (*see* Relationships)
Futility, sense of
    in depressed patients, 20
    in therapist, 136

Gender issues, in substance abuse groups,
    105–106
Genogram method, of taking family history,
    113
Gestalt therapy groups, 12
Global evaluation, for medical illness groups,
    128
Goals, of group (*see* Group goals)
''Go-around'' technique
    at end of first session, 67–68
    origins of, 5, 62
Group-centered analytic therapy, 10
Group climate, in substance abuse group, 101
Group cohesion, 25–26, 37
    in brief therapy groups, 82–83
    and initial session, 63
    in substance abuse groups, 95–96, 99
Group composition, 9, 15, 19
    and altruism, 21–22
    in brief therapy groups, 83–85
    for couples groups, 118–119
    explained in pregroup orientation, 41
    and initial screening/evaluation, 33–39
    in substance abuse groups, 104–106
Group construction, 29–52
Group goals
    in brief group therapy, 81–82
    for medically ill patients, 130–131
    outlined in pregroup orientation, 41
    for psychiatric patients, 144–146
    reviewed in first session, 53
    in substance abuse groups, 93–97,
        94t–95t
Group leader/leadership (*see* Leader;
    Leadership)
Group membership, issues of, 17–18
    in substance abuse groups, 101–102
    (*See also* Group composition)

Group Psychology and the Analysis of the
    Ego (Freud), 4
Group psychotherapy
    classification of, 13–18, 16t
    clinically oriented definition of, 9
    clinical principles of, 19–27
    formats of, 9–13
    future directions in, 153–154
    literature on, development of, 6
    motives for seeking, 35–39
    origins of, ix, 3–7
    as part of broader treatment plan, 48–49
Group rules, 46–47, 50, 54, 63
    in couples therapy, 110–111
    in substance abuse groups, 63t, 101
Group stages (*see* Developmental stages)
Group themes, 72
    in brief group therapy, 83
    in couples group therapy, 120
    in initial session, 63–64
    for medically ill patients, 130–132
    for psychiatric patients, 145
    in substance abuse groups, 96, 102
Guilt feelings
    of medically ill patients, 131–132
    of therapist, 136

Health care reform, ix
    (*See also* Managed mental health care)
Heterogeneity, of group members, 14–15,
    84–85
    (*See also* Group composition)
HIV/AIDS patients
    bereavement feelings of, after death of
        group member, 132–133
    continuum model of, 127–128
    depression/suicide risk in, 127
    families of, 130, 134
    guilt feelings of, 132
    and personal values of therapist, 138–139
    therapy goals of, 130–131
Homework
    given in brief therapy groups, 67, 84
    for medically ill patients, 130
Homogeneity, of group members, 15, 83, 85,
    125, 142
    (*See also* Group composition)
Hopefulness, realistic, in groups, 20–21, 37,
    98, 133
Horizontal transference, 23, 120

Hospitalization
  discussed in pregroup orientation, 48–49
  for chronic psychiatric patients (*see*
      Acute patient groups, for chronic
      psychiatric patients)
  for medically ill patients, 129
  for substance abuse patients, 103–104
Humor, use of, in groups, 66

Illness (*see* Medically ill patients, group
      therapy with)
Imitative behavior, in groups, 24–25, 120
Inclusion criteria, vs. exclusion criteria, for
      group membership, 34
Independence vs. dependence, as group
      theme, 64, 131
Individual/intrapsychic level, of interaction,
      56
Induction phase, in substance abuse groups,
      99
Information, dissemination of, groups for,
      19–20
Informed consent, for observation of groups,
      43
Initial group session
  common themes in, 63–64
  ending, 67–68
  leadership issues/considerations in,
      53–61
  patient roles during, 64–67
  vs. second group session, 69
  starting, 62–63
Initial interview
  of couple/family, 108–117
  of group members, 29–31
  questions used in, 35–39
Inpatient therapy
  for chronic psychiatric patients, 141,
      143–145
  early origins of, 4
  large groups in, 18
  for medically ill patients, 129
Insight, acquisition of, in therapy process,
      25, 98
Insurance (*see* Managed mental health care)
Interaction, multiple levels of, in group,
      56–57
Interdisciplinary leadership, of medical
      illness groups, 126
Intermediate group therapy, 88–89

Interpersonal functioning
  of medically ill patient, 128, 130–131
  of prospective group member, 30, 32–33
Interpersonal/group level, of interaction, 56
Interpersonal model, of group stages, 72
Interview
  family, for substance abuse patients, 102
  initial
      of couple/family, 108–117
      of group members, 29–31
      questions used in, 35–39
"I" statements, vs. "you" statements, 109

Lateness, rules about, in group, 47, 62
Lazell, Edward, and group therapy origins, 4
Leader
  addressed by name or title, 58–61
  and countertransference, 23, 75
      in couples therapy, 121
      with medically ill patients, 131,
          134–139
  as evaluator, of prospective group
      members, 29–30
  need for trust in, 64
  personal values of, 138–139
  role modeling by, 24
  role/posture of, 19–20
      explained in pregroup orientation,
          42–43
      reviewed in first session, 53–55
      (*See also* Group psychotherapy,
          formats of)
  self-reflectiveness of, 75
  session summary by, 68
  solo vs. co-, in substance abuse groups,
      100–101
  testing/challenging of, by group
      members, 64–66
  theoretical orientation of, 13–15, 16t
      in brief group therapy, 85–86
Leadership
  in brief group therapy, 82, 85–87
  with chronic psychiatric patients, 146
  in couples therapy, 120–121
  multidisciplinary, for medical illness
      groups, 126
  styles of, and group outcomes, 6
  in substance abuse groups, 100–101,
      104
Learning, in groups, 25, 98, 123

Learning theory, and behavior/cognitive
    therapy, 10
Long-term therapy groups, 44–46
    developmental stages of, 72–73
    end of first session of, 67–68
    inclusion criteria for, 34
    leader's role in, 54
    termination of, 75–77, 76t
Loss
    of group members, 45–46
        through death, 132–133
    issues of, and group psychotherapy,
        36
        (*See also* Bereavement groups)
    therapist's feelings of, 138
Love (*see* Relationships)

Magical thinking, of therapist, in medical
    illness groups, 137
Maintenance group therapy, 88–89
Managed mental health care, ix, 90, 153
    and brief group therapy, 7, 81, 88
    and confidentiality, 50, 87
    and group stages, 74
    and pregroup orientation, 47–48
Marital therapy (*see* Couples therapy groups)
Marsh, Cody, and group therapy origins, 4
Matching, of leader to groups, 7, 9
Medically ill patients
    group therapy with, 20
        and countertransference, 134–139
        and death of member, 132–133
        general principles of, 125–127
        selection of modality, 128–129
        treatment considerations in, 127–134
        types of, 129–131
    in non-medical illness group, 135
Medication groups, 11, 90, 149–150
    origins of, 6
Medications (*see* Medication groups;
    Psychotropic medications)
Membership in groups, types of, 17–18
Mixed addictions, and detoxification, 95
"Monopolizing" group member, 65
Mood disorder, comorbid with substance
    abuse, 98
Moreno, Jacob, and origins of psychodrama,
    4, 10
Motivation, patient
    in brief therapy groups, 83–84
    in substance abuse groups, 106

Motives, for seeking therapy, 35–39
Mourning (*see* Bereavement, after death of
    group member)
Multidisciplinary leadership, of medical
    illness groups, 126
Multiple family group psychotherapy, 11,
    122–124
Mutual-help groups, 6, 11, 16t, 37

Names, use of, in group, 58–61
Narcissistic personality disorder, in
    prospective group members, 42
National Registry of Certified Group
    Psychotherapists, 154
Networking, of peers, 104
    (*See also* Extragroup contact/
        socialization)
Nonpsychotic vs. psychotic patients, group
    therapy with, 142t
Nonverbal vs. verbal level, of group
    behavior, 67
Notes, taking of, in group therapy, 44

Observation, of group sessions, 43–44
Open-ended therapy groups (*see* Long-term
    therapy groups)
Open membership groups, 17, 45–46, 101
Orientation
    pregroup (*see* Pregroup orientation, of
        members)
    theoretical (*see* Theoretical orientation, of
        group leader)
Original family (*see* Family of origin)
Origins, of group psychotherapy, ix, 3–7
Out-of-session assignments (*see* Homework)
Outpatient groups
    for chronic psychiatric patients, 146–148
    for medically ill patients, 129, 141–142

Paranoid patients, as prospective group
    members, 33
Partner-to-partner transference, in couples
    groups, 120
Patient responsibility, for change, in brief
    therapy groups, 83–84
Patient role(s)
    denial of, 59
    during first session, 65–68

Patient selection (*see* Group composition; Initial interview)

Patient turnover, in substance abuse groups, 101–102

Peer group relationships, of prospective group member, 30

Perls, Fritz, and Gestalt therapy, 12

Personality disorders
and brief group therapy, 87–88
in prospective group members, 32, 42

Physical illness (*see* Medically ill patients, group therapy with)

Posttraumatic stress disorder (PTSD)
group therapy goals for, 41
and group therapy origins, 5

Power, issues of, in couples/families, 114

Pratt, Joseph, and group therapy origins, 3

Pregroup orientation, of members, 39–52, 86–87

Preparation, of group members (*see* Pregroup orientation, of members)

Previous relationships, history of, 115

Previous therapy, and couples/families groups, 115

Process notes, in group therapy, 44

Promptness, rules about, in group, 47, 62, 106

Psychiatric patients (*see* Chronic psychiatric patients; Inpatient therapy)

Psychoanalysis, group applications of, 9–10
leader's role in, 54
origins of, 4–5, 62

Psychoanalysis in Groups (Wolf and Schwartz), 62

Psychodrama groups, 10–11
origins of, 4

Psychodynamic/analytic model, of group stages, 72–73

Psychodynamic group therapy, 9–10, 16t
learning in, 25
for medically ill patients, 130

Psychoeducational groups, 19–20, 84

Psychotherapy, vs. self-help groups, 93–97, 94t–95t, 103

Psychotic vs. nonpsychotic patients, group therapy with, 142t

Psychotropic medications
and chronic psychiatric patients, 142, 147, 149–150
development of, 6
discussed in pregroup orientation, 48–49
for substance abuse patients, 102–103

Question-and-answer period, during pregroup orientation, 51

Realistic hopefulness, in groups, 20–21, 37, 98, 133

Reality testing
in couples group therapy, 119
in substance abuse groups, 37
videotape playback and, 43–44

Recording, of group sessions, 43–44

Recovered user, as co-leader, in substance abuse group, 100–101

Rehabilitative phase, of illnesses, therapy during, 126

Relationship-oriented diagnostic aids, for couples therapy, 117

Relationships
capacity for forming
of prospective group member, 31, 36
by substance abusers, 105
extramarital, and couples/families therapy, 115
previous, history of, 115

Role modeling
in couples group therapy, 120
by group leader, 24
in substance abuse groups, 37

Role-playing, origins of, 4

"Round robin" technique
at end of first session, 67–68
origins of, 5, 62

Rules (*see* Group rules)

Same-sex groups, for substance abusers, 105–106

Scapegoating, of group member(s), 66, 82, 97, 111

Schilder, Paul, and group psychoanalysis, origins of, 4

Schwartz, Emanuel, and group therapy origins, 5, 62

Screening
for couples therapy, 117–118
of prospective group members, 29–31, 83
pregroup orientation as, 40, 43, 49

Seating arrangement, for first group session, 55–57

Second group session, 68–69

Selection, of patients, for groups (*see* Group composition; Initial interview)

Self-help groups, 6, 11, 16t, 37
    for chronic psychiatric patients, 151–152
    for substance abuse, 93, 94t–95t, 96, 103
Self-image, of medically ill patients, 131
Self-monitoring techniques, and substance
    abuse groups, 97
Self-reflectiveness, of group leader, 75
Sensitivity groups, origins of, 6
Session summary, by leader, 68
Session time, length/extensions of, 17,
    44–45, 83
Setting, for group therapy
    and first session, 55–57
    shown in pregroup orientation, 44
"Sharing," in AA meetings, vs. group
    feedback, 96
"Shell shock," and group therapy origins, 5
Short-term therapy groups (*see* Brief group
    psychotherapy)
"Silent" group member, 65
Similarities, among group members (*see*
    Group cohesion; Homogeneity, of
    group members; Universality, feeling
    of, in groups)
Size of groups, 17–18
Slavson, Samuel, and group therapy origins,
    5
Smoking, during group sessions, 57
Socialization, outside group sessions (*see*
    Extragroup contact/socialization)
Social skills, development of, in groups, 22
Splitting, used by borderline personality, 48,
    60
Stabilization, in substance abuse groups, 99
Strengths, assessment of, in couples/families,
    113–114
Structured group experiences, 11
Substance abuse groups
    age factors in, 104–105
    clinical orientation of, 97–99
    and confrontational format, 12
    and extra-group socialization, 24, 49,
        104
    family involvement in, 102
    gender issues in, 105–106
    goals in, 95–97
    group cohesion in, 95–96
    and group membership, 101–102
    group rules in, 63t, 101
    leadership in, 100–101
    multifamily group therapy and, 122–124

    and patient hospitalization, 103–104
    and patient motivation, 36–37
    post-Vietnam War, 6
    and psychotropic medications, 102–103
    self-help vs. psychotherapy, 93–97,
        94t–95t, 103
    stages of, 99–100
Suicide risk
    of HIV/AIDS patients, 127
    of psychiatric patients, 144
Summary, of session, by leader, 68
Supportive group therapy, 11, 16t, 123, 129
Symptom description, in initial session, 65
Symptoms, function of, in family system,
    111–112
Systems-oriented approach, to couples/
    families therapy, 109–111

Team leadership (*see* Cotherapy)
Technical eclecticism, 7, 14, 82, 85, 127
Teenagers (*see* Adolescents)
Telephone network
    for medical illness groups, 133
    for substance abuse groups, 104
Termination stage, of group, 75–77, 76t
Testing/challenging, of leader, by group
    members, 64–66
Themes, 72
    in brief group therapy, 83
    in couples group therapy, 120
    in initial session, 64–65
    for medically ill patients, 130–132
    for psychiatric patients, 145
    in substance abuse groups, 96, 102
Theoretical orientation, of group leader,
    13–15, 16t
    in brief group therapy, 85–86
Therapeutic alliance, in brief group therapy,
    86–87
Therapeutic climate, in substance abuse
    group, 101
Therapeutic communities
    origins of, 6
    for substance abuse, 12
Therapeutic drugs (*see* Psychotropic
    medications)
"Therapeutic factors," in groups, 7, 19, 27,
    98
Therapeutic plan, 19, 27
    group therapy as part of, 48–49

Therapist
    group (*see* Leader; Leadership)
    outside
        and coordination with group therapy,
            48–49
        and referral to group therapy, 38–39
Therapy (*see* Group psychotherapy)
Third-party payers (*see* Managed mental
    health care)
Time-extended groups, 17
Time factors
    in brief group therapy, 87–91
    in group therapies, 17, 44–45, 50, 83
Time-limited groups (*see* Brief group
    psychotherapy)
Time-unlimited groups (*see* Long-term
    therapy groups)
Timing
    of group member additions, 46
    of group therapy choice, 35–37, 71
Titles, use of, by group members, 58–61
Total abstinence, as group rule, in substance
    abuse groups, 101
Transactional analysis groups, 12
Transference
    in couples therapy, 120
    in group therapy, 23, 25
Transitional groups, for chronic psychiatric
    patients, 141, 145–146
Transition, out of substance abuse group, 99
Transition times, in families, 111–112

Treatment plan, 19, 27
    group therapy as part of, 48–49
Trust, as group goal, 64
Tuberculosis patients, and early
    psychotherapy, 3
12-step groups, 6, 11, 37, 95–96
Two-therapist model (*see* Cotherapy)

Universality, feeling of, in groups, 21, 98

Verbal vs. nonverbal level, of group
    behavior, 67
Vertical transference, 23, 120
Videotaping, of group sessions, 43–44
Vietnam War, and group psychotherapy, 5–6

War, and group therapy, 5–6
Wender, Louis, and group psychoanalysis,
    origins of, 4
"Whole-group" level, of interaction, 56
Wolf, Alexander, and group therapy origins,
    5, 62
Working group phase, in substance abuse
    groups, 99
World War II, and group therapy, ix, 5

"You" statements, vs. "I" statements, 109